T0324324

TRADE RELATIONS

BETWEEN

COLOMBIA AND

THE UNITED STATES

TRADE RELATIONS

BETWEEN

COLOMBIA AND

THE UNITED STATES

Jeffrey J. Schott, editor

INSTITUTE FOR INTERNATIONAL ECONOMICS
Washington, DC
August 2006

Jeffrey J. Schott, senior fellow, joined the Institute in 1983. He was a senior associate at the Carnegie Endowment for International Peace (1982–83) and an international economist at the US Treasury (1974–82). He is the author, coauthor, or editor of *NAFTA Revisited: Achievements and Challenges* (2005), *Free Trade Agreements: US Strategies and Priorities* (2004), *Prospects for Free Trade in the Americas* (2001), *The WTO after Seattle* (2000), *Western Hemisphere Economic Integration* (1994), and *NAFTA: An Assessment* (rev. ed. 1993), among others.

INSTITUTE FOR
INTERNATIONAL ECONOMICS
1750 Massachusetts Avenue, NW
Washington, DC 20036-1903
(202) 328-9000   FAX: (202) 659-3225
www.iie.com

C. Fred Bergsten, *Director*
Valerie Norville, *Director of Publications and Web Development*
Edward Tureen, *Director of Marketing*

Typesetting by BMWW
Printing by United Book Press, Inc.

Copyright © 2006 by the Institute for International Economics. All rights reserved. No part of this book may be reproduced or utilized in any form or by any means, electronic or mechanical, including photocopying, recording, or by information storage or retrieval system, without permission from the Institute.

For reprints/permission to photocopy please contact the APS customer service department at Copyright Clearance Center, Inc., 222 Rosewood Drive, Danvers, MS 01923; or email requests to: info@copyright.com

Printed in the United States of America
08 07 06   5 4 3 2 1

Library of Congress Cataloging-in-Publication Data

Trade relations between Colombia and the United States / Jeffrey J. Schott, editor.
     p. cm.
     Includes bibliographical references and index.
     ISBN 0-88132-389-6 (978-0-88132-389-4 : alk. paper)
     1. Free trade—Colombia.   2. Free trade—United States.   3. Tariff—Colombia.   4. Tariff—United States.   5. Colombia—Commerce—United States.   6. United States—Commerce—Colombia.   7. Colombia—Foreign economic relations—United States.   8. United States—Foreign economic relations—Colombia.   I. Schott, Jeffrey J., 1949–

HF1966.T73 2006
382.09861073—dc22   2006023570

The views expressed in this publication are those of the authors. This publication is part of the overall program of the Institute, as endorsed by its Board of Directors, but does not necessarily reflect the views of individual members of the Board or the Advisory Committee.

Contents

Figures

Boxes

Preface

For the past two decades the Institute has pursued an extensive research agenda on the costs and benefits of prospective US free trade agreements (FTAs) for the signatory countries and for regional integration and the world trading system. Our initial work focused primarily on North America, with in-depth studies of the US-Canada FTA and the North American Free Trade Agreement (NAFTA). In those and subsequent studies, we have analyzed inter alia the extent to which the bilateral or regional pact would complement, and even reinforce, efforts to strengthen the multilateral trading system through a process of "competitive liberalization." This body of work was collectively assessed in a 2004 volume, *Free Trade Agreements: US Strategies and Priorities*, edited by Institute Senior Fellow Jeffrey J. Schott.

Our FTA studies are primarily designed to help inform public debate in the participating countries. In some cases, Institute analyses have explored the desirability of launching FTA negotiations, including possible US-Korea (2001), US-Egypt (2004), and US-Switzerland pacts (2006)—with differing impacts. Talks with Korea began in 2006; Egyptian leaders have pushed for negotiations, but talks were shelved due to their country's backtracking on political reform; and Swiss leaders subsequently decided that talks were not politically feasible for them. Institute analyses of talks that came to fruition have been widely cited during the ratification debates in the respective legislatures, as occurred in all three signatories to the NAFTA in 1993.

This study has had two specific objectives: to examine trade relations between the United States and Colombia and the economic implications of an FTA between them and to inform the ratification debate in both countries. The analysis has been pursued in parallel with the start and conclusion of the free trade negotiations, spanning a period from May 2004 to July 2006. During that time, the authors held meetings in both Washington and Bogotá to review drafts and receive comments from representatives of business, academia, and government. The entire manuscript was provided to both negotiating teams well before the talks were concluded earlier this year. President George W. Bush and President Alvaro Uribe shook hands on a deal in late February 2006, but it took an additional five months to translate their political commitment into legal text. President Bush is expected to sign the FTA in the fall of 2006, making it likely that the US Congress will vote to ratify and implement the pact in 2007.

While the United States conducted negotiations with three members of the Andean Community—Colombia, Ecuador, and Peru—our study focuses primarily on Colombia because of the exceptional circumstances in which those trade talks were pursued. Most trade initiatives seek to achieve a mixture of economic and foreign policy goals. In this case, cementing the already strong political alliance, and especially complementing US support for Plan Colombia against narco-trafficking and civil insurrection in Colombia, has been a central focus of the exercise. The trade pact is part of the ongoing commitment of both governments to stop the cultivation and trade in illegal drugs, open new opportunities for production and employment, particularly in rural areas of Colombia where drug trade and armed insurgency commingle, and thus foster peace, stability, and economic prosperity in Colombia.

The Institute for International Economics is a private, nonprofit institution for the study and discussion of international economic policy. Its purpose is to analyze important issues in that area and to develop and communicate practical new approaches for dealing with them. The Institute is completely nonpartisan.

The Institute is funded by a highly diversified group of philanthropic foundations, private corporations, and interested individuals. Major institutional grants are now being received from the William M. Keck, Jr. Foundation and the Starr Foundation. About 33 percent of the Institute's resources in our latest fiscal year were provided by contributors outside the United States, including about 16 percent from Japan.

This project is part of the Institute's overall program of research on possible free trade agreements between the United States and developing countries, supported by the Ford Foundation and the GE Foundation. Partial funding for this particular study was also provided by the United Nations Development Program. The authors express gratitude for the substantial access to information about Colombia that they received from agencies of the Colombian government as well as from current and former officials and academics in that country. I am especially grateful to Luis Moreno, former ambassador of Colombia to the United States and now president of the Inter-American Development Bank, for inspiring the project and facilitating those contacts.

The Institute's Board of Directors bears overall responsibilities for the Institute and gives general guidance and approval to its research program, including the identification of topics that are likely to become important over the medium run (one to three years) and that should be addressed by the Institute. The director, working closely with the staff and outside Advisory Committee, is responsible for the development of particular projects and makes the final decision to publish an individual study.

The Institute hopes that its studies and other activities will contribute to building a stronger foundation for international economic policy around the world. We invite readers of these publications to let us know how they think we can best accomplish this objective.

C. FRED BERGSTEN
Director
August 2006

INSTITUTE FOR INTERNATIONAL ECONOMICS
1750 Massachusetts Avenue, NW, Washington, DC 20036-1903
(202) 328-9000   Fax: (202) 659-3225

*C. Fred Bergsten, *Director*

BOARD OF DIRECTORS

*Peter G. Peterson, *Chairman*
*Reynold Levy, *Chairman,*
  Executive Committee
*George David, *Vice Chairman*

Leszek Balcerowicz
Bill Bradley
The Lord Browne of Madingley
Chen Yuan
*Jessica Einhorn
Stanley Fischer
Jacob Frenkel
Maurice R. Greenberg
*Carla A. Hills
Nobuyuki Idei
Karen Katen
W. M. Keck II
*Caio Koch-Weser
Lee Kuan Yew
Donald F. McHenry
Mario Monti
Minoru Murofushi
Hutham Olayan
Paul O'Neill
David O'Reilly
*James W. Owens
Frank H. Pearl
*Joseph E. Robert, Jr.
David Rockefeller
David M. Rubenstein
Renato Ruggiero
Edward W. Scott, Jr.
*Adam Solomon
Lawrence H. Summers
Jean Claude Trichet
Laura D'Andrea Tyson
Paul A. Volcker
*Dennis Weatherstone
Edward E. Whitacre, Jr.
Marina v.N. Whitman
Ernesto Zedillo

Ex officio
*C. Fred Bergsten
Nancy Birdsall
Richard N. Cooper

Honorary Directors
Alan Greenspan
Frank E. Loy
George P. Shultz

Honorary Chairman,
  Executive Committee
*Anthony M. Solomon

ADVISORY COMMITTEE

Richard N. Cooper, *Chairman*

Isher Judge Ahluwalia
Robert Baldwin
Barry P. Bosworth
Menzie Chinn
Susan M. Collins
Wendy Dobson
Juergen B. Donges
Barry Eichengreen
Kristin Forbes
Jeffrey A. Frankel
Daniel Gros
Stephan Haggard
David D. Hale
Gordon H. Hanson
Takatoshi Ito
John Jackson
Peter B. Kenen
Anne O. Krueger
Paul R. Krugman
Roger M. Kubarych
Jessica T. Mathews
Rachel McCulloch
Thierry de Montbrial
Sylvia Ostry
Tommaso Padoa-Schioppa
Raghuram Rajan
Dani Rodrik
Kenneth Rogoff
Jeffrey D. Sachs
Nicholas H. Stern
Joseph E. Stiglitz
William White
Alan Wm. Wolff
Daniel Yergin

*Member of the Executive Committee

Acknowledgments

This book reflects the hard work of not only the authors who contributed individual chapters but also the Institute's highly competent publications team, led by Valerie Norville. Particular thanks are due to Madona Devasahayam and Marla Banov for their diligence in preparing the manuscript for publication and to Agustin Cornejo for his able research assistance.

JEFFREY J. SCHOTT
July 2006

Free Trade Between the United States and Colombia: Analysis of the Issues

JEFFREY J. SCHOTT

On May 19, 2004, the United States joined Colombia and its Andean Community partners, Ecuador and Peru, in negotiations on a free trade agreement (FTA).[1] The initiative was a natural progression in the deepening relations between the trading partners over the past two decades, building on the trade and investment framework agreements signed in the 1980s; the Andean Trade Preference Act (ATPA), which has provided US trade preferences to the Andean region (excluding Venezuela) since 1992; and joint efforts to craft a Free Trade Area of the Americas (FTAA) pursuant to the mandate of the Summit of the Americas and to negotiate multilateral trade reforms in the Doha Round of the World Trade Organization (WTO).

On December 7, 2005, US and Peruvian trade negotiators concluded negotiations on a bilateral FTA; that pact, called The US-Peru Trade Promotion Agreement, was signed on April 12, 2006. Negotiations on the US-Colombia FTA lagged those with Peru. However, following last-minute intervention by Colombian President Alvaro Uribe, trade ministers of the United States and Colombia shook hands on a similar deal on February 27, 2006, although officials were still reviewing the details of the commit-

Jeffrey J. Schott is a senior fellow at the Institute for International Economics.

1. Bolivia is participating as an observer but is not yet ready to undertake and enforce the terms of the prospective accord. Venezuela was excluded from the initiative because of the policies of the Hugo Chávez government.

ments to agricultural liberalization in June 2006, even after releasing the FTA text the previous month.[2] Negotiations with Ecuador were suspended in April 2006 following the expropriation of Ecuadorian assets of Occidental Petroleum.

Under the terms of the Trade Act of 2002, the US-Colombia agreement cannot be signed until at least 90 days after US officials notify the Congress of their intent to enter into the accord. Assuming the US-Colombia pact is notified in July 2006, the earliest date it could be signed would be October 2006. After signature, the US-Peru and US-Colombia trade pacts must then be ratified by the legislatures in both countries before the agreements can enter into force. In the United States, the Congress will consider the FTAs under the expedited procedures of trade promotion authority and probably will vote on each pact separately. Congressional consideration of the US-Colombia pact probably will continue into 2007 due to the truncated congressional calendar prior to the November mid-term elections. However, because it has already been signed, the US-Peru agreement conceivably could proceed to votes in one or both houses of Congress in 2006.

US relations with the Andean region have progressed markedly over the past decade, despite frictions arising from narcotics production and trafficking, investment disputes, and inadequate protection of intellectual property rights. Overall, US merchandise exports and imports with the Andean Community exceed trade with all other partners in Latin America and the Caribbean except Mexico (table 1.1). However, that comparison includes US-Venezuelan trade, which is dominated by US petroleum imports. Excluding Venezuela, which is not engaged in current FTA negotiations, US-Andean trade totaled about $30 billion in 2005, less than US trade with Argentina, Brazil, Paraguay, and Uruguay, the four members of the Southern Cone Common Market (Mercosur), or with its partners in the Central American Free Trade Agreement–Dominican Republic (CAFTA-DR). US-Colombia trade accounts for almost 50 percent of the Andean total (excluding Venezuela), or about $14.2 billion—higher than current or prospective US FTA partners Chile, Jordan, Morocco, Bahrain, Panama, the Dominican Republic, or the Southern African Customs Union, but smaller than Singapore, Israel, Australia, or Thailand.[3]

Similarly, US foreign direct investment (FDI) in the Andean region (again excluding Venezuela) reached almost $8 billion on a historical cost basis by year-end 2004; this total, however, is less than US placements in either Brazil, Argentina, or Chile. US FDI in Colombia (on a historical-cost basis) was valued at $3 billion, down from a historic peak of $3.8 billion in 1999 (table 1.2).

---

2. See *Inside US Trade*, May 12, 2006, 1.

3. See US International Trade Commission, *US Trade by Geographic Regions*, www.dataweb.usitc.gov. (accessed May 22, 2006).

Table 1.1   US merchandise trade by region, 2005 (billions of dollars)

Country/region	US exports to:	US imports from:	Total trade
Total Latin America and Caribbean	192.2	293.0	485.2
Andean Community	16.3	54.0	70.3
Mercosur	20.7	29.8	50.5
Chile	5.2	6.7	11.9
CAFTA-DR	16.8	18.1	34.9
Caribbean Community	6.3	9.3	15.6
Mexico	120.1	170.2	290.2
Andean Community (excluding Venezuela)	9.9	20.0	29.9
Of which, Colombia	5.4	8.8	14.2
Of which, Peru	2.3	5.1	7.4

CAFTA-DR = Central American Free Trade Agreement–Dominican Republic
Mercosur = Mercado Comùn del Sur (Southern Cone Common Market)

Sources: US International Trade Commission, *US Trade by Geographic Regions*, www.dataweb. usitc. gov (accessed May 22, 2006).

In short, despite the fillip of trade preferences under the ATPA and marked improvements in relations, US-Andean trade and investment remain modest. While US-Andean trade ties are a key component of the larger hemispheric trade mosaic, and a prospective FTA could perhaps be an important stepping stone to the FTAA, the trade talks have not been headline news in the United States or been given priority by the US business community.

Why, then, does the Andean region, and Colombia in particular, merit exceptional attention? And, more pointedly, why does this study focus primarily on US-Colombia free trade?

What makes US-Colombian relations exceptional is the context in which trade negotiations are taking place. Both governments share common objectives in strengthening economic growth through trade and investment, and both recognize the importance of using trade to promote economic growth and cement political relations between the two countries.

Historically, the United States has pursued bilateral FTAs for a variety of economic and foreign policy reasons. The first US FTA—with Israel in 1985—was primarily a political initiative designed to bolster ties with an ally facing precarious security threats. The North American Free Trade Agreement (NAFTA) survived a close congressional vote because then General Colin Powell argued persuasively that the trade pact would promote economic growth and political stability not only in Mexico but also

Table 1.2   US foreign direct investment in Latin America and the Caribbean, 2004

Country/region	Billions of dollars[a]
Total Latin America and Caribbean	325.9
Andean Community[b]	16.2
Mercosur[c]	44.9
Chile	10.2
Central America[d] and Dominican Republic	9.9
Mexico	66.6
Other[e]	178.1
Andean Community (excluding Venezuela)	7.7
Of which, Colombia	3.0

Mercosur = Mercado Comùn del Sur (Southern Cone Common Market)

a. On a historical-cost basis.
b. Colombia, Ecuador, Peru, and Venezuela.
c. Argentina and Brazil.
d. Includes Panama.
e. Mostly in offshore financial centers.

Source: US Department of Commerce, Bureau of Economic Analysis, www.bea.gov (accessed May 2006).

in the entire troubled Central American region. The FTAA was conceived soon after at the Summit of the Americas in Miami in December 1994 as a crucial part of a broad agenda for hemispheric cooperation on economic, political, social, and cultural issues. Similar rationales underpin the Middle East FTA initiative launched by President George Bush in May 2003.

US-Colombia FTA talks fit the same pattern. As the largest economy and the largest US trading partner among the Andean participants in the FTA negotiations, Colombia clearly stands out from its neighbors. But the primary reason that Colombia merits the attention of US policymakers is the link between trade talks and the ongoing commitment of both governments to stop the cultivation and trade in illegal drugs and to foster peace, stability, and economic prosperity in Colombia and the region. If properly crafted and implemented in conjunction with new Colombian economic programs, an FTA could facilitate economic adjustment and growth, particularly in rural areas of Colombia where the drug trade and armed insurgency commingle.

Production and trafficking of illicit drugs pose threats both to political stability in the Andean region and to security in the hemisphere. Colombia is today the main theater of operations in the war on drugs. The problem is that production easily shifts from one country to another, and consumption in North America continues to encourage more production in South America. The United States and Colombia need to learn the lessons of past drug eradication programs in Bolivia and Peru, which successfully reduced national production but failed to establish viable economic alternatives for the affected farmers. Coca cultivation simply migrated north to Colombia. Proceeds from this black economy, estimated a decade ago to generate revenues equal to about 10 percent of GDP, now finance significant paramilitary operations and contribute to corruption in government and the judiciary. The cost to the economy and to the political and social fabric of the country is significant. The recent Bolivian experience, where damage to the rural economy fed political revolt and destabilized the elected government, is a precedent that needs to be avoided.

The United States and Colombia have common goals regarding drug interdiction and stemming the flow of illicit funds to paramilitary and terrorist organizations. *Plan Colombia* has been a central part of the political and military response. A trade pact obviously cannot solve this problem, but the opportunities created by the new trade regime, in conjunction with effective domestic adjustment programs, can contribute to the overall resolution of the crisis. The hard part is to find viable economic alternatives to drug cultivation that promote economic development and rural employment and stem the flow of illicit funds to paramilitary and terrorist groups. Ultimately, the success of the US-Colombia trade initiatives will turn on progress in these areas.

With these overarching objectives in mind, we now examine specific US and Colombian interests in pursuing a free trade pact.

Colombia's Negotiating Objectives

Colombian officials have taken a pragmatic approach to the FTA negotiations, which they sought for several years prior to the launch of talks in May 2004. Colombia is already highly dependent on merchandise trade with the United States, which accounts for more than 40 percent of Colombian exports (down from a 54 percent share in 1999) and about a quarter of its imports (table 1.3). By comparison, intra–Andean Community trade represented only 15 percent of Colombia's total merchandise trade in 2004 (20 and 11 percent of exports and imports, respectively). Deeper trade relations with its Andean partners, or with Brazil and other South American neighbors, while desirable, cannot substitute for the country's important trade and investment ties with the United States.

What does Colombia stand to gain from an FTA with the United States? In the short run, an FTA would provide only slightly better access to the US market than Colombian exporters already enjoy as a result of trade

Table 1.3 Colombian trade, 1995–2005

	Exports to:					Imports from:					Trade balance	Current account	
Year	World total (billions of dollars)	United States[a] Billions of dollars	Percent share	Andean countries Billions of dollars	Percent share	World total (billions of dollars)	United States[b] Billions of dollars	Percent share	Andean countries Billions of dollars	Percent share	(billions of dollars)	Billions of dollars	Percent of GDP
1995	10.2	3.8	.37	2.0	.19	13.9	4.6	.33	1.9	.13	-3.7	-4.5	-5.0
1996	10.6	4.3	.40	1.8	.17	13.7	4.7	.34	1.8	.13	-3.0	-4.6	-4.8
1997	11.5	4.7	.41	2.1	.18	15.3	5.2	.34	2.2	.14	-3.8	-5.8	-5.4
1998	10.9	4.7	.43	2.1	.20	14.7	4.8	.33	1.9	.13	-3.8	-4.9	-4.9
1999	11.6	6.3	.54	1.7	.14	10.7	3.5	.33	1.4	.14	1.0	0.7	0.8
2000	13.2	7.0	.53	2.2	.17	11.8	3.7	.31	1.6	.14	1.4	0.7	0.7
2001	12.3	5.7	.46	2.8	.22	12.8	3.6	.28	1.4	.11	-0.5	-1.1	-1.5
2002	12.0	5.6	.47	2.3	.20	12.7	3.6	.28	1.4	.11	-0.7	-1.4	-1.9
2003	13.1	6.4	.49	1.9	.15	13.9	3.8	.27	1.5	.11	-0.8	-1.2	-1.8
2004	16.7	7.3	.44	3.2	.19	16.7	4.5	.27	1.9	.11	0	-1.0	-1.0
2005	21.2	8.9	.42	4.2	.20	21.2	5.4	.26	2.3	.11	0	-2.1	-1.7

a. Based on US general imports.
b. Based on total US exports.

Sources: Colombia's Administrative Statistics Department (DANE), 2006; US International Trade Commission, www.dataweb.usitc.gov (accessed May 2006).

preferences under the ATPA, as amended. Those products currently excluded from ATPA coverage would likely be those subject to longer transition periods to free trade, if not outright exclusion, under an FTA, since protection for those products commands strong political support in Washington. In this regard, FTAs are mislabeled—they should be called "freer" trade pacts, with some notable exceptions to the rule.

The negotiations bore out this pragmatic assessment. For example, Colombia was not offered free access to the US sugar market; instead, at the end of the negotiations, US officials agreed to an incremental increase from 25,000 to 75,000 metric tons in the existing tariff-rate quota, plus a small annual growth rate. Overquota tariffs on sugar were not liberalized.[4] Nonetheless, the US offer to Colombia exceeded the modest quota increases accorded the Central American countries in their free trade pact with the United States and elicited strong opposition from the US sugar lobby.

An FTA would provide contractual guarantees regarding the permanency of the trade preferences, in stark contrast to the uncertainty that surrounds whether the US Congress will reauthorize the ATPA before it expires at the end of 2006. Such uncertainty imposes costs on bilateral trade and investment and has contributed to the lackluster FDI in Colombia by US firms—just as it did in previous years when the continuation of trade preferences turned on annual US government decisions whether to "decertify" Colombia for inadequate cooperation in the war on drugs. To be sure, other factors—including Colombia's macroeconomic policies, security environment, and domestic regulatory policies—may be of equal or greater importance in investment decisions. Colombian officials need to make progress on trade liberalization as well as these other issues to spur increased investment in the economy.

While Colombia has undertaken significant economic reforms since the financial crisis in 1999, it still faces important challenges to improve its investment climate and to provide viable alternatives to drug cultivation in rural areas. Chapter 3 examines the country's progress over the past decade on macroeconomic policy and trade and other regulatory reforms as measured by a set of "readiness indicators" originally developed by Hufbauer and Schott (1994). Essentially, these indicators measure the adaptability of an economy to the increased competition that arises from globalization and FTAs. By this standard, Colombia does not fare much better than its negotiating partners in the Andean region.

To an important extent, attracting investment is the key objective of the FTA. If implemented in conjunction with domestic policies that promote macroeconomic stability and enhance productivity, an FTA could make Colombia a much more attractive host for new investment not only by foreign companies but by Colombians as well.

---

4. See *Inside US Trade*, March 3, 2006, 1.

At the same time, an FTA with the United States could provide part of Colombia's policy response to the competitive challenge now posed by China in both home and third-country markets—especially in textiles and apparel. The textiles, clothing, and footwear sector has been a primary beneficiary of the expanded ATPA preferences implemented in 2002. Colombian exports to the United States of these products totaled $641 million in 2005, an increase of 65 percent over 2001–02 average annual levels. The sector now accounts for about 16 percent of Colombia's nonoil exports to the United States. However, with the expiration of apparel quotas under the Multi-Fiber Arrangement at year-end 2004, the competition for US market share among foreign suppliers of textiles and apparel has become more intense. Reinforcing the existing tariff preferences, which still provide a modicum of advantage over East Asian products that are levied the most favored nation rate, and strengthening buyer-supplier relationships with US firms are two ways that an FTA could help blunt the Chinese drive to wrest sales away from Colombian producers.

In sum, the FTA should be seen as part of Colombia's overall development strategy. Many of the reforms that will likely be required by FTA obligations may well parallel changes in domestic economic policies that were sought by the government but were blocked or diluted because there has been insufficient political support to gain legislative approval. In other words, the trade and investment incentives built into the FTA could provide the catalyst to move ahead on the domestic reform agenda. To sustain and augment domestic political support for its market-oriented policies, however, the Colombian government needs to demonstrate that domestic reforms and new trade initiatives will benefit both the rich and the poor.

US Negotiating Objectives

In the US Trade Act of 2002, the Congress included an extensive list of negotiating objectives that US officials must pursue in the course of trade talks for the resulting agreement to qualify for "fast track" implementing procedures (box 1.1). The congressional mandate covers both traditional and nontraditional issues, including some that have been excluded from WTO discussions, such as competition policy and labor standards. The long list explains why US officials require comprehensive coverage of goods, services, and investment in FTAs—combining extensive liberalization of tariff and nontariff barriers to trade with rule-making obligations on labor and environmental policies, government procurement, electronic commerce, and intellectual property rights into what are labeled "gold standard" trade pacts. In brief, what is being sought in the negotiations with Colombia and its Andean partners is an agreement much like the CAFTA-DR but adapted to fit the conditions of US-Colombian trade and the specific domestic economic policies of the Andean partners.

Box 1.1 Principal US negotiating objectives

- Trade barriers and distortions: reciprocally eliminate tariff and nontariff barriers
- Trade in services: reduce or eliminate regulatory and other barriers
- Foreign investment: reduce trade-distorting barriers and reciprocal investment protection
- Intellectual property: accelerate full implementation of the World Trade Organization Agreement on Trade-Related Aspects of Intellectual Property Rights (TRIPS)
- Transparency: public access, timely publication
- Anticorruption: antibribery, equal treatment
- Improvement of WTO and multilateral agreements: expand sector/product coverage and participation in the information technology agreement
- Regulatory practices: promote consultation on proposed rules, transparency and nondiscrimination, and sound science criteria
- Reciprocal trade in agriculture: reduce tariffs and subsidies, support a reasonable adjustment period, and maintain export credit programs
- Electronic commerce: support the most liberal treatment possible and a moratorium on duties
- Labor and the environment: promote greater protection and ensure enforcement
- Dispute settlement and enforcement: strengthen WTO dispute mechanism, improve compliance provisions and standard of review in antidumping.
- Textile negotiations: promote equivalent competitive opportunities for US exports
- Worst forms of child labor: prohibit practice, enforce laws, and cooperate with the International Labor Organization
- Trade remedy laws: preserve US antidumping and countervailing duty and safeguard laws, remedy market distortions
- Border taxes: redress direct taxation disadvantage in WTO rules.

US officials hope that reforms undertaken as part of an FTA will open new export opportunities for US firms, workers, and farmers by reducing Colombia's applied tariffs, which average about 14 percent for imports from the United States, and by opening access for US firms to public procurement tenders and contracts for infrastructure, air transport, and other services. Existing barriers are significant in a limited range of products and services, as reported in chapter 2. Perhaps the most contentious involve agricultural products (chapter 5). In the rule-making area, the most sensitive issues involve labor issues and the enforcement of internationally recognized labor standards—reflecting US concern about the need to make further progress in reducing violence against trade unionists—plus the protection of intellectual property rights, particularly in pharmaceuticals (chapters 6 and 7).

Removal of barriers to trade and investment in goods and services would bolster commercial interests in both countries, and the resulting fillip to Colombian economic growth is also an important US objective of the FTA initiative. A more prosperous Colombia would be better able to address the socioeconomic problems that confront the nation, fuel political unrest, and facilitate the spread of drug cultivation and paramilitary forces. The "deconstruction" of the drug economy will only succeed, however, if there are parallel efforts to generate new economic opportunities in Colombia. That was a prime rationale for passing the original ATPA. US Trade Representative Robert Zoellick argued that extending and augmenting that legislation in 2002 "would serve as a natural complement to *Plan Colombia*." In passing the legislation, the US Congress recognized that the "enhancement of legitimate trade with the United States" would provide economic alternatives to drug cultivation and thus provide "an alternative means for reviving and stabilizing the economies in the Andean region" (as cited in Zoellick 2003).

Both the US and Colombian governments have invested substantial political capital, resources, and manpower to implement *Plan Colombia*. From the US perspective, the FTA can be seen as an important complement to the extensive military cooperation extended to Colombia in 2001 and since renewed and increased by Congress in October 2004 as part of the 2005 National Defense Authorization Act. Much of the US assistance is targeted at counter-narcotics operations, including equipment and training for the Colombian army and police. Other US programs provide funds for alternative economic development and support for human rights and judicial reform. Clearly, US economic assistance cannot be expected to fund the redevelopment of large segments of the Colombian countryside—nor need it do so. The aim of the FTA, coupled with capacity-building initiatives by the US government and domestic and regional development agencies, is to provide the means to produce goods and services and the ability to sell them in both domestic and foreign markets.

Finally, an FTA with Colombia and its Andean partners is part of the incremental process of building a hemisphere-wide free trade regime that has been slowed by numerous setbacks in recent years. The FTAA talks themselves have ground to a halt since the FTAA ministerial meeting in Miami in November 2003. More recently, Bolivia has joined Venezuela in seeking "Bolivarian" alternatives to both the FTAA and the Andean Community. Nonetheless, the rationale for integrating the key economies of North and South America remains compelling—especially for the Pacific nations facing competitive challenges from China and its East Asian neighbors. Given their own recent trade pact with the Mercosur countries, the Andeans could provide a bridge between North and South American participants in the hemispheric talks, which in turn would contribute to progress on the broad socioeconomic, political, and cultural initiatives tasked by the Summit of the Americas declarations. To that end, and to their credit, Colombian officials agreed at the Mar del Plata Summit in November 2005 to undertake consultations with FTAA participants on how to revive the moribund talks. We return to this issue in chapter 8.

Lessons from US FTA Experiences

As of April 2006, the United States had concluded FTAs with 17 countries, listed here chronologically: Israel, Canada, Mexico, Jordan, Singapore, Chile, Australia, Morocco, CAFTA-DR (Costa Rica, El Salvador, Dominican Republic, Guatemala, Honduras, and Nicaragua), Oman, Bahrain, and Peru. Negotiators learn by doing, and over time they have incrementally improved and supplemented coverage and rule-making provisions of the resulting agreements. The US pacts differ somewhat by region, reflecting the particular economic circumstances affecting bilateral trade and investment, but within a geographic region, the FTAs usually follow a similar template. In the Western Hemisphere, the most recent negotiation—on the CAFTA-DR—provides general guidelines for what the United States expects to achieve in its negotiations with Colombia and its Andean partners.

From the recent experience of US free trade pacts with developing countries, one can derive several important lessons that should prove instructive for negotiators of the US-Colombia FTA. Because trade deals require more extensive changes in trade protection and domestic economic policies of the developing-country partner, most of these points highlight what that country needs to do to undertake and sustain FTA obligations with its much richer US partner.

First, FTA negotiations largely involve what the US partner country needs to do to make its market more accessible to trade and investment. What does this mean? Above all, it means ensuring a stable macroeconomic environment, pursuing trade and regulatory reforms, strengthening legal protection (including intellectual property rights), and promoting greater transparency of administrative and regulatory processes. FTAs offer improved access to the US market, but inefficient domestic policies can impose additional costs on production and trade that can price a country's goods or services out of the US market. This lesson is so fundamental that all of chapter 3 is devoted to the "readiness" of Colombia and its Andean partners to make their economies more open to foreign competition.

Second, unlike NAFTA, rights and obligations on labor and environmental policies are now integrated into the body of the trade agreement and are subject to the procedures and disciplines of that FTA's dispute settlement system. The most recent FTAs also include labor and environmental cooperation agreements, appended to the trade pact, that are designed to develop an agenda of concrete projects to proactively redress problems before they adversely affect production, trade, or investment in the country. In most respects, these topics are not on the agenda of WTO discussions or other trade arrangements. In addition, FTAs to which the United States is a party generally seek to expand on the commitments and rule-making obligations undertaken in the WTO, particularly in areas such as services, government procurement, and intellectual property rights. Even when these issues are covered by international accords—such as those administered by the International Labor Organization or the World Intellectual Property Organization—cases of noncompliance with rights and obligations are often not actionable, for political or legal reasons, under dispute resolution procedures. The integration of new rule-making obligations with dispute settlement procedures is both a source of strength of the FTA regime and a source of friction among the partner countries.

Third, each FTA has focused extensively on problems in the agricultural economy of the partner countries. This is not surprising, since farm trade has been subject to less multilateral reform in the postwar trading system than industrial products and because most countries—rich and poor—support and protect their farmers through trade-distorting programs. Each agreement has segregated a class of farm products for special treatment that has ranged from granting an extended implementation period for agreed-upon reforms to outright exemption from the free trade regime (for example, sugar in the US-Australia FTA). Since farm lobbies represent a core element of the supporters of trade reform in the United States, progress in this area is a prerequisite for US negotiators to conclude a trade deal. US trading partners need to make virtue of necessity and develop a strategy to both expand their own agricultural exports, accommodate increased imports of US grains and poultry/meat products, and attract new investment in agricultural processing industries to benefit from higher-value-added production and to foster alternative sources of income and employment in rural areas.

Fourth, US FTAs generally have avoided rules on subsidies and contingent protection measures. The US-Canada FTA deferred action on industrial subsidies pending progress in the then current Uruguay Round of multilateral trade negotiations (and never followed through on promises to revisit the issue after those global trade talks ended). The FTA did not address new rules on farm subsidies at all—which is understandable, since the disciplines would likely be unworkable without parallel restraint by subsidizing countries not signatory to the regional pact. Both the US-Canada FTA and NAFTA did provide special provisions on antidumping and countervailing duties, but only with regard to the review of final administrative determinations by national authorities (basically to replace or expedite judicial review of those rulings). Those trade pacts also gave preferences to Canada and Mexico under US safeguard measures; as a result, trade from the two partners has been exempted from most duties and quotas pursuant to US section 201 cases (for example, in the recent steel safeguards case). However, the special treatment accorded the NAFTA partners has not been replicated in subsequent trade pacts.

In sum, the FTAs to which the United States is a party are comprehensive in coverage and scope of trade reform—though a few notable exceptions mar the record. They offer significant advantages in terms of security of access to the US market, but they often require significant restructuring and adjustments in the partner's domestic economy due to the increased competition in the domestic marketplace. These adjustment burdens involve the public as well as the private sector, since new rule-making obligations often tax the administrative and regulatory capabilities of the partner country. For that reason, technical assistance and other capacity-building initiatives have become a necessary complement to the negotiation of a free trade pact.

Overview of Chapters

This study examines the major issues and the prospective impact of a US-Colombia free trade agreement. While the emphasis throughout is generally on the economic aspects of the proposed FTA, political and security considerations also color the analysis.

Chapter 2 examines bilateral trade and investment between the United States and Colombia and assesses areas of trade complementarities and points of trade friction (including antidumping cases and WTO disputes). Chapter 3 reports on the "readiness" of Colombia and its Andean Community partners for entering into a free trade regime with the United States in terms of the "Hufbauer-Schott" indicators of economic and political stability. Chapter 4 presents the quantitative analyses undertaken for the study using applied general equilibrium (AGE) and gravity models to assess the magnitude of the trade and welfare impacts of a US-Colombia FTA on both countries. The next three chapters then turn to detailed analysis of the most contentious issues in the negotiations: agriculture, labor, and intellectual property rights, respectively. The final chapter summarizes the main findings, offers some lessons for Colombia on how the FTA can support its development strategies, and concludes with the implications of the US-Andean FTAs for broader hemispheric trade integration.

2

Bilateral Trade and Investment

DEAN A. DeROSA, PAUL L. E. GRIECO,
and JEFFREY J. SCHOTT

This chapter examines the current pattern of bilateral trade and investment between the United States and Colombia and identifies those issues that should be given priority in the FTA. The two countries already have strong trade ties; Colombia is second only to Venezuela as the largest trading country in the Andean region, and the United States is its primary importing and exporting partner. However, US investment in Colombia is modest and relatively small compared with US foreign direct investment (FDI) in Peru and Venezuela, as well as other Latin American countries.

The chapter presents summary statistics on US-Colombian trade and investment, as well as calculations of the revealed comparative advantage of US and Colombian product sectors to highlight where an FTA would be most likely to expand trade. Not surprisingly, many of the products identified benefit from high levels of trade protection. In that regard, however, the adage "no pain, no gain" still rings true: The more that sensitive sectors are pushed toward liberalization in the US-Colombia FTA, the more both countries stand to benefit. The chapter also describes the current regimes of tariffs and administrative protection, identifies key barriers to bilateral trade in goods and services that should be reduced or dismantled by the FTA, and examines specific areas of past trade friction between the United States and Colombia and the likelihood that these problems will affect the agreement.

Dean A. DeRosa is a visiting fellow at the Institute for International Economics. Paul L. E. Grieco, doctoral student at Northwestern University's Department of Economics, was a research assistant at the Institute. Jeffrey J. Schott is a senior fellow at the Institute.

Table 2.1   Andean-3 exports, 2005 (millions of dollars)

Country/region	Colombia[a]	Peru[b]	Ecuador[c]	Andean-3 total
The Americas	15,323	8,804	7,932	32,059
United States	8,850	4,760	4,878	18,488
Andean Community	4,181	973	1,486	6,640
Brazil	166	454	88	709
Rest of the Americas	2,125	2,617	1,480	6,222
Rest of the world	5,863	6,788	1,887	14,537
European Union	2,767	2,594	1,216	6,577
China	192	1,983	7	2,182
Japan	353	630	71	1,055
All other destinations	2,551	1,580	592	4,723
Total exports	21,186	15,592	9,818	46,596

a. Data compiled by the Foreign Trade Statistical System of Colombia's National Customs Agency (DIAN).
b. Preliminary data at an annualized rate (based on the first three quarters of 2005).
c. Data reported by Colombia's Exports and Imports Promotion Corporation (CORPEI).

Sources: CORPEI; DIAN; IMF's *Direction of Trade Statistics* database, 2006.

Trade and Investment Overview

Colombia has recorded substantial growth in its exports and imports over the past few years, fueled by strong commodity prices and robust investment in the domestic economy. Exports have increased at an annual rate of 27 percent since 2003, while imports have grown almost as rapidly. Trade with the United States grew briskly as well, but as noted in chapter 1, the US share of Colombian trade has fallen from its peak levels at the end of the last decade (table 1.3).

Bilateral Merchandise Trade

Tables 2.1 and 2.2 present the principal markets for merchandise exports and imports for Colombia, Peru, and Ecuador. The United States is Colombia's leading trading partner by far; US trade with Colombia is larger than the combined exports and imports of Colombia with the rest of the Western Hemisphere and accounts for about 35 percent of total Colombian merchandise trade. By contrast, the Andean Community accounts for 15 percent and the European Union for 13 percent of total Colombian trade. A similar story applies to US trade with Peru, where the US trade share is almost 27 percent, followed by the European Union (15 percent) and the Andean countries (11 percent). Interestingly, the Chinese share of

Table 2.2   Andean-3 imports, 2005 (millions of dollars)

Country/region	Colombiaa	Perub	Ecuadorb	Andean-3 total
The Americas	12,994	7,608	6,376	26,978
United States	6,006	2,536	2,195	10,737
Andean Community	2,290	2,056	2,264	6,610
Brazil	1,383	968	554	2,905
Rest of the Americas	3,316	2,048	1,363	6,727
Rest of the world	8,210	4,248	3,022	15,480
European Union	2,922	1,431	1,121	5,474
China	1,617	886	467	2,969
Japan	705	399	362	1,466
All other destinations	2,965	1,532	1,073	5,570
Total imports	21,204	11,856	9,398	42,458

a. Data from the Foreign Trade Statistical System of Colombia's National Customs Agency (DIAN). Values differ from estimates in table 2.4 by roughly $1 billion. About one-third of the discrepancy arises from cost, insurance, and freight (c.i.f.) and free on board (f.o.b.) valuations; in addition, there are different estimates for chapter 88 (aircraft).

b. Preliminary data at an annualized rate (based on the first three quarters of 2005).

Sources: DIAN; IMF's Direction of Trade Statistics database, 2006.

Peruvian trade has almost equaled that of intra-Andean trade; in Colombia, however, China accounted for only 4 percent of trade in 2005.

According to Colombian customs statistics, the United States is Colombia's principal export market ($8.8 billion in 2005), followed by the Andean Community ($4.2 billion) and the European Union ($2.8 billion). Together, these three partners accounted for about three-fourths of Colombia's total export earnings of $21.2 billion in 2005. The remaining share of the country's exports go chiefly to its trading partners in the rest of Latin America (mainly Mexico and Brazil). Colombia exports comparatively little to Japan or other countries in East Asia (table 2.1).

Colombia's total merchandise imports in 2005 amounted to $21.2 billion, of which $6 billion, or 28 percent, originated in the United States. Following the United States, leading import sources were the European Union ($2.9 billion), Andean Community partners ($2.3 billion), China ($1.6 billion), and Brazil ($1.4 billion). Together, these countries accounted for about two-thirds of Colombia's total import bill (table 2.2).

Tables 2.3 and 2.4 present annual US-Colombian trade broken down by two-digit Harmonized Schedule (HS) classifications for 2003–05. As shown in table 2.3, US exports to Colombia were predominantly manufactures (81 percent). In 2005, the most important US exports of manufactures to Colombia were chemicals and plastics (29 percent) and electrical machinery and equipment (28 percent). Agricultural products represented

Table 2.3   US exports to Colombia, 2003–05 (millions of dollars)

Category/HS classification	2003	2004	2005	Percent share of total, 2005
I. Agricultural products (HS 01-24, 5201-03)	497	575	657	13
Corn (maize)	173	213	231	5
Wheat and meslin	108	106	129	3
Cotton	47	57	52	1
Soybeans, whether or not broken	31	34	42	1
Soybean oilcake and other solid residues from soybean oil	10	20	38	1
Flours and meals of oil seeds or oleaginous fruits	1	24	19	0
Food preparations nesoi	11	14	18	0
Preparations of a kind used in animal feeding	22	14	17	0
II. Petroleum oil, coal, and minerals (HS 25-27)	65	77	169	3
Petroleum oils other than crude	50	59	151	3
III. Manufactures (HS 28-97)	2,874	3,423	4,034	81
A. Chemical and plastic industries (HS 28-40)	1,016	1,274	1,441	29
Organic chemicals (HS 29)	459	622	667	13
Plastics and articles thereof (HS 39)	190	242	297	6
Miscellaneous chemicals (HS 38)	87	93	110	2
Pharmaceuticals (HS 30)	37	60	84	2
Fertilizers (HS 31)	57	61	69	1
Cosmetics, perfumery, soaps, and waxes (HS 33-34)	57	60	65	1
B. Electrical machinery and mechanical appliances (HS 84-85)	1,021	1,221	1,375	28
Bulldozers and other lifting machinery and parts (HS 8425-31)	181	238	287	6
Data processing and other office machinery and parts (HS 8469-73)	221	209	236	5
Television, radio, and transmission equipment (HS 8525-29)	122	191	195	4
Air conditioners, vacuum pumps and ventilators, dryers (HS 8413-24)	107	124	132	3
Engines and turbines (HS 8406-12)	57	71	84	2
C. Transport equipment[a]	180	220	344	7
Motor vehicles other than railway (HS 87)	81	144	191	4
D. Measuring and precision instruments (HS 90)	133	161	223	4
E. Textiles and clothing	160	177	170	3
F. Pulp, paper, and printed material (HS 47-49)	139	124	150	3
G. Articles of base metal (HS 72-83)	80	91	147	3
H. All other manufactured products	144	155	183	4
IV. Imports for repairs or small value transactions (HS 98-99)	107	127	154	3
Total exports (I + II + III + IV)	3,496	4,145	4,962	100

nesoi = not elsewhere specified or included

a. In general, US statistics mirror closely values reported by Colombian authorities, except for a significant discrepancy in HS classification 88 (aircraft). For that chapter, the Colombia's National Customs Agency (DIAN) reports imports from the United States of $500 million (f.o.b.), while the US International Trade Commission (USITC) records US exports worth only $100 million.

Source: US International Trade Commission, www.dataweb.usitc.gov (accessed May 22, 2006).

Table 2.4   US imports from Colombia, 2003–05 (millions of dollars)

Category/HS classification	2003	2004	2005	Percent share of total, 2005
I. Agricultural products (HS 01-24)	1,115	1,254	1,511	17
Coffee	374	406	628	7
Flowers and plants	348	422	425	5
Bananas, fresh or dried	164	165	196	2
Sugar	64	68	70	1
Prepared foods (HS 15-23)	43	54	65	1
Tobacco	55	59	39	0
Fish and crustaceans	31	36	37	0
II. Petroleum and coal (HS 27)	3,096	3,803	4,817	55
Petroleum oils, crude	2,135	2,634	3,140	36
Coal and solid fuels manufactured from coal	440	583	951	11
Petroleum oils other than crude	521	585	727	8
III. Manufactures (HS 28-97)	1,752	1,905	1,982	23
A. Clothing, textiles, and footwear (HS 52-64)	543	644	631	7
Men's or boys' suits, blazers, trousers, not knitted or crocheted. (6203)	191	205	257	3
Women's or girls' suits, dresses, skirts, not knitted or crocheted (6204)	100	117	90	1
Pantyhose, tights, stockings, socks, and other hosiery knitted or crocheted (6115)	22	31	37	0
Sweaters, sweatshirts and similar articles, knitted or crocheted (6110)	32	39	30	0
Women or girls' pajamas, negligees and similar articles, knitted or crocheted (6108)	24	30	25	0
Track suits, ski-suits, and swimwear, knitted or crocheted (6112)	20	18	18	0
Bed linen, table linen, toilet linen, and kitchen linen (6302)	18	24	17	0
Men's or boys' pajamas, bathrobes, and similar articles, knitted or crocheted (6107)	18	17	17	0
Brassieres, girdles, corsets, braces, and similar articles (6212)	11	15	16	0
Gimped yarn and strip nesoi, including manmade textile yarn (5606)	14	16	15	0
B. Gold, precious stones, and jewelry (HS 71)	560	508	408	5
Gold unwrought or in semimanufactured forms, or in powder form	469	419	297	3
Precious and semiprecious stones (no diamonds)	54	48	56	1
Waste and scrap of precious metal	11	16	28	0
C. Base metals and articles thereof (HS 72-83)	125	212	286	3
Tubes, pipes of iron and steel	28	62	99	1
Ferroalloys	24	41	46	1
Articles of aluminum	21	32	45	1

(table continues next page)

Table 2.4   US imports from Colombia, 2003–05 (millions of dollars)
(continued)

Category	2003	2004	2005	Percent share of total, 2005
D. Construction materials (HS 2523; 4409-12; HS 69-70)	157	185	202	2
Portland cement	65	84	96	1
Ceramic sinks, baths, bidets, and similar sanitary fixtures	21	32	38	0
E. Chemical and plastic industries (HS 28-40)	115	148	201	2
F. Travel goods and leather items (HS 41-42)	31	32	36	0
G. All other manufactured products	220	177	217	2
IV. Imports for repairs or small value transactions (HS 98-99)	383	399	461	5
Total exports (I + II + III + IV)	6,346	7,361	8,770	100

Source: US International Trade Commission, www.dataweb.usitc.gov (accessed May 22, 2006).

13 percent of total US exports to Colombia, of which about half were corn and wheat.

By contrast, table 2.4 shows that Colombian exports to the United States are dominated by petroleum and other fuels, which were valued at almost $5 billion, or 55 percent of total shipments to the United States in 2005. Agricultural products accounted for 17 percent of Colombian exports to the United States. Interestingly, sugar exports have averaged about $70 million annually for the past few years, less than 1 percent of US imports from Colombia. Shipments of coffee, cut flowers, and bananas have been far more important, totaling $1.25 billion in 2005. Colombian manufactures accounted for 23 percent of exports in 2005, led by the textile, clothing, footwear ($631 million, or 7 percent of exports), and precious stones ($408 million) sectors.

Trade in Services

As the fourth largest economy in South America, Colombia has a relatively developed and increasingly modern services sector, particularly in the major urban areas of the country such as Bogotá, Cali, and Medellín. Services comprise nearly 60 percent of the Colombian economy.

Like merchandise trade, Colombia's exports and imports of services were sluggish until 2004. Colombia ran persistent services trade deficits over 2000–2004 that averaged about $1.5 billion annually. In 2004, exports of services amounted to $2.2 billion (table 2.5). Travel services (in-country meals, lodging, and transport consumed by tourists and other short-term visitors to the country) accounted for almost half of Colombia's service exports (46 percent), followed by transport services (30 percent) and other

Table 2.5   Colombia: Trade in services, 2000–2004 (millions of dollars)

Sector	2000	2001	2002	2003	2004
Total exports	2,049	2,190	1,867	1,900	2,236
Transport	588	567	539	623	680
Travel	1,030	1,217	967	869	1,032
Other private business services	366	339	293	339	467
Total imports	3,300	3,549	3,294	3,322	4,009
Transport	1,307	1,414	1,202	1,260	1,613
Travel	1,060	1,164	1,075	1,036	1,290
Other private business services	876	912	957	982	1,084
Trade balance	–1,251	–1,359	–1,427	–1,422	–1,773
Transport	–719	–847	–663	–637	–933
Travel	–30	53	–108	–167	–258
Other private business services	–510	–573	–664	–643	–617

Source: Statistics from the Andean Community, 2006.

private business services (21 percent). Imports of services by Colombia in 2004 totaled $4 billion, or about 24 percent of merchandise imports. Transport services (40 percent) accounted for the largest share of these imports, with the remainder divided between travel services (32 percent) and other private business services (27 percent).

On a unilateral basis during the 1990s, and in concert with the World Trade Organization's General Agreement on Trade in Services (GATS) and Decision 439 of the Andean Community establishing a framework for regional free trade in services, Colombia appreciably opened its market to foreign service providers, especially in such areas as financial services, telecommunications, accounting, energy, and tourism (Dangond 2000, USTR 2003a, Coalition of Services Industries 2004). Progress, however, has been more modest in liberalizing other areas of traded services, including legal services, insurance, distribution services, advertising, and data processing. Colombia has not yet undertaken multilateral commitments in the GATS to liberalize access in retail distribution, education, environmental, health care, sports and recreation, or transportation services (WTO 2004).

A common problem in a number of cases is Colombia's requirements for partnership with local services firms or professionals (e.g., legal services) and for limited employment of foreign personnel, especially in the financial services sector. Other "local content" requirements include a commercial presence for insurance and data processing activities and local content requirements for television programming (as high as 70 percent during prime-time broadcasting hours).

Despite the government's support for removing possible barriers, including efforts in cooperation with the United States, electronic commerce in Colombia has progressed at a slower rate than in most other Latin

Table 2.6 Total stock and sectoral distribution of FDI in the Andean-3, 1995–2004

Sector	Colombia	Ecuador	Peru
Total FDI stock in 2004[a] (millions of dollars)	22,278	12,482	13,310
Sectoral distribution[b] (percent of total stock)			
Agriculture	0	2	0
Oil and mining	25	77	14
Manufactures	18	4	14
Electricity	16	0	13
Construction	1	6	1
Commerce	6	5	8
Communications and transport	11	3	31
Other services	2	4	4
Financial services	21	0	14

a. As reported by the UN Conference on Trade and Development (UNCTAD).
b. For Colombia and Ecuador, sectoral distribution is estimated from accumulated FDI flows during 1995–2004, as reported by each country's central bank to the Andean Community. Values for Peru correspond to the sectoral composition of FDI reported by Proinvertir.

Sources: Proinvertir Peru, Andean Community, and UNCTAD.

American countries. However, improvement in phone service, along with wider acceptance of personal computers and Internet hosting, is expected to bring faster growth of e-commerce in the future. US telecommunications firms have a strong interest in participating in this future development, especially in the "unbundled" elements of basic networks and services, including cellular phone networks.

Foreign Direct Investment

Total FDI in Colombia was $22.3 billion at year-end 2004, with almost half of it in extractive industries and financial services and another third in manufacturing industries and electricity (table 2.6). While Colombia attracts substantially more FDI than Peru and Ecuador, its cumulative stock is still substantially lower than in the other major trading countries in Latin America, including Mexico ($165 billion), Brazil ($128 billion), and Chile ($46 billion). In addition, Colombia's FDI stock seems lower than might be expected based on its population (nearly 43 million) and its potential as a lucrative market for foreign goods and services and as a pool of manpower for production and export (UNCTAD 2004).

Foreign direct investment is generally accorded national treatment in Colombia, with only routine screening of proposed long-term foreign in-

Table 2.7 US foreign direct investment in the Andean-3, 2004
(millions of dollars on a historical-cost basis)

Sector	Colombia	Ecuador	Peru	Andean-3 total
Mining	590	499	1,830	2,919
Utilities	21	(*)	(D)	n.a.
Total manufacturing	995	22	250	1,267
Food	82	38	70	190
Chemicals	457	9	107	573
Primary and fabricated metals	12	–3	–70	–61
Machinery	0	0	(*)	0
Computers and electronic products	(*)	0	0	0
Electrical equipment and components	14	0	(*)	14
Transportation equipment	(D)	(D)	–1	n.a.
Wholesale trade	387	95	77	559
Information	69	2	86	157
Professional, scientific, and technical services	26	–2	39	63
Depository institutions	(D)	(D)	(D)	n.a.
Finance and insurance[a]	296	19	143	458
Other industries	(D)	(D)	(D)	n.a.
US total	2,987	814	3,934	7,735

(*) = less than 500,000 (+/–)
(D) = suppressed to avoid disclosure of data of individual companies
n.a. = not available

a. Except depository institutions.

Source: US Commerce Department, Bureau of Economic Analysis, www.bea.gov.

vestments on a nondiscriminatory basis.[1] Complete foreign ownership is permitted, except in activities related to national security and the disposal of hazardous waste. Rights to repatriate profits and remittances are guaranteed under Colombian law, so long as the foreign investment is registered with the country's central bank.

The stock of US foreign direct investment in Colombia was valued at $3 billion at year-end 2004 (table 2.7) and accounted for 13 percent of Colombia's total FDI stock. This is a much smaller proportion of total long-term investment in Colombia than US multinational firms and other investors accounted for during the 1980s, when US investment accounted for as much as half or more of total FDI in Colombia. Total US investment

1. See Coinvertir (2004). For an extensive technical review of legal and other issues surrounding foreign investment in Colombia, see Kenworthy (2003).

in Colombia pales by comparison to US FDI in other South American countries such as Brazil ($33.3 billion), Argentina ($11.6 billion), and Venezuela ($8.5 billion). Even Chile, a considerably less populous but more outward-oriented country with an FTA with the United States, hosts much more US FDI ($10.2 billion) than Colombia.

US FDI in Colombia is concentrated in mining, chemicals, and wholesale trade, which, as shown in table 2.7, together account for nearly half of the country's current stock of US FDI. Compared with other Latin American countries, US FDI in other manufacturing sectors in Colombia seems low in proportion to the country's population and potential market size. For instance, Argentina and Chile attract much greater US long-term investment in fabricated metals and machinery than does Colombia. Attracting more US and other foreign investment in such sectors would spur Colombia's industrialization and industry-based employment.

According to the Office of the US Trade Representative (USTR) (2003b, 2004a), the principal barriers to US foreign direct investment in Colombia are in the petroleum sector. In particular, Colombia requires all foreign investment in petroleum exploration and development to be carried out in association with the state oil company, Ecopetrol. In order to increase oil exploration, Ecopetrol's mandatory share in joint ventures with multinational corporations was recently reduced to 30 percent, along with complementary reform to royalties. Ecopetrol was also restructured, and in mid-2003 it was placed under the control of the new National Hydrocarbon Agency, which henceforth will administer petroleum exploration and development contracts with multinational corporations. The USTR maintains that television broadcast laws and regulations in Colombia also limit US FDI because they require that US and other foreign investors be actively engaged in television operations in their home country and, moreover, that foreign investment in television broadcasting in Colombia involve some transfer of broadcast industry or related technology to the country.

Revealed Comparative Advantage

Using the metric of revealed comparative advantage (RCA) can shed light on those industries that are best positioned to benefit from a US-Colombia FTA. Simply put, comparative advantage suggests that countries specialize in goods that they make relatively efficiently (in terms of the production cost of all other goods) compared with the costs of other nations and then trade for the goods they make less efficiently. Importantly, even if a country is absolutely more efficient (in terms of resources expended in production) compared with other nations in the creation of every possible good, it still stands to gain from specialization in those goods where it is most efficient. Under comparative advantage, it is the differences in country cost structures that provide gains from trade.

How can policymakers identify where a country has comparative advantage? Ideally, analysts could compare production costs across different industries throughout the world. Unfortunately, cost data are rarely available. Instead, Balassa (1965) introduced a measure that relies on propensity to export as a representation of revealed comparative advantage. Revealed comparative advantage is indicated by the ratio of a country's share of exports in a given industry to that industry's share of world exports. If the RCA value of a good is above unity, the country is more likely than average to export—a revealed comparative advantage. If the value is less than unity, it reveals a comparative disadvantage.

While RCA is an indicator of comparative advantage, it suffers several drawbacks. Rather than being a calculation based on production costs, it relies on exports under the current trading regime. If production or export of a particular good is subsidized, that good's revealed comparative advantage will rise, while there is no effect on comparative advantage. Conversely, tariffs or barriers to exports will falsely lower the RCA index of a good. Also, RCA treats all industries equally and does not consider the possibility of expansion. Certain sectors that rely on the presence of natural resources (such as petroleum) face limits to production, while other industries (such as manufacturing) are easier to expand by shifting labor and capital endowments from other sectors. These marginal production costs are important when considering what industries are likely to expand as a result of trade liberalization. Finally, RCA is a past statistic that does not predict future developments. In particular, foreign investment can play an important role in turning an industry from a comparative disadvantage position to one of comparative advantage by spurring technology transfer and augmenting capital and human resources in the local industry.

Keeping these limitations in mind, the RCA indices for Colombia and the United States are presented in table 2.8, calculated at the HS two-digit level.[2] RCA values usually change slowly over time, although they may be affected by one-off factors (such as commodity price spikes). The data are presented here using a three-year average for 2001–03 in order to mitigate the influence of temporary surges or declines in exports.

In the context of a US-Colombia FTA, in which categories of traded goods do the countries have significant comparative advantage? And to what extent do the categories of comparative advantage in one country correspond to those of comparative disadvantage in the other? Strong negative correlation of RCA values between the two countries across

---

2. RCA indices become more indicative of comparative advantage and specialization opportunities as industry disaggregation gets finer. However, the two-digit level allows for a broad look at the structure of US and Colombian exports.

Table 2.8 Revealed comparative advantage of Colombia and the United States in world trade, 2001–03

Harmonized Schedule (HS) classification	Colombia				United States			
	2001	2002	2003	Average, 2001–03	2001	2002	2003	Average, 2001–03
01 Live animals	1.15	.40	.29	.61	.98	.63	.91	.84
02 Meat and edible meat offal	.21	.07	.07	.12	1.50	1.28	1.47	1.42
03 Fish, crustaceans, mollusks, aquatic invertebrates, nes	1.54	1.52	1.32	1.46	.52	.53	.56	.54
04 Dairy products, eggs, honey, edible animal products, nes	1.56	1.04	1.01	1.20	.30	.23	.25	.26
05 Products of animal origin, nes	.48	.44	.36	.42	1.32	1.41	1.49	1.41
06 Live trees, plants, bulbs, roots, cut flowers, etc.	32.94	35.02	34.75	34.24	.25	.24	.27	.25
07 Edible vegetables and certain roots and tubers	.76	.35	.31	.48	.72	.71	.77	.73
08 Edible fruit, nuts, peel of citrus fruit, melons	6.55	6.72	5.98	6.42	1.02	1.08	1.17	1.09
09 Coffee, tea, mate, and spices	32.32	34.96	34.30	33.86	.19	.27	.30	.25
10 Cereals	.01	.02	.02	.01	3.32	2.79	3.08	3.06
11 Milling products, malt, starches, inulin, wheat gluten	1.42	1.67	3.32	2.14	.99	1.15	1.16	1.10
12 Oil seed, oleagic fruits, grain, seed, fruit, etc, nes	.05	.09	.09	.08	2.87	3.07	3.53	3.16
13 Lac, gums, resins, vegetable saps and extracts, nes	.02	.01	.03	.02	1.03	1.06	1.10	1.06
14 Vegetable plaiting materials, vegetable products, nes	.35	.21	.56	.38	.36	.59	.53	.49
15 Animal, vegetable fats and oils, cleavage products, etc.	1.97	1.20	1.65	1.61	.80	.78	.79	.79
16 Meat, fish, and seafood food preparations, nes	.76	.96	1.05	.92	.51	.50	.52	.51
17 Sugars and sugar confectionery	12.31	11.62	11.69	11.88	.46	.37	.42	.42
18 Cocoa and cocoa preparations	1.16	1.13	1.07	1.12	.52	.40	.41	.44
19 Cereal, flour, starch, milk preparations and products	1.58	1.33	1.15	1.35	.84	.72	.76	.77
20 Vegetable, fruit, nut, etc. food preparations	.44	.50	.44	.46	.93	.89	.86	.90
21 Miscellaneous edible preparations	3.52	3.40	2.94	3.29	1.47	1.34	1.41	1.41
22 Beverages, spirits, and vinegar	.26	.29	.30	.28	.42	.39	.44	.42
23 Residues, wastes of food industry, animal fodder	.35	.15	.16	.22	1.76	1.46	1.53	1.58
24 Tobacco and manufactured tobacco substitutes	.86	1.31	1.74	1.31	1.86	1.31	1.38	1.52

25	Salt, sulphur, earth, stone, plaster, lime, cement	2.62	2.64	2.70	2.65	.80	.69	.73	.74
26	Ores, slag, ash	.04	.07	.10	.07	.33	.33	.34	.33
27	Mineral fuels, oils, distillation products, etc.	3.72	3.75	3.69	3.72	.19	.18	.19	.19
28	Inorganic chemicals, precious metal compounds, isotopes	.45	.41	.41	.42	1.28	1.21	1.21	1.24
29	Organic chemicals	.25	.20	.21	.22	1.05	1.02	1.16	1.08
30	Pharmaceutical products	1.11	.82	.65	.86	1.01	.77	.86	.88
31	Fertilizers	.26	.37	.39	.34	1.21	1.24	1.31	1.25
32	Tanning, dyeing extracts, tannins, derivatives, pigments, etc.	4.45	3.51	.50	2.82	1.06	1.04	1.09	1.06
33	Essential oils, perfumes, cosmetics, toiletries	1.24	1.40	1.27	1.30	1.22	1.15	1.21	1.19
34	Soaps, lubricants, waxes, candles, modeling pastes	1.47	1.36	1.26	1.36	1.27	1.16	1.24	1.22
35	Albuminoids, modified starches, glues, enzymes	1.10	1.16	1.14	1.13	1.52	1.42	1.22	1.39
36	Explosives, pyrotechnics, matches, pyrophorics, etc.	.26	.20	.19	.22	1.67	1.67	2.09	1.81
37	Photographic or cinematographic goods	.04	.04	.05	.04	1.30	1.53	1.68	1.50
38	Miscellaneous chemical products	2.03	1.84	1.64	1.84	1.78	1.60	1.67	1.68
39	Plastics and articles thereof	1.05	1.17	1.28	1.17	1.27	1.24	1.24	1.25
40	Rubber and articles thereof	.68	.54	.52	.58	1.02	.95	.90	.96
41	Raw hides and skins (other than fur skins), leather	2.17	2.21	2.27	2.21	1.10	1.05	1.11	1.08
42	Articles of leather, animal gut, harness, travel goods	1.04	.88	.84	.92	.16	.20	.22	.19
43	Fur skins and artificial fur, manufactures thereof	.03	.02	.10	.05	.54	.53	.47	.51
44	Wood and articles of wood, wood charcoal	.21	.25	.21	.23	.68	.64	.64	.65
45	Cork and articles of cork	.15	.13	.08	.12	.26	.29	.33	.29
46	Manufactures of plaiting material, basketwork, etc.	.05	.05	.09	.07	.09	.16	.16	.14
47	Pulp of wood, fibrous cellulosic material, waste, etc.	.02	.01	.02	.02	1.57	1.71	1.78	1.69
48	Paper and paperboard, articles of pulp, paper, and board	1.24	1.25	1.30	1.26	.97	.91	.95	.94
49	Printed books, newspapers, pictures, etc.	2.93	2.52	2.54	2.66	1.59	1.48	1.53	1.53
50	Silk	.07	.03	.02	.04	.11	.14	.17	.14
51	Wool, animal hair, horsehair yarn, and fabric thereof	.23	.23	.25	.24	.09	.10	.11	.10
52	Cotton	.59	.43	.47	.50	1.19	1.12	1.42	1.24
53	Vegetable textile fibers nes, paper yarn, woven fabric	.02	.01	.01	.01	.11	.15	.10	.12

(table continues next page)

Table 2.8 Revealed comparative advantage of Colombia and the United States in world trade, 2001–03 (continued)

Harmonized Schedule (HS) classification	Colombia				United States			
	2001	2002	2003	Average, 2001–03	2001	2002	2003	Average, 2001–03
54 Manmade filaments	.55	.44	.47	.49	.70	.67	.65	.67
55 Manmade staple fibers	.62	.56	.45	.54	.65	.65	.69	.66
56 Wadding, felt, nonwovens, yarns, twine, cordage, etc.	1.90	1.72	1.75	1.79	1.11	1.12	1.25	1.16
57 Carpets and other textile floor coverings	.21	.17	.25	.21	.82	.81	.82	.82
58 Special woven or tufted fabric, lace, tapestry, etc.	1.04	1.25	1.30	1.20	1.21	1.21	.92	1.11
59 Impregnated, coated, or laminated textile fabric	1.74	.62	.91	1.09	1.14	1.09	1.24	1.16
60 Knitted or crocheted fabric	1.66	1.40	1.44	1.50	.73	.84	1.10	.89
61 Articles of apparel, accessories, knit or crochet	1.14	1.01	1.12	1.09	.36	.31	.29	.32
62 Articles of apparel, accessories, not knit or crochet	1.57	1.63	1.86	1.69	.19	.20	.17	.19
63 Other made textile articles, sets, worn clothing, etc.	1.46	1.26	1.21	1.31	.45	.43	.41	.43
64 Footwear, gaiters and the like, parts thereof	.37	.26	.27	.30	.11	.12	.12	.11
65 Headgear and parts thereof	.39	.35	.31	.35	.28	.27	.26	.27
66 Umbrellas, walking-sticks, seat-sticks, whips, etc.	.02	.03	.01	.02	.06	.07	.06	.06
67 Bird skin, feathers, artificial flowers, human hair	.02	.03	.03	.03	.11	.15	.16	.14
68 Stone, plaster, cement, asbestos, mica, etc. articles	.83	.77	.75	.79	.66	.64	.68	.66
69 Ceramic products	1.74	2.11	2.00	1.95	.45	.42	.39	.42
70 Glass and glassware	1.08	1.45	1.33	1.28	1.11	.99	.98	1.03
71 Pearls, precious stones, metals, coins, etc.	.67	1.04	3.13	1.61	1.01	1.01	1.21	1.08
72 Iron and steel	1.28	1.43	1.63	1.45	.39	.37	.42	.39
73 Articles of iron or steel	.69	.63	.55	.62	.81	.78	.77	.79
74 Copper and articles thereof	.29	.31	.41	.34	.52	.56	.64	.57
75 Nickel and articles thereof	.29	.25	.25	.26	.70	.62	.50	.61

76	Aluminum and articles thereof	.70	.76	.75	.73	.70	.69	.68	.69
78	Lead and articles thereof	.76	.63	1.02	.80	.47	.44	.80	.57
79	Zinc and articles thereof	0	0	.01	.01	.16	.18	.21	.18
80	Tin and articles thereof	.04	.02	.01	.02	.39	.41	.41	.40
81	Other base metals, cermets, articles thereof	0	.02	.02	.01	1.51	1.60	1.73	1.61
82	Tools, implements, cutlery, etc. of base metal	.79	.55	.49	.61	.96	.99	.98	.97
83	Miscellaneous articles of base metal	.39	.42	.27	.36	1.06	1.09	1.06	1.07
84	Nuclear reactors, boilers, machinery, etc.	.11	.09	.08	.09	1.06	1.33	1.31	1.32
85	Electrical, electronic equipment	.10	.11	.09	.10	1.01	1.14	1.11	1.09
86	Railway, tramway locomotives, rolling stock, equipment	.05	.01	0	.02	1.43	1.10	1.38	1.30
87	Vehicles other than railway, tramway	.39	.30	.10	.26	.92	.92	.92	.92
88	Aircraft, spacecraft, and parts thereof	.17	.07	.15	.13	3.93	3.64	3.61	3.73
89	Ships, boats, and other floating structures	.07	.04	.05	.05	.93	.60	.56	.70
90	Optical, photo, technical, medical, etc. apparatus	.06	.07	.06	.06	1.94	1.93	1.94	1.94
91	Clocks and watches and parts thereof	.03	.02	.19	.08	.13	.20	.22	.18
92	Musical instruments, parts, and accessories	.01	.01	.01	.01	.89	.98	1.03	.97
93	Arms and ammunition, parts and accessories thereof	.02	.01	0	.01	5.90	3.77	3.36	4.34
94	Furniture, lighting, signs, prefabricated buildings	.43	.35	.46	.41	.60	.58	.54	.58
95	Toys, games, sports requisites	.14	.18	.18	.16	.49	.54	.60	.54
96	Miscellaneous manufactured articles	1.15	1.04	1.05	1.08	.62	.68	.69	.67
97	Works of art, collector's pieces, and antiques	.04	.07	.46	.19	1.21	2.03	2.54	1.93
99	Commodities, nes	0	0	0	0	1.32	1.78	1.32	1.47

nes = not elsewhere specified

Source: Authors' calculations based on 2004 data from the UN Commodity Trade Statistics (Comtrade) database, unstats.un.org/unsd/comtrade (accessed May 22, 2006).

traded-goods categories would indicate substantial complementarity of trade and hence scope for significant welfare-enhancing trade creation under a bilateral free trade agreement.

Colombian Advantages

The RCA indices show that Colombia has a large comparative advantage in trees, plants, and cut flowers (HS 06, with an RCA of 34.24) and coffee, tea, and spices (HS 09, 33.86).[3] Colombia also enjoys a significant advantage in sugars (HS 17, 11.88) and fruits and nuts (HS 08, 6.42). In all of the above cases, Colombia enjoys a natural endowment (its climate) for producing scarce goods that are popular throughout the world. Another obvious case of natural endowments is mineral fuels, oils, and distillation products (HS 27, 3.72), which include petroleum.

Because of its different natural endowments, the United States has a significant comparative disadvantage in these goods.[4] This illustrates complementarities—and potential gains from trade—between Colombia and the United States. However, barriers may be difficult to remove in many of these sectors. Although domestic production of these products in the United States does not fully supply domestic demand, some industries have historically strong lobbies that would surely provoke trade friction if barriers to Colombian imports were to be lowered. The US sugar industry is the most obvious example.

The RCA data also indicate Colombian advantage beyond natural resources: raw hides and leather (HS 41, 2.21), printed books and newspapers (HS 49, 2.66), and ceramic products (HS 69, 1.95). Colombia also holds comparative advantage in certain parts of the textiles and apparel sectors: wadding, felt, nonwovens, yarns (HS 56, 1.79), knitted or crocheted fabric (HS 60, 1.50), and articles of apparel, not knit (HS 62, 1.69).[5] High revealed comparative advantage in these products probably indicates an abundance of unskilled labor.

Of these categories, the United States is at a strong comparative disadvantage in ceramic products (HS 69, 0.42) and articles of apparel, not knit (HS 62, 0.19). Again, complementarity indicates that these products gen-

---

3. A lower disaggregation would probably reveal a comparative advantage in cut flowers and coffee—which are major traditional Colombian exports—and less of an advantage in the other goods within these aggregations.

4. Oil is something of an exception. The United States is a large oil producer, but it consumes oil at an even higher rate and exports little. Thus, the United States has a comparative disadvantage in this category (HS 27, 0.19).

5. Production of these goods is not limited by environmental factors, so it is not surprising that the RCA scores are substantially lower than for natural endowment goods such as coffee.

erate the strongest gains from trade and are also the products most likely to provoke political friction in the United States. In this case, the US textile and apparel industry (particularly its trade unions) are threatened by even stronger import competition if barriers are reduced. On the other hand, the United States has a comparative advantage relative to the world in printed books and newspapers (HS 49, 1.53) and is roughly neutral in raw hides and leather (HS 41, 1.08), knitted or crocheted fabric (HS 60, 0.89), and wadding, felt, and yarns (HS 56, 1.16), indicating that markets other than the United States may be more lucrative targets for Colombian products in these sectors.

Colombian Disadvantages

Colombia's RCA data indicate comparative disadvantages in some natural resource goods such as silk (HS 50, 0.04) and capital-intensive goods such as aircraft (HS 88, 0.13), boilers and machinery (HS 84, 0.09), and electronic equipment (HS 85, 0.10). In all these cases, world export shares exceed Colombian export shares by roughly a factor of 10.

Given differences in natural resource endowments between Colombia and the United States, the RCA data indicate that Colombia stands to gain from importing meat (HS 02, 0.12), cereals (HS 10, 0.01), and oilseeds (HS 12, 0.08) from the United States (1.42, 3.06, and 3.16, respectively). Note, however, that this result conflates true comparative advantage and farm support in the United States. US farm subsidies complicate the analysis of the prospective impact of FTA agricultural tariff cuts, though Colombian farming is not naturally disposed to the large-scale production of grains.

The gains from trade are also apparent where the United States has a comparative advantage in capital-intensive goods, such as aircraft (HS 88, 3.73), optical, photo, technical, and medical equipment (HS 90, 1.94), and arms and ammunition (HS 93, 4.34). Colombia is at a large disadvantage in all of these product categories and stands to gain from lowering barriers to imports from the United States. As Colombian production in these categories is very small, trade friction should be less of a problem in these sectors.

Tariffs and Administered Protection

Traditionally, tariffs and other border measures applied to merchandise trade have been the focus of preferential trading arrangements between countries. As these barriers have come down through negotiated and unilateral liberalization, distortions imposed by nontariff barriers have increased in importance. Starting with the Uruguay Round, negotiators have placed significant emphasis on reducing nontariff barriers as part of trade negotiations, and the FTA with the United States addresses these types of trade barriers as well.

Calculating the protective effect of nontariff barriers is difficult. To provide some sense of the pervasiveness of such measures, "frequency ratios" are used here to identify the incidence (but not the effective rate of protection) of such barriers in specific product sectors (table 2.9). Although the average tariff rate applied to imports is only about 13 percent in Colombia and about 6 percent in the United States, both countries restrict imports through the application of nontariff barriers at high frequency ratios (computed across all nontariff barrier measures), especially in agriculture but also for manufactures (Colombia: 86 and 46 percent, respectively; United States: 75 and 30 percent, respectively). "Core" nontariff barriers covering mainly price and quantity measures restricting imports are appreciably lower for both countries (Bora, Kuwahara, and Laird 2002).

How Colombia's Tariffs and Protection Relate to US Negotiating Goals

Since 1995, the tariff structure of Colombia has conformed to the common external tariff (CET) of the Andean Community customs union, which became fully operational in December 2003 (though Peru only fully implemented the common tariff regime as of January 2006).[6] The CET involves four bands: zero and 5 percent for raw materials and for intermediate and capital goods not produced in Colombia; 10 and 15 percent for goods in the above categories with domestic production registered in Colombia; 20 percent for finished consumer goods; and exemptions for some favored sectors (for example, 35 percent for autos) and for agricultural goods that are covered by the Andean Community price band system. Through that scheme, Colombia enforces tariff rates between 27 and 107 percent for 13 basic agricultural commodities, including wheat, sorghum, corn, rice, barley, milk, and chicken parts, with the avowed purpose of insulating domestic prices from alleged excessive international price fluctuations (chapter 5).[7] Furthermore, not all goods are traded duty-free among mem-

---

6. Peru suspended its trade commitments in 1992 but subsequently agreed in July 1997 to reinstate the Andean free trade area in incremental steps by year-end 2005. See Andean Community, press release, "Peru Fully Incorporated into the Andean Free Trade Area," January 10, 2006, available at www.comunidadandina.org.

7. The Andean Community price band system is also applied to 159 commodities considered substitute or related products. For each product covered, a floor and ceiling price is specified. If the reference import price falls outside the price band, a surcharge or discount may be applied before the tariff is assessed in order to achieve a target domestic price. As reported by USTR (2003b, 2004a), this system lacks transparency and is subject to manipulation to produce arbitrary levels of protection.

bers, and the exemptions list from the customs union agreement has yet to be finalized. If the exemptions list is extensive or covers a number of important products, it would reflect a weak commitment by Colombia and its Andean partners to the new customs union, not unlike the situation surrounding free trade areas established in other developing regions.

In 2004 Andean leaders proposed a unified and somewhat more liberal CET, with zero duties on capital goods, 5 percent on industrial goods and raw materials, 10 percent on manufactured goods (with some exceptions), and 20 percent on "ultra-sensitive" goods. This scheme was scheduled to be implemented in May 2005 but has been deferred.[8] Instead, at their meeting in Lima, Peru in July 2005, the leaders of the Andean countries committed to adopt by mid-December "a common tariff policy . . . incorporating a Common External Tariff with flexibility and convergence criteria among the five countries."[9] This objective has been rendered moot, however, by Venezuela's notification to the Andean Community Secretariat in April 2006 of its intent to repudiate the Cartagena Agreement that created the Andean Community.[10]

Andean Community–wide protection—particularly the variable duties on agricultural imports—has been a central US focus in the FTA negotiations. The United States has vigorously pressed for the elimination or radical reform of those practices.

For nontariff barriers, two areas of particular US concern are the openness of government procurement tenders and protection of intellectual property rights in Colombia (USTR 2003b, 2004a). Although Colombia has recently introduced a number of reforms to its government procurement practices, including eliminating a 20 percent surcharge on foreign bids and streamlining bureaucratic procedures, it has still not signed the WTO Government Procurement Agreement that would require still greater transparency in the tendering of government contracts. In addition, Colombia has been included in recent years on the US Special 301 "watch list" for its failure to protect intellectual property rights, thereby jeopardizing returns to US exporters and investors of a variety of products protected by US and international copyrights, patents, and trademarks, as well as other

---

8. Andean Community Decision 580 (repealing Decision 577), May 4, 2004. Text available at www.ita.doc.gov (accessed March 7, 2005). See also Andean Community, press release, "Andean Ministers Agree to Postpone the Effective Date of the CET and Deepen Commercial Integration," March 5, 2004, available at www.comunidadandina.org (accessed March 7, 2005).

9. Conclusions of the Presidential Discussion at the 16th Andean Council of Presidents, Lima, July 18, 2005, available at www.comunidadandina.org (accessed August 15, 2005).

10. However, Article 135 of the Cartagena Agreement requires that countries that repudiate the pact must still maintain the free trade area for at least five years. See Andean Community, press release, "CAN General Secretariat Receives Official Communication of Venezuela's Withdrawal," April 22, 2006, available at www.comunidadandina.org (accessed May 22, 2006).

Table 2.9 Protection in Colombia and the United States, by HS classification, 1999–2002 (percent)

HS classification	Most favored nation rate Minimum	Most favored nation rate Maximum	Average most favored nation rate	Average applied rate World	Average applied rate Andean Community	Average applied rate United States	Frequency of nontariff barriers[a] "Core" measures	Frequency of nontariff barriers[a] All nontariff barriers
Colombia								
Live animals, animal products	5	20	15.2	14.9	n.a.	14.9	54.1	86.7
Vegetable products	5	20	12.3	11.9	n.a.	12.1	8.7	86.3
Fats, oils	5	20	18.3	18.1	n.a.	17.6	54.8	83.1
Manufactured foodstuffs	5	20	18.2	18.3	n.a.	18.7	12.8	80.7
Mineral products	0	15	5.7	5.9	n.a.	5.6	0	20.6
Chemicals	0	20	9.2	9.5	n.a.	9.1	4.3	76.2
Rubber, plastics	0	20	13.6	14.7	n.a.	13.6	3.8	25.7
Hides, leather products	5	20	12.3	16.0	n.a.	16.1	0	41.3
Cork, wood articles	5	20	13.4	14.7	n.a.	13.5	0	91.8
Pulp, paper products	0	20	10.7	11.5	n.a.	10.5	0	5.1
Textiles, apparel	0	20	17.3	18.4	n.a.	18.1	4.8	89.9
Footwear, made-up articles	15	20	18.6	19.3	n.a.	19.1	29.3	50.0
Stone, mineral products	5	20	14.3	15.1	n.a.	14.3	0	10.4
Precious stones, jewelry	5	20	10.9	16.3	n.a.	12.3	0	0
Base metals, metal products	0	20	9.6	10.2	n.a.	10.1	1.4	18.9
Machinery	0	20	9.6	9.6	n.a.	9.7	0	12.2
Transport equipment	0	35	10.2	10.3	n.a.	10.1	3.8	24.7
Professional equipment	0	20	6.7	7.7	n.a.	7.2	0	11.2
Arms, ammunition	10	20	18.3	18.4	n.a.	18.2	75.0	78.6
Miscellaneous manufactures	5	20	18.1	18.3	n.a.	18.0	2.0	10.0
Works of art	20	20	20.0	20.0	n.a.	20.0	0	14.3
All agriculture	5	20	15.3	15.0	n.a.	14.8	30.5	86.2
All minerals	0	15	5.7	5.9	n.a.	5.6	0	20.6
All manufactures	0	35	13.2	14.3	n.a.	13.7	3.5	45.6
					n.a.	13.6	6.1	49.0

United States

Live animals, animal products	26.4	3.7	2.2	0	0.9	92.9
Vegetable products	163.8	3.5	1.4	0	1.5	65.0
Fats, oils	19.1	3.4	2.0	0	1.4	7.2
Manufactured foodstuffs	350.0	26.9	11.9	3.1	10.0	66.2
Mineral products	7.0	0.3	0.1	0	3.4	4.4
Chemicals	9.2	2.2	1.6	0	2.0	13.2
Rubber, plastics	14.0	3.2	2.4	0	7.1	7.1
Hides, leather products	20.0	3.7	3.1	1.4	0	11.5
Cork, wood articles	18.0	1.8	1.8	0.3	0	49.1
Pulp, paper products	3.4	0.2	0.3	0	0	0
Textiles, apparel	32.5	7.3	7.5	7.3	1.0	57.9
Footwear, made-up articles	48.0	5.7	4.9	4.1	0	5.4
Stone, mineral products	38.0	3.6	3.3	0	0.2	0.9
Precious stones, jewelry	13.5	2.1	1.5	0	0	0
Base metals, metal products	15.0	2.3	1.7	0	20.7	21.3
Machinery	15.0	1.5	1.0	0	11.3	22.7
Transport equipment	25.0	2.4	1.1	0	5.2	62.1
Professional equipment	16.0	2.8	2.1	0	1.4	4.7
Arms, ammunition	5.7	0.9	0.7	n.a.	n.a.	70.0
Miscellaneous manufactures	32.0	2.6	2.0	0.1	0.4	13.5
Works of art	0	0	0	0	0	7.1
All agriculture	163.8	3.5	1.9	0	1.2	74.5
All minerals	7.0	0.3	0.1	0	3.4	4.4
All manufactures	350.0	4.3	2.9	1.1	6.1	29.3
All products	**350.0**	**5.6**	**3.6**	**1.7**	**5.5**	**33.7**

n.a. = not available

a. Frequency ratios cover nontariff barriers on imports from the world in 2001 for Colombia and in 1999 for the United States. Core nontariff barriers cover price control measures, restrictive finance measures, and quantity control measures (excluding tariff quotas).

Source: Authors' calculations based on UNCTAD's Trade Analysis and Information System (TRAINS) database, www.unctad-trains.org.

protection for industrial and other inventions and products (including against piracy of audio, visual, and software products). In 2002, Colombia passed a decree to fully implement Article 39.3 of the WTO Agreement on Trade-Related Aspects of Intellectual Property Rights (TRIPS), taking an important step in protecting test or other data in different forms. This issue is discussed in more detail in chapter 7.

How US Protection Relates to Colombian Negotiating Goals

Because of the Andean trade preferences, the average US applied tariff on Colombian exports is very low (about 1.7 percent; see table 2.8). However, the United States has used other measures to protect its "sensitive" industries in the past. In addition to controls on bilateral trade in apparel, US antidumping measures applied to Colombia's exports of roses and other cut flowers, beginning during the 1980s and ending in 1994, were particularly irksome. However, with removal of the last antidumping measures against Colombian cut flower exports to the United States in 1999, and the final inclusion of cut flowers in the coverage of the expanded Andean trade preference program, trade in this sector has become much less restricted.

There remain, however, numerous other US protection measures covering agricultural products that are politically sensitive in the United States but economically important for Colombia. Recalling the significant revealed comparative advantage found previously for Colombia's sugar exports as well as fruits and nuts, US controls on imports of these products need to be addressed, and at least partially mitigated, during the FTA negotiations. Indeed, given US sensitivity to liberalizing its trade in sugar in previous bilateral FTA negotiations (especially with Australia), even limited expansion of US sugar quotas came grudgingly in the negotiations with Colombia (as well as with Peru).[11]

From Colombia's perspective, US tariffs are not a major problem due in large measure to duty-free preferences extended to imports from Colombia by the United States under the US Generalized System of Preferences (GSP) and the US Andean Trade Promotion and Drug Enforcement Act of 2002 (ATPDEA), which amended and expanded the coverage of the US Andean Trade Preference Act of 1991. Indeed, in terms of the trade, employment, and foreign direct investment supported by these initiatives, Colombia has been a major beneficiary of the Andean trade promotion program. To be sure, the GSP and Andean trade promotion program are

---

11. In 1997, Colombia and Peru were among the top 10 sources of raw sugar imported to the United States, with import market share of 2.3 and 4 percent, respectively (Skully 1998). Though these percentages are small, elimination of the US quota on imports of sugar from Colombia alone could appreciably lower US domestic sugar prices by some 10 percent, according to impact estimates by Tanner (1994) using 1990 data and a range of price elasticity values for US import demand and Colombian export supply of sugar.

subject to important limitations and safeguard measures and can be withdrawn by the United States at any time. By entering into FTA negotiations with the United States, Colombia is seeking to expand and lock in to the fullest extent possible the US trade preferences that it presently enjoys before the ATPDEA's scheduled expiration in December 2006.

Bilateral Trade Friction

For countries whose bilateral merchandise trade exceeded $14 billion in 2005, the United States and Colombia have few serious trade problems. Most involve the use of broad trade policy instruments such as public procurement preferences, farm subsidies and price bands, and protection of intellectual property.

For Colombia, the main problem is US sugar quotas and conditions for access to Andean trade preferences for textiles and apparel products. For fiscal 2005, Colombia's share of the US sugar quota was 25,273 metric tons (compared with 45,175 metric tons for Peru and 11,583 metric tons for Ecuador).[12] As noted above, Colombia would like to expand and make permanent the benefits of the program in all sectors—including all of apparel and footwear and manufactured foodstuffs (including refined sugar). Colombia will also want to negotiate the elimination of nontariff barriers faced by its exports to the United States. These would include, in particular, US barriers to actual or potential exports of animal products, vegetable products (including cut flowers), refined sugar and other manufactured foodstuffs, and wood manufactures.

US complaints against Colombia, as summarized in the USTR's annual report on foreign trade barriers, cover import tariff barriers; import licenses; phytosanitary standards, labeling and certification; government procurement; export subsidies; performance requirements; intellectual property rights protection; services barriers; investment barriers; electronic commerce restrictions; and other barriers (USTR 2004a). The USTR report catalogues a long list of trade complaints, including tariff peaks and agricultural border measures. While Colombia significantly cut import duties on capital and industrial goods as well as manufactured goods, high import tariffs of 35 percent on automobiles and of nearly 100 percent on agricultural products remain. In addition, while Colombia is the largest market for US agricultural exports in South America, US exporters voice concern about import licenses used to restrict agricultural imports of wheat, corn, and chicken, as well as variable agricultural import duties across the Andean Community that established regulated price bands (chapter 5). Moreover, processed food exports from Chile and other Andean Community members (Peru, Ecuador, Bolivia, and Venezuela) enter

---

12. See *Inside US Trade*, November 5, 2004, 16.

Colombia duty-free, while US agricultural exports are subject to high variable duties.

Another implicit tariff barrier that concerns the United States is the 35 percent excise tax on whiskey aged for less than 12 years, considerably higher than the rate of 20 percent for European whiskey aged for 12 or more years (USTR 2005). In effect, these differences discriminate against US imports compared with like products from other countries. However, Colombian officials report that the tax was changed in 2002 and now applies to all liquors regardless of origin and is based on the alcoholic content.

A related concern for the US business community is the poor enforcement of intellectual property rights. The International Intellectual Property Alliance (2003), an influential lobbying group representing 1,300 US-based copyright companies, estimates that Colombian piracy cost US firms about $118 million in lost sales in 2002. However, according to Maskus (2000a), such estimates are probably exaggerated because they assume that current sales levels would not fall if prices rose as a result of eliminating piracy. Specific growing areas of concern are pharmaceuticals and motion pictures. While the Colombian government issued Decree 2085 in 2002, which protects the health certification of pharmaceuticals, US officials remain concerned about counterfeit pharmaceutical products, especially in rural areas (USTR 2005, 135). Intellectual property issues are discussed in more detail in chapter 7.

US firms also seek national treatment and access to bid on government procurement contracts in Colombia.[13] In 2003, the Colombian government established Law 816 to protect national industries and provide preferential treatment for bids that include Colombian goods or services. As a result, US suppliers have been effectively prevented from participating in or competing for Colombian government procurement contracts to supply various services, including express delivery, financial services, and telecommunications.

While there are concerns over numerous areas of bilateral trade, there have been few formal legal disputes between the United States and Colombia. The United States does not have any outstanding antidumping or countervailing duty orders against Colombia. Since 1980, the United States has initiated six antidumping investigations against Colombian exports, four of which involved trade in fresh cut flowers. Half of these cases ended with negative determinations of dumping or injury; two cases were terminated; and duties were actually applied in only one case, fresh cut flowers, initiated in 1986. Those duties were revoked in 1999 (table 2.10).

Colombia has pursued only three antidumping investigations against US products and has imposed duties only twice since 1990 (table 2.10). All

---

13. See Deputy US Trade Representative Peter Allgeier's speech, Importance of US-Andean Trade Accord, September 29, 2004, available at www.ustr.gov (accessed June 28, 2006).

Table 2.10 US-Colombia trade cases

US products subject to Colombian antidumping investigations

Product	Initiation	Provisional measures	Final measures	Notes
Orthophosphoric acid	August 14, 1991	April 22, 1992 Provisional margin: 77.76 percent	August 14, 1992 Final margin: 77.76 percent	Duties were imposed on imports from the United States and Belgium
	Antidumping reviews: January 26, 1998 October 1, 2002		July 13, 1998 Revised margin: 56.26 percent December 19, 2002	2002 antidumping review terminated duties
Homopolymer polypropylene	June 18, 1993	November 3, 1993 Provisional margin: 27.62 percent	March 18, 1994 Final margin: 29.55 percent	
	Antidumping review: October 25, 2002		October 27, 2003 Revised margin: 44.22 percent	Antidumping order subject to annual review
Polyvinyl chloride	September 8, 1998	November 3, 1998 Provisional margin: 19.10 percent	Case suspended: March 5, 1999	No action since 1999

Table 2.10 US-Colombia trade cases *(continued)*

Colombian products subject to US antidumping investigations

Product	Case no.	Year	Investigation outcome	Status
Oil country tubular goods	AD-995	2002	Terminated	
Fresh cut roses	AD-684	1994	Negative	
Portland cement	AD-356	1987	Negative	
Fresh cut flowers	AD-329	1986	Affirmative	Duty revoked in May 1999
Fresh cut roses	AD-148	1983	Negative	
Fresh cut roses	AD-43	1981	Terminated	

WTO disputes involving Colombia and the United States

Case number	Year	Complainant	Respondent	Product	Status
WT/DS78/1	1996	Colombia, Mexico	United States	Safeguard measure against imports of broom-corn brooms	Terminated in January 1999

Sources: World Trade Organization, www.wto.org; personal communication with Diane Mazur, US International Trade Commission (USITC), February 2005; and USITC Web site, ia.ita.doc.gov/trcs/foreignadcvd/colombia.html (accessed May 22, 2006).

the Colombian cases initiated against the United States involved chemical products. Duties of almost 80 percent were imposed in 1992 on imports of orthophosphoric acid; the dumping margins were reduced in 1998 and the order was terminated in 2002. Colombia also imposed antidumping duties of almost 30 percent on US shipments of polypropylene; these duties were increased after a 2002 review to 44 percent and remain in effect. The third case, which involved polyvinyl chloride, was suspended in March 1999.

Nor have there been many bilateral disputes between the two countries under the WTO. The United States has not filed any WTO disputes against Colombia, while Colombia has filed just one case against the United States, the *Broom-Corn Brooms* case (WT/DS78/1) in 1996, which was terminated in January 1999.

3

Colombia's Readiness for a Free Trade Agreement

PAUL L. E. GRIECO and JEFFREY J. SCHOTT

The ultimate objective of regional integration is to promote a higher standard of living for all citizens. A free trade agreement can contribute to that desired result, but the trade pact alone is not sufficient to ensure sustained growth. Reaping the benefits of an FTA requires a sustained commitment to economic reform and to structural adjustments in the economy. Trade agreements create opportunities; they do not guarantee sales.

To take advantage of new trade and investment reforms, countries need to implement domestic economic policies that promote stable macroeconomic policies and a tax and regulatory climate conducive to sustained investment and employment generation. Governments must be prepared to allow greater international competition in domestic markets and to manage the adverse effects on local firms, workers, and communities that arise due to shifts in production and employment between and within sectors of the economy. Even if an FTA gives impetus to new investment and economic growth, if a country is ill prepared to address adjustment problems, the political consensus for economic reform could collapse and generate a reform backlash (as occurred in recent years in Bolivia and Venezuela, with repercussions now felt throughout South America).

In an era of globalization, countries cannot afford to defer policy reforms that allow them to make better use of their own resources and attract investment from abroad. Regardless of whether they engage in FTAs,

Paul L. E. Grieco, doctoral student at Northwestern University's Department of Economics, was a research assistant at the Institute for International Economics. Jeffrey J. Schott is a senior fellow at the Institute.

countries that do not keep pace with the competition in global markets will come under increasing pressure to maintain export shares and slow import penetration in the domestic market. Countries that stand pat fall behind. FTAs are not magic bullets to cure competitiveness problems, but they can contribute as part of a broader development strategy.

This is not to suggest, however, that FTAs are a cost-free strategy for political leaders. Because FTAs often require reforms of border barriers and domestic policies that distort trade and investment in goods and services, they can spur substantial restructuring of the domestic economy; indeed, they *should* pose adjustment challenges because their goal is to remove obstacles to trade and create a more competitive domestic market.

Due to their comprehensive coverage, FTAs with the United States tend to be the most welfare enhancing but also the most demanding of broad adjustments by the developing-country partner. Indeed, one of the most important US criteria for selecting FTA partners is the political commitment to undertake domestic reforms needed to implement a comprehensive and reciprocal free trade pact. For that reason, countries need to gauge their "readiness" to undertake economic reforms that will enable them to take advantage of a prospective FTA, especially one involving the United States.

The definition of readiness developed here draws heavily on readiness indicators originally developed by Hufbauer and Schott (1994). The key is stability and sustainability: A country with a track record of structural strength is not likely to plunge into crisis in the event of economic turbulence. This chapter surveys Colombia's readiness and compares it to that of its Andean partners. We start with a brief comment on Colombia's economic performance over the past decade and then turn to how the country fares under the Hufbauer-Schott readiness indicators.

Broad Measures of the Colombian Economy

Colombia is a middle-income developing economy whose GDP is less than 1 percent the GDP of the United States. Table 3.1 presents basic figures on Colombia's GDP and unemployment over the past decade. For most of this period, economic growth has been sluggish, though the commodity price boom of the past few years has fueled more robust performance and boosted per capita income (which had not significantly changed over the previous decade). Based on purchasing power parity, the average Colombian income in 2004 was less than one-fifth that of the average US citizen and 71 percent of that of the average Mexican.[1]

---

1. Like most developing countries, market exchange rates severely underestimate purchasing power in Colombia due to low prices for nontradable goods and services. Therefore, when considering Colombian living standards, the purchasing power parity measure is the better metric. In 2004 per capita gross national income was $6,820 in Colombia, $9,590 in Mexico, and $39,710 in the United States (data from World Bank 2006).

Table 3.1 Colombia: GDP and unemployment, 1996–2005

Indicator	1996	1997	1998	1999	2000	2001	2002	2003	2004	2005
Indicators of economic activity										
Real GDP growth (percent)	2.1	3.4	0.6	-4.2	2.9	1.5	1.9	3.9	4.8	5.1
Unemployment[a] (percent)	11.2	12.4	15.3	19.4	17.2	18.2	17.6	16.7	15.4	13.9
Size of the economy (billions)										
GDP, current pesos	100,711	121,708	140,483	151,565	174,896	188,559	203,451	228,517	254,405	283,848
GDP, current dollars at market exchange rate	97	107	98	86	84	82	81	79	97	122
Per capita income										
Constant pesos	1,915,679	1,945,793	1,919,323	1,803,375	1,821,446	1,814,376	1,817,455	1,854,729	1,909,467	1,973,590
Dollars based on purchasing power parity	6,252	6,456	6,439	6,138	6,334	6,461	6,585	6,874	7,216	7,565
Prices										
Exchange rate (pesos/dollar)	1,037	1,141	1,427	1,759	2,087	2,300	2,508	2,876	2,628	2,322
Annual inflation rate (percent)	20.8	18.5	18.7	10.9	9.2	8.0	6.3	7.1	5.9	5.0

a. Based on data for 13 metropolitan areas. Reported data corresponds to annual averages of monthly observations and includes estimates of "hidden unemployment."

Sources: IMF (2006); ECLAC (2005); Colombia's Administrative Statistics Department (DANE) household survey.

Colombia's weak economic performance for most of the past decade contributed to an unhealthy increase in urban unemployment, which reached almost 20 percent at the end of the 1990s. Since then, the economic revival of the past few years has mitigated this problem somewhat, though the unemployment rate still hovered around 14 percent in 2005. Moreover, while the urban unemployment statistics are troubling, they probably underestimate the national problem given the prevalence of underemployment in rural areas—reflected by the high levels of poverty in the rural population. In 1999, the rural poverty rate was 79 percent of the population, while urban poverty stood at 55 percent.[2]

Table 3.2 presents national and sectoral growth rates for 1995–2005 based on Colombian data denominated in real pesos. Average annual real GDP growth over the period was 2.35 percent but was very uneven—in part due to the substantial contraction in 1999 following the 1998–99 financial crisis and an earthquake that hit central Colombia in January 1999. Real GDP fell 4.2 percent in 1999, with contractions in every sector, with the exceptions of mining and community services. After the crisis, the Colombian economy was slow to recover; however, annual growth has averaged about 4 percent since 2003 (table 3.2).

At the sector level, construction has been Colombia's most volatile sector, with heavy downturns in 1996 and 1998–99. Construction has grown by an annual average of 11 percent since 2002. Mining and petroleum boomed during the 1990s, then crashed in 2000–2001. After a sharp recovery in 2003, growth in this sector has been sluggish, despite favorable price trends. The financial sector has gone through deregulation and has seen a steep increase in foreign ownership during the last decade. After severe contraction as a result of financial crisis, the financial intermediation sector also has rebounded sharply since 2003. The agricultural sector stagnated for much of the decade but has grown by 2.6 percent per year since 2003, benefiting largely from increases in commodity prices, particularly coffee, Colombia's largest agricultural export.

Turning to the relative size of sectors within the economy, table 3.3 shows the relative sector shares of value added in 1995, 2000, and 2005. Overall, Colombian shares of value added have been stable over the past decade. There has been only a small drop in the share of the low-productivity agricultural sector, which accounts for 13 percent of total production. Manufacturing and construction, two sectors that might be expected to expand as part of development, have been stagnant or shrunk modestly. There has been some growth in mining and petroleum—from 3.7 to 4.8 percent of production—most likely due to higher energy prices and some increased investment. The largest gains were in the community

---

2. Based on the national poverty line. The national poverty estimate was 64 percent. See World Bank, *World Development Indicators 2005*, for details on methodology.

Table 3.2 Colombia: Real GDP growth by sector, 1995–2005 (annual percent change)

Sector	1995	1996	1997	1998	1999	2000	2001	2002	2003	2004	2005[a]
Agriculture	3.7	-1.2	0.7		0	3.8	-0.4	0.1	2.7	4.2	2.1
Mining and petroleum	14.6	7.3	3.7	15.6	18.5	-10.3	-6.1	-0.5	13.7	3.0	3.0
Electricity, gas, water	2.6	4.9	1.0	1.8	-4.2	0.9	3.0	0.8	2.2	2.7	3.2
Manufacturing	5.5	-1.4	0.5	-0.2	-8.6	11.8	1.3	2.6	4.5	7.0	4.0
Construction	1.9	-12.9	2.2	-7.2	-27.0	-3.9	3.9	12.4	13.3	10.6	12.6
Wholesale/retail trade, repair, hotel/restaurant services	3.8	-0.9	1.7	-1.6	-15.4	7.3	3.1	1.9	5.4	6.1	9.2
Transport, storage, and communications	6.5	3.8	5.8	2.5	-1.9	1.5	4.0	2.4	2.9	5.4	5.1
Financial establishments, insurance, business services	8.6	5.2	4.9	-1.3	-4.9	-1.0	2.2	2.3	5.7	4.5	3.5
Community and personal social services	9.0	16.2	7.2	1.8	3.3	0.6	0.7	-0.3	-0.2	2.7	4.0
Financial intermediation	26.0	16.7	2.7	-7.3	-19.5	-15.1	2.5	-6.9	11.8	11.9	8.5
GDP	5.2	2.1	3.4	0.6	-4.2	2.9	1.5	1.9	3.9	4.8	5.1

a. Annualized estimate (based on first three quarters of the year).

Source: Colombia's Administrative Statistics Department (DANE), Directorate for Analysis and National Accounts, 2005.

Table 3.3 Colombia: Sector shares of value added, 1995, 2000, and 2005 (percent)

Sector	1995	2000	2005[a]
Agriculture	13.3	13.0	13.3
Mining and petroleum	3.7	4.9	4.8
Electricity, gas, water	3.1	3.1	2.9
Manufacturing	14.6	14.4	14.3
Construction	7.1	4.0	5.4
Wholesale/retail trade, repair, hotel/restaurant services	12.1	10.6	11.5
Transport, storage, and communications	7.2	7.9	8.2
Financial establishments, insurance, business services	17.3	17.3	17.4
Community and personal social services	16.3	20.9	19.4
Financial intermediation	5.3	3.9	2.7

a. Annualized estimate (based on first three quarters of the year).

Source: Colombia's Administrative Statistics Department (DANE), Directorate for Analysis and National Accounts, 2005.

and personal services sector, which rose from 16.3 to 19.4 percent of the economy. An FTA is likely to cause a shift in production between sectors—one of the aims of such an agreement would be to increase foreign direct investment in Colombia in more productive sectors.

The financial crisis is also the dominating event in the current account history (table 3.4). Colombia maintained a current account deficit of 5 percent of GDP during the mid-1990s and suffered during the financial crises that pervaded Latin America in 1998–99. Subsequently, the current account corrected to a surplus of 1 percent of GDP, primarily due to a 27 percent decline in merchandise imports between 1998 and 1999. After the crisis, the current account again went into deficit in 2001, reaching almost 2 percent of GDP in 2002–03. Recent strong commodity prices, particularly oil, have boosted export earnings and helped narrow the current account deficit to 1 percent of GDP in 2004.

For foreign exchange, Colombia is highly dependent on shipments of petroleum, which account for about a quarter of all merchandise exports. The value of coffee exports has declined sharply from its 1997 peak and now accounts for only 6 percent of merchandise exports, down from almost 25 percent in the mid-1990s. Over the past decade, foreign transfers, presumably in the form of household remittances from emigrants, have become an important source of foreign income. In 2003, nearly $3.5 billion in transfers came into Colombia, an amount roughly equivalent to Colombia's petroleum income.

Table 3.4 Colombia: Current account, 1994–2005[a] (millions of dollars)

	1994	1995	1996	1997	1998	1999	2000	2001	2002	2003	2004	2005p
Current account balance	−3,674	−4,528	−4,642	−5,751	−4,858	671	779	−1,089	−1,359	−974	−938	−1,930
(percent of GDP)	(−4.5)	(−4.9)	(−4.8)	(−5.4)	(−4.9)	(0.8)	(0.9)	(−1.3)	(−1.7)	(−1.2)	(−1.0)	(−1.6)
Goods balance	−2,229	−2,546	−2,092	−2,638	−2,450	1,775	2,648	579	238	555	1,346	1,594
General commerce	−2,526	−2,739	−2,211	−2,768	−2,686	1,664	2,444	407	141	141	1,119	1,384
Exports	8,546	10,155	10,539	11,534	10,930	11,563	13,099	12,233	11,794	12,933	16,442	20,815
Coffee	1,990	1,832	1,577	2,259	1,893	1,324	1,069	764	772	809	949	1,471
Petroleum and derivatives	1,313	2,185	2,895	2,707	2,329	3,757	4,569	3,285	3,275	3,383	4,227	5,559
Carbon products	550	596	849	886	936	848	861	1,179	990	1,422	1,854	2,598
Iron	119	185	169	161	120	154	211	235	272	416	628	738
Nontraditional exports[b]	4,575	5,358	5,050	5,521	5,653	5,481	6,388	6,770	6,484	6,902	8,784	10,449
Imports	11,072	12,894	12,750	14,302	13,616	9,900	10,655	11,826	11,653	12,792	15,324	19,431
Consumer goods	1,818	2,476	2,365	2,732	2,621	1,858	1,991	2,296	2,465	2,425	2,818	3,530
Intermediate goods	4,456	5,653	6,041	6,058	5,710	4,565	5,425	5,290	5,331	5,844	7,268	8,629
Capital goods	4,798	4,766	4,344	5,511	5,285	3,477	3,239	4,240	3,857	4,523	5,237	7,271
Special operations of the commercial sector	297	193	119	130	236	111	204	172	96	414	227	210
Exports	513	438	427	531	550	474	639	615	521	879	782	912
Imports	216	245	308	401	314	363	435	443	425	466	554	702

(table continues next page)

Table 3.4 Colombia: Current account, 1994–2005[a] (millions of dollars) *(continued)*

	1994	1995	1996	1997	1998	1999	2000	2001	2002	2003	2004	2005p
Services	-1,055	-1,185	-1,193	-1,501	-1,462	-1,204	-1,259	-1,412	-1,435	-1,439	-1,679	-2,089
Exports	1,571	1,700	2,192	2,155	1,955	1,940	2,049	2,190	1,867	1,921	2,255	2,666
Imports	2,626	2,885	3,385	3,656	3,416	3,144	3,308	3,602	3,302	3,360	3,934	4,755
Factor rents	-1,458	-1,596	-2,062	-2,326	-1,697	-1,355	-2,283	-2,610	-2,867	-3,398	-4,332	-5,525
Income	702	678	716	920	949	923	1,054	919	717	553	671	1,075
Outflows	2,161	2,274	2,778	3,246	2,646	2,278	3,337	3,529	3,584	3,951	5,003	6,600
Current transfers	1,069	799	706	713	750	1,455	1,673	2,354	2,706	3,309	3,727	4,089
Income	1,262	1,033	924	931	912	1,703	1,911	2,656	3,010	3,565	3,996	4,349
Outflows	193	234	218	217	162	248	238	302	304	256	270	260

p = preliminary

a. After 1994, methodology conforms to the IMF's *Balance of Payments Manual*.
b. Exports of nonmonetary gold and emeralds are classified under nontraditional exports.

Source: Banco de República, Colombia.

In summary, broad economic measures reveal that the Colombian economy stagnated for much of the past decade until a combination of good luck and good policy contributed to a solid record of 4 percent growth from 2003–05. The structure of the economy is not substantially different from 1995. The financial crisis in the late 1990s produced a jarring current account correction and erased what little gains had accrued prior to that point. Unemployment remains extremely high, even though levels have dropped significantly since the peak in 2000.

As a result of the financial crisis, subsequent weak economic performance, an expanding amount of external debt, and high fiscal deficits, Colombia's current president, Alvaro Uribe, entered into a two-year stand-by arrangement with the International Monetary Fund (IMF) worth $2.3 billion in January 2003. The IMF plan called for fiscal austerity to reduce Colombia's debt burden, lower inflation, and improve financial supervision. In July 2004 the IMF reported that the program was on track and was expected to reduce the public debt burden to 52 percent of GDP by year-end 2004 (IMF 2004). Colombia did not draw on the IMF funds for the duration of the stand-by arrangement. A new and smaller IMF tranche ($613 million) was approved in May 2005 for a period of 18 months.[3]

In this environment, FTA-induced reforms can help strengthen economic performance. At the same time, further opening of the economy to trade and investment in goods and services will exert additional pressure on firms to restructure their operations, and on workers and farmers to adjust to the more competitive environment. Examining a composite of more specific indicators can serve to gauge how Colombia might cope with these changes.

Hufbauer-Schott Readiness Indicators

To better quantify the concept of readiness, Hufbauer and Schott (1994) developed a composite readiness indicator, later updated by Schott (2001). While not comprehensive, the readiness indicators establish a policy metric gauging the adaptability of an economy to economic reform, including the opening of domestic markets to foreign competition under an FTA.

The overall indicator is divided into three components that measure macroeconomic stability, microeconomic flexibility, and political sustainability. These components are weighted equally in the computation of the readiness indicator. For the most part, the readiness indicators are developed using a three-year average for each of the included series.[4] Each series

---

3. See IMF press release 05/95, revised May 2, 2005.

4. With the following exceptions: one component of the macroeconomic indicator—currency stability—is concerned with exchange rate volatility rather than appreciation or depreciation, so a three-year standard deviation is used rather than the three-year average; one component

is scored on a 0 to 5 scale, calibrated in Hufbauer and Schott (1994) and updated in Schott (2001), with zero being not ready and 5 being most ready. Table 3.5 provides a summary of the calibration of the readiness indicators.

The indicator serves two purposes. First, it broadly sums up the competitive strength of an economy. A poor showing in any single component of the indicators does not necessarily imply structural weakness, but it is a useful red flag. From this point of view, the overall indicator represents a useful tally of red (and orange) flags. It is easier for a government to rationalize a low savings rate as its cultural fate if it does not have to consider a spendthrift government on the same page. This is important because structural problems (an entrenched poor population, overregulation or misguided regulation, a spendthrift government) are likely to impact several components and have a large effect on the indicator. One-off circumstances will impact a narrower set of components, and therefore produce a smaller effect on the readiness score.[5] The indicator's second strength comes from examining the underlying data. While the indicator serves as a "service engine" light, the warning could be due to any combination of problems. To fix the problem, policymakers must look under the hood. Considering the set of indicator components that drag down an economy's score and determining what policies can address that set of problems is a first step in the investigation.

Macroeconomic Indicator

The macroeconomic indicator covers five core aspects of economic activity: price stability, budget discipline, national savings, external debt, and exchange rate stability. It attempts to quantify the attractiveness of the broad economy to foreign investment, especially long-term direct investment. The variability of the real exchange rate provides a measure of exchange risk to investors. At home, price stability—a modest level of inflation—will encourage savings and investment and is an indicator of economic well being. The indicators also consider a country's levels of external debt and national savings, which could signal a country's dependence on international capital and vulnerability to currency and interest rate fluctuations.[6] A large public deficit is also susceptible to these risks,

---

of the microeconomic indicator—market-oriented policies—is a subjective determination based on policy history and so has no underlying series; finally, the policy sustainability indicators are concerned with the current political and social environment rather than recent changes, so they rely on the most recent data available rather than three-year averages.

5. An important corollary to this argument is that small differences in the indicator (either across economies or across time) are not very significant. Large shifts and differences—a consequence of several components—are much more important.

6. Schott (2001) added gross national savings to the macroeconomic indicator.

Table 3.5 Readiness indicator scales

Indicator	Metric	Measurement	Score 0	1	2	3	4	5
Macroeconomic								
Price stability	December-on-December inflation	3-year average	Over 45 percent	35 to 45 percent	25 to 35 percent	15 to 25 percent	5 to 15 percent	Less than 5 percent
Budget discipline	Nonfinancial public sector balance	3-year average	Over 8 percent deficit	6.5 to 8 percent deficit	5 to 6.5 percent deficit	3.5 to 5 percent deficit	2 to 3.5 percent deficit	Less than 2 percent deficit or surplus
Gross national savings	Percent of GDP	3-year average	Under 6 percent	6 to 12 percent	12 to 18 percent	18 to 24 percent	24 to 30 percent	Over 30
External debt	Percent of exports of goods and services	3-year average	Over 430 percent	360 to 430 percent	290 to 360 percent	220 to 290 percent	150 to 220 percent	below 150 percent
Currency stability	Real effective exchange rate	3-year standard deviation	Over 25 percent volatility	20 to 25 percent volatility	15 to 20 percent volatility	10 to 15 percent volatility	5 to 10 percent volatility	0 to 5 percent volatility
Microeconomic								
Market-oriented policies	Subjective appraisal		A score is awarded based on policies with respect to government regulation, privatization, and barriers to trade and investment. Proposed policy changes that have not yet been implemented are not taken into account.					
Reliance on trade taxes	Trade taxes as percent of total revenue	3-year average	Over 25 percent	20 to 25 percent	15 to 20 percent	10 to 15 percent	5 to 10 percent	Less than 5 percent
Political sustainability								
Human development	UN Human Development Index	Most recent year	Under .50	1.0: .50 to .55 1.5: .55 to .60	2.0: .60 to .65 2.5: .65 to .70	3.0: .70 to .75 3.5: .75 to .80	4.0: .80 to .85 4.5: .85 to .90	Over .90
Freedom House indices	Freedom House political rights and civil liberties indices	Average of political rights and civil liberties scores for most recent year	7	6	5	3.0: 4 3.5: 3	2	1

Source: Schott (2001).

with the added danger that direct pressure on the government balance sheet may lead to recidivist policies.[7] The simple average of these five scores is the macroeconomic indicator.

Microeconomic Indicator

The microeconomic indicator measures the strength of the government's commitment to market-oriented policies. The first component is reliance on trade taxes.[8] Tariffs are one of the easiest taxes for a developing nation to collect; a free trade agreement will necessarily slash tariff revenue from bilateral trade. If tariff revenue is a large share of government revenue, it may be difficult to replace. Unless accompanied by tax reform and restructuring, countries could face budget shortfalls that could make it difficult to finance the requisite adjustment policies needed to complement FTA trade reforms. Of course, tariff cuts generally are phased in over time, with the highest (on the most import-sensitive products) accorded the longest transition, which minimizes the fiscal risk and allows time for the phased implementation of tax reforms. The second component is a subjective evaluation of the country's commitment to market-oriented policies—which in turn contributes to investor confidence. Included in this component is the size of the private sector, recent privatization and deregulation, and liberalization of tariff and nontariff barriers to trade. The microeconomic indicator is the average of these two components.

Policy Sustainability Indicator

The final component of the readiness indicator is a hybrid of political and socioeconomic factors. The policy sustainability indicator tries to measure the ability of the domestic political process to distribute the gains from trade and maintain support for liberalization. National "quality of life" indicators can help determine how gains will be distributed. Unfortunately, the concept of quality of life itself is extraordinarily difficult to measure; the United Nations Development Program's (UNDP) Human Development Index (HDI) is used here as a proxy for national quality of life, a composite index of health, education, and per capita incomes. The

---

7. The readiness indicators measure the nonfinancial public sector balance, which unifies federal and subnational budgets. This is important in the case of Colombia because a portion of the central government deficit is traditionally offset by a surplus in local budgets (partially due to revenue transfers from the central government).

8. This component, like the macroeconomic indicators, is scored as a three-year average calibrated to a five-point scale in Hufbauer and Schott (1994).

HDI is produced at a two-year lag, so by necessity the index of the latest year available is used to compute the policy sustainability indicator.[9]

After basic living standards, political and economic freedom are used as essential indicators of policy sustainability. The proper functioning of an open-market economy requires a responsive government and the free dissemination of information. The Freedom House indicators of political rights and civil liberties are used for proxies.

To compute the policy sustainability indicator, each of the proxy indicators is converted onto a five-point scale, and the HDI is then weighed equally against the combined political rights and civil liberties indicator from Freedom House.

Limitations of the Readiness Indicators

The readiness indicator comprises a broad array of data, but it is not all-encompassing. There are several important influences in the readiness of a country that are not measured in the indicator's components. National infrastructure (roads, ports, pipelines, and telecommunications) and institutional and administrative capacity (police, courts, tax collection, and effective regulatory institutions) are large and underrepresented contributors to readiness. Poor performance in these areas threatens to both dampen the effect of an FTA (when perceived as nontariff barriers that remain in place after the agreement) and hinder the distribution and allocation of gains in an efficient manner. Unfortunately, there are no proxies for these components of readiness in the indicators.

Despite these imperfections, the indicator presents a policy tool for tracking progress toward productive integration with the world economy. In addition to the overall readiness score, its components illuminate areas where more progress is needed. What do these readiness indicators say about the Colombian economy? The data and readiness scores for Colombia are reported in table 3.6 and examined in the section that follows.

Readiness in Colombia

Macroeconomic Indicator

Price Stability. A key component thus far in the success of Colombia's stand-by arrangement with the IMF has been low inflation. After recording inflation rates well over 20 percent throughout the early 1990s, Colombia seems to have achieved reasonable price stability by Latin American standards. The central bank (Banco de la República) was given independence

---

9. As would be expected of a quality of life indicator, the HDI is very stable, so a two-year lag does not represent a major deficiency in the readiness indicators.

Table 3.6 Colombia's readiness, 1991–2005

Indicator	1991	1992	1993	1994	1995	1996	1997	1998	1999	2000	2001	2002	2003	2004	2005
Price stability	26.8	25.1	23.0	22.6	19.5	21.6	17.7	16.7	9.2	8.8	7.6	7.0	6.5	5.5	5.1
Budget discipline	0.2	–0.2	0.1	0.1	–0.3	–1.7	–2.8	–3.7	–4.1	–4.2	–4.1	–3.6	–2.7	n.a.	n.a.
National savings	22.9	19.1	17.2	18.6	20.8	17.3	15.5	14.4	13.7	14.5	13.6	13.0	13.7	n.a.	n.a.
External debt	190.5	186.9	190.1	205.6	214.0	236.0	242.0	273.0	263.0	229.0	260.0	263.1	242.0	202.0	150.0
Real exchange rate	114.6	113.8	107.3	90.8	88.0	83.0	77.9	83.6	92.2	100.0	104.3	107.5	121.6	111.7	n.a.
Averages/standard deviations, previous three years															
Price stability				25.0	23.6	21.7	21.2	19.6	18.7	14.5	11.6	8.5	7.8	7.0	6.3
Budget discipline				0	0	0	–0.6	–1.6	–2.7	–3.5	–4.0	–4.1	–4.0	–3.5	–2.3
National savings				19.7	18.3	18.9	18.9	17.9	15.7	14.5	14.2	13.9	13.7	13.4	13.4
External debt				189.2	194.2	203.2	218.5	230.7	250.3	259.3	255.0	250.7	250.7	255.0	235.7
Real exchange rate				4.0	11.9	10.4	4.0	5.1	3.1	7.2	8.2	6.1	3.8	9.2	7.2
Score															
Price stability				3.0	3.0	3.0	3.0	3.0	3.0	4.0	4.0	4.0	4.0	4.0	4.0
Budget discipline				5.0	5.0	5.0	5.0	5.0	4.0	3.0	3.0	3.0	3.0	3.0	4.0
National savings				3.0	3.0	3.0	3.0	2.0	2.0	2.0	2.0	2.0	2.0	2.0	2.0
External debt				4.0	4.0	4.0	4.0	3.0	3.0	3.0	3.0	3.0	3.0	3.0	3.0
Real exchange rate				5.0	3.0	3.0	5.0	4.0	5.0	4.0	4.0	4.0	5.0	4.0	4.0
Macro indicator				4.0	3.6	3.6	4.0	3.4	3.4	3.4	3.2	3.2	3.2	3.2	3.4

Reliance on trade taxes	12.9	8.7	8.4	9.4	9.2	7.6	8.1	9.9	7.3	5.7	5.7	5.2	5.1	4.5
Previous 3-year average				10.0	8.8	9.0	8.7	8.3	8.5	8.5	7.7	6.2	5.5	4.9
Score														
Market-oriented	4.0	4.0	4.0	4.0	4.0	4.0	4.0	4.0	4.0	4.0	4.0	4.5	4.5	4.5
Reliance on trade taxes	4.0	4.0	4.0	4.0	4.0	4.0	4.0	4.0	4.0	4.0	4.0	4.0	4.0	4.0
Market indicator	4.0	4.0	4.0	4.0	4.0	4.0	4.0	4.0	4.0	4.0	4.0	4.25	4.25	4.25
HDI	0.81	0.84	0.84	0.85	0.76	0.76	0.77	0.76	0.77	0.77	0.78	0.77	n.a.	0.79
Indicator score	4.0	4.0	4.0	4.0	3.5	3.5	3.5	3.5	3.5	3.5	3.5	3.5	3.5	3.5
FH political rights	3.0	2.0	2.0	2.0	3.0	4.0	4.0	4.0	3.0	4.0	4.0	4.0	4.0	4.0
Indicator score	3.5	4.0	4.0	4.0	3.5	3.0	3.0	3.0	3.5	3.0	3.0	3.0	3.0	3.0
FH civil liberties	4.0	4.0	4.0	4.0	4.0	4.0	4.0	4.0	4.0	4.0	4.0	4.0	4.0	4.0
Indicator score	3.0	3.0	3.0	3.0	3.0	3.0	3.0	3.0	3.0	3.0	3.0	3.0	3.0	3.0
FH score	3.25	3.5	3.5	3.5	3.25	3.0	3.0	3.0	3.25	3.0	3.0	3.0	3.0	3.0
Political sustainability index	3.63	3.75	3.75	3.75	3.38	3.25	3.25	3.25	3.38	3.25	3.25	3.25	3.25	3.25
Readiness indicator	**3.63**	**3.75**	**3.75**	**3.92**	**3.66**	**3.62**	**3.75**	**3.55**	**3.59**	**3.48**	**3.48**	**3.57**	**3.63**	**3.63**

Note: See table 3.5 for units of measurement.

FH = Freedom House

HDI = Human Development Index

n.a. = not available

Sources: ECLAC (2005), IMF's International Financial Statistics, UNDP (2004), Freedom House (2005), and authors' calculations.

from the government as part of the 1991 constitution (although the minister of finance sits on its board of directors). The bank currently uses an inflation targeting system and has successfully held inflation under 10 percent for the past six years, with the rate declining each year. Inflation averaged less than 5.5 percent over 2004–05. Colombia's average December-on-December inflation rate for 2003–05 was 5.7 percent, earning a component score of 4 out of 5.

Budget Discipline. Due to a confluence of factors, including El Niño, earthquakes, and the increase in obligations due to the new constitution, the Colombian public balance sheet deteriorated during the late 1990s, with the deficit topping 4 percent of GDP over 1999–2001. Since then, escalation of Colombia's 40-year armed insurrection has prompted the government to increase military spending significantly during the Pastrana and Uribe administrations. In addition, the pension system continues to be a sizable drain on public finances. Under the stand-by agreement, President Uribe has pledged to maintain a primary budget surplus. He has initiated a series of reforms aimed at stemming government corruption. While the failure of a October 2003 referendum that included anticorruption provisions and a public expenditure freeze was a setback,[10] Uribe still guided tax increases and spending limitations through Congress in December 2003. However, an attempt to expand the package—most notably by expanding the base of the value-added tax—failed to win approval in 2004. The government has been helped in its effort to control deficits by the combination of low interest rates and large price increases for Colombia's exports. As a result, the nonfinancial public sector deficit fell to 2.7 percent of GDP in 2003 and declined further in 2004–05, raising Colombia's budget deficit score from 3 to 4.

Gross National Savings. Gross domestic savings in Colombia fell from 23 percent of GDP in 1991 to a low of 13 percent in 2002, before rising to 13.7 percent in 2003. The country's low gross national saving rate—a characteristic it shares with much of Latin America—increases the importance of and need for foreign investment in the economy. The 1990s saw a significant expansion in government expenditure, prompted by new requirements of the 1991 constitution and the increased intensity of the civil war. Public expenditure increases probably had an adverse effect on public as well as private savings through increased taxes.[11] Colombia receives a score of 2 for this indicator, its lowest component score.

---

10. Although most referendum measures received the support of at least 80 percent of the voters, turnout was below the required 25 percent of the electorate needed to implement the reforms.

11. Lopez (1997) attributes the decline in private savings in Colombia during the first half of the 1990s to a reduction in disposable income, not an increase in private consumption.

External Debt. Fiscal deterioration coincided with a significant increase in external debt, which peaked in 2002 at 263.1 percent of total exports. In part, this increase was due to the 9.6 percent decline in exports of goods and services in 2002 from their peak of $15 billion in 2000, reflecting the slowdown in the US economy and severe contraction in Venezuela, Colombia's top export markets. The situation subsequently improved, and the external debt ratio fell to 202 percent of GDP at year-end 2004 as high commodity prices boosted export earnings. One of the key features of the IMF stand-by arrangement is a reduction of Colombia's public external debt burden to more sustainable levels, and the steady decline is a positive sign. For now, Colombia has a score of 3 for external debt, unchanged since 1998, although it has migrated from the high to the low end of the range. In 2005 government buybacks of external debt further reduced the debt ratio to around 150 percent (ECLAC 2005). Given that improvement, Colombia's score will improve on this indicator in the future.

Currency Stability. The Colombian peso operated in a currency band until the 1998–99 financial crisis, when the peso band was adjusted to allow devaluation several times before being abandoned altogether on September 25, 1999. Following the crisis, the free-float peso remained remarkably stable, with a three-year standard deviation of only 1.4 from 2000–2002, earning the highest currency stability score of 5. More recently, however, the currency has been more volatile, with a large depreciation followed by a moderate appreciation. As a result, currency volatility in 2002–04 came in at 7.2 percent, for a score of 4. As of June 2005, the central bank maintained more than $13 billion in foreign reserves, up sharply from the $10 billion to $11 billion level of recent years (which the IMF described as an "adequate reserves cushion"). The central bank increased exchange reserves in the second half of 2005 and used the interest on foreign reserves to pay back some of its external debt.

Average Macroeconomic Score. The average of Colombia's macroeconomic scores is 3.4, only a slight increase from its score of 3.2 in the postcrisis years, and well below its peak score of 4 in 1994 and 1997. There has been a major improvement both in the budget discipline category, where Colombia has brought its three-year average nonfinancial public-sector deficit to 2.3 percent of GDP, and in its external debt ratio. If these gains can be sustained, Colombia's readiness score will improve significantly in 2006. On the other hand, if the Uribe administration continues to have difficulty implementing year-by-year tax and spending reforms, these improvements could be short-lived. Colombia's weakest component is gross national savings, which has been in steady decline since the mid-1990s. To reverse this decline, Colombia will have to find a way to promote private savings.

Microeconomic Indicator

Reliance on Trade Taxes. Colombia is not heavily reliant on trade taxes. Since 1991, tariffs have consistently declined as a source of tax revenue to about 5 percent of total public revenue, or about 1 percent of GDP. As a result, Colombia scores a strong 4 for reliance on trade taxes. The Uribe administration is seeking to increase tax revenue from other sources; if successful, Colombia's ratio of trade taxes to total tax revenue would fall below 5 percent, and increase its readiness score to 5.

How would a free trade agreement with the United States affect this indicator? Because Colombia is such a heavy trading partner with the United States, the loss of tariff revenue resulting from an FTA with the United States could be substantial. In 2002, Colombian imports from the United States were about $3.6 billion; the average trade-weighted tariff on US goods was 13.6 percent (chapter 2). As a back-of-the-envelope calculation, the immediate elimination of tariffs on US goods could cost Colombia $490 million, or 0.6 percent of 2002 GDP. To be sure, tariffs generally are phased out over time under FTAs, so the budget hit would not be so large. Nonetheless, revenue loss should be kept in mind when negotiating tariff reduction schedules; tariff lines that produce significant revenue (often *not* those that provide industries with the highest protection) should be phased out gradually to allow the government to replace revenue from other sources.

Market-Oriented Policies. Since the advent of the readiness indicators, Colombia has received high marks for market openness. Its score in this category is higher than its Andean partners and many other Latin American countries. Recent reform efforts, however, have brought mixed results.

Colombia liberalized its financial system in the early 1990s, prompting a heavy influx of foreign investment led by Spanish banks BBVA and Santander and by Citibank. During the 1999 financial crisis, the government stepped in to buy several troubled Colombian banks. These have been restructured and are being sold to the private sector. In February 2004, 55 percent of Bancafé was scheduled for auction, but no bids were received. In October 2004 the government abandoned its attempt to sell Bancafé, which it will instead use to provide loans to small businesses.[12] In March 2005, the bank was split into two entities, Granbanco-Bancafé and Granahorrar. The latter was sold in October 2005 to BBVA Colombia for 970 billion pesos,[13] allowing the government to restructure its labor contract. The government hopes that lower compensation levels will allow the other half, Granbanco-Bancafé, to eventually be privatized, although no target

---

12. See *IMF Morning Press*, October 22, 2004.

13. See BBVA press release, October 31, 2005, http://press.bbva.com (accessed May 22, 2006).

date has been set (IMF 2005). Granbanco-Bancafé and Banco Agrario are now the only two Colombian banks remaining in government hands.

Since the financial crisis, Colombia has moved to privatize several state-owned enterprises. In February 2005, as part of negotiations for an extension of the IMF stand-by agreement, the government announced its intention to fully privatize the national natural gas company (ECOGAS), which primarily operates the gas transportation system, and five electric utilities. The value of the total privatization plan is estimated at $811 million.[14] The government announced that revenue from the privatization would be used to bolster the pension system and for infrastructure investment.

Unlike its neighbors, Colombia has been partnering with foreign oil and natural gas companies since the mid-1960s. The state oil firm, Ecopetrol, controls oil production and offers association contracts to enter into joint projects with foreign firms; the primary investors are Occidental Petroleum and BP Amoco. By law, Ecopetrol must control a 30 percent stake in any energy project beyond the exploratory stage. Concerns about low investment in energy led the government to reduce the public stake requirement from 50 percent in 1999. This policy change sparked renewed interest in investment, and 13 new contracts were awarded in 2000. However, foreign investors remain cautious due to pipeline sabotage by the Revolutionary Armed Forces of Colombia (FARC) and the National Liberation Army (ELN). Colombian oil exports by volume fell 25 percent between 2002 and 2003 to 195,000 barrels a day and have only recovered slightly since then. Without increased investment in exploration and development, Colombia may become a net oil importer in the medium term (Energy Information Administration 2005).

Despite deregulation of the telecommunications sector in 1997, there remain strict barriers to market entry in land-based telephony. As a result, the growth of mobile telephony, where foreign investment is unencumbered, has been rapid. The primary players are Mexico's America Móvil and Spain's Telefónica (which bought BellSouth's cellular operations in 2004).

For business and investment, Colombia generally offers an above average environment compared to the Latin American region as a whole. According to the World Bank (2003), it generally takes an average of 43 days to comply with regulations establishing a business in Colombia, and the estimated cost of starting a business (including licenses and registration fees) is 27 percent of annual per capita income. In Latin America as a whole, starting a business takes, on average, 70 days and 60 percent of per capita income.[15] Colombia's friendlier business environment is a competitive advantage in the region.

---

14. See *Business News Americas*, February 10, 2005.

15. As a reference, the averages for member countries of the Organization for Economic Cooperation and Development are six days and 8 percent of per capita income.

In December 2004, Colombia deviated from its market-oriented approach by introducing capital controls on short-term investments, requiring money invested in Colombia to be kept there for at least a year. Skeptics charged that the controls were not primarily a safeguard against inflows of "hot money," but instead a play to preserve export competitiveness by weakening the peso. Analysts further questioned the effectiveness of the controls, maintaining that most inward investment into Colombia was long term.[16] Later that month, the government offered further support to the export sector by introducing export subsidies for bananas and fresh cut flowers.[17]

In summary, Colombia's score for market-oriented policies is 4.5, the same score it has received since 2002. Recent reforms in the energy and financial sectors consolidate the score, but continuing protection in agriculture and the imposition of capital controls bar a score of 5. Therefore, the overall microeconomic indicator—the average of the trade taxation and market-orientation scores—comes to 4.25 out of 5.

Policy Sustainability Indicator

Human Development. Colombia ranks 69th among countries graded in the UNDP's Human Development Index (HDI) for 2003 (latest year available).[18] Ranked by purchasing power parity GDP per capita alone, Colombia would rank 77th. The country's development ranking is improved by its relatively high life expectancy of 72.4 years and an adult literacy rate of 94 percent (UNDP 2004). Colombia's HDI score of .785 translates to a 3.5 on the five-point scale being used in this chapter.

Political and Civil Liberties. The hangover from four decades of civil strife continues to hamper Colombia's prospects for long-term political stability. The Revolutionary Armed Forces of Colombia (FARC) and the National Liberation Army (ELN) fund themselves through the drug trade and conduct sabotage attacks on the infrastructure. The right-wing paramilitary organization, United Self-Defense Forces of Colombia (AUC), once tacitly allied with the government, also runs drugs and uses death-squad tactics to disrupt civil society. President Uribe launched talks aimed at decommissioning the AUC, but progress has been slow.[19] In June 2005,

---

16. See *The Financial Times*, December 21, 2004, 38.

17. See *The Wall Street Journal*, January 7, 2005, A11.

18. The UNDP also issued a special report on human development in Colombia (UNDP 2003).

19. The AUC, many of whose members double as extremely successful narcotics traffickers, are requesting blanket amnesty and official validation of their assets in exchange for decommissioning (*The New York Times*, November 27, 2004, 3).

after almost two years of debate, the Colombian Congress passed the Justice and Peace Law aimed at demobilizing terrorist organizations. Whether the politically delicate balance of limited amnesty and punishment can promote national reconciliation will be the key challenge for President Uribe and for future administrations.

The armed insurrections and the narcotics trafficking that accompany them are among the most significant threats to the Colombian economy. President Uribe himself survived an assassination attempt in April 2002, one month prior to his election, and the presidential complex received mortar fire during his inauguration. The president's "democratic security" policy, which strengthens the hand of the military and police to the point of giving them judicial powers, has caused concern among the human rights community.[20] On the other hand, negotiations with Marxist rebel groups during the Pastrana administration delayed needed structural reforms within the economy. More directly, the rebels are responsible for infrastructure bombings and kidnappings that have dampened foreign interest in doing business in Colombia. Another problem is persistent violence against trade unionists. In a survey of global labor rights in 134 countries, the International Confederation of Free Trade Unionists declared Colombia "the most hostile country in the world for trade unionists" (ICFTU 2004, 87). While the number of such homicides has dropped significantly over the past four years, the Colombian government still reported 89 murders of union members in 2004. This issue is discussed in more detail in chapter 6.

In the October 2003 elections, 26 mayoral or gubernatorial candidates were assassinated. Government control often does not extend beyond major cities, according to Freedom House; 150 mayors reportedly attempt to govern their municipalities from provincial capitals out of fear for their own safety.

So far, Uribe's attempts to strengthen governance, improve security, and reduce corruption have had mixed results. Corruption is estimated to cost roughly $2.2 billion annually, or 2.8 percent of GDP (Freedom House 2005), despite the best attempts of the Uribe administration, which has waged an anticorruption campaign. Despite concerns from human rights groups about "democratic security," the Freedom House indicators for political and civil liberties have been stable since the mid-1990s. Translated into the scoring system used in this chapter, they combine for a score of 3.

Overall, Colombia's political sustainability indicator comes to 3.25 out of 5. With the exception of a brief blip in 1999, the indicator has been stable since 1996, with no movement in any of the components.

---

20. Legislation passed in December 2003 gives the military the authority to make arrests and conduct searches for four years. See "You Do the Math—Colombia's Security Policy," *The Economist*, January 10, 2004.

Colombia's Readiness Indicator

Overall, Colombia's readiness indicator comes to 3.63 (table 3.6). Movement in the indicator has been basically stagnant over the last 10 years.[21] Colombia receives high marks on the microeconomic indicator (4.25), but the macroeconomic indicator is weighed down by a low level of domestic savings and receives a score of 3.4 (a deterioration from the early 1990s, despite recent improvement owing to smaller budget deficits). Note, however, that recent reductions in external debt coupled with a stronger fiscal performance should produce higher readiness scores in the coming years. Colombia scores lowest (3.25) on the political sustainability indicator. The low score is primarily due to the Freedom House indicators, which reflect the government's continuing inability to provide security to many parts of the country. If anything, the lack of security is underrepresented in the readiness indicator score. Improving the security environment has been a major focus of the Uribe administration, but continued commitment is required if Colombia is to be in a position to benefit from an FTA though increased foreign investment and export activity.

How does Colombia compare with its Andean neighbors? Figure 3.1 graphs the overall readiness score for Bolivia, Colombia, Ecuador, and Peru. Colombia's readiness score has moved very little over the past decade. By contrast, Peru and Ecuador have improved their readiness scores over the past decade (tables 3.7 and 3.8), though from a lower base. Bolivia's score improved in the 1990s but has deteriorated badly since 2002 (table 3.9).

Peru has been the outstanding performer in the region over the past decade, substantially improving its overall score. In 1994, Peru lagged behind all other Andeans with a readiness score of 2.47, but it has improved steadily since the mid-1990s and now scores 3.56, only slightly lower than Colombia on the overall readiness scale. Peru's improvements in the political sustainability indicator after the defeat of the Shining Path played a significant role. Another important Peruvian success has been the control of inflation, which Colombia's inflation target system seems poised to replicate.

Ecuador's readiness score has recorded wide fluctuations over the past decade. It was hardest hit by the financial crisis of the late 1990s: Ecuador's readiness score plunged from 3.28 in 1997 to 2.61 in 2000. Roughly two-thirds of the fall was due to the combination of higher inflation, exchange rate volatility, and higher government deficits. Since then, and de-

---

21. The decline between 1994 and 1995 is partially due to the substantial increase in exchange rate instability. In addition, there was a discontinuity in the calculation of the HDI, which does not reflect a decline in readiness.

Figure 3.1 Andean readiness indicators, 1994–2005

readiness index

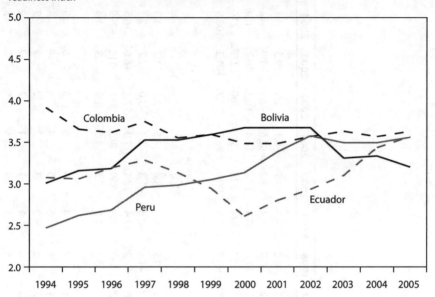

spite unstable presidential terms, the indicator has slowly recovered and stands today at 3.57, only slightly below Colombia.[22]

Although Bolivia has improved its readiness score since 1994, over the past five years it has fallen from 3.68 to 3.20. Today, Bolivia lags behind its Andean partners by about 0.3 points. The Bolivian decline has been spread evenly across the macroeconomic, microeconomic, and political sustainability indicators. Bolivia has experienced a large increase in its nonfinancial public-sector deficit, which stood at 7.9 percent of GDP in 2003, and currently receives a component score of 0. The microeconomic indicator has fallen as the government has reacted to the country's growing antiprivatization climate, in which protests forced the government to block or end energy and utility contracts. Foreign investors also responded to the threatening climate, reducing foreign investment inflows from $1 billion in 1999 to $134 million in 2004.[23] Most troubling has been the decline in the

---

22. Due to the unavailability of data on Ecuador's collection of customs duties and other trade taxes since 2002, this component of the readiness score is highly speculative. A one-point change in the component that measures reliance on trade taxes would result in a change of 0.17 in the overall readiness score.

23. See "Latin America Fails to Deliver on Basic Needs," *The New York Times*, February 22, 2005, 1.

Table 3.7 Peru's readiness, 1991–2005

Indicator	1991	1992	1993	1994	1995	1996	1997	1998	1999	2000	2001	2002	2003	2004	2005
Price stability	139.2	56.7	39.5	15.4	10.2	11.8	6.5	6.0	3.7	3.7	-0.1	1.5	2.5	4.1	n.a.
Budget discipline	-0.9	-1.5	-1.2	-2.8	-3.1	-1.0	0.2	-0.9	-3.2	-3.2	-2.6	-2.3	-1.9	n.a.	n.a.
National savings	13.8	11.7	13.4	16.9	17.1	16.3	18.2	17.6	18.5	17.2	16.4	16.3	16.7	n.a.	n.a.
External debt	491	476	630	533	504	464	342	391	374	329	319	300	279	210	n.a.
Real exchange rate	88.8	90.5	97.5	93.3	92.8	91.6	91.5	93.3	101.8	100.0	98.0	97.7	101.2	102.9	n.a.
Averages/standard deviation, previous three years															
Price stability				78.5	37.2	21.7	12.5	9.5	8.1	5.4	4.5	2.5	1.7	1.3	2.7
Budget discipline				-1.2	-1.8	-2.4	-2.3	-1.3	-0.6	-1.3	-2.4	-3.0	-2.7	-2.3	-2.1
National savings				13.0	14.0	15.8	16.8	17.2	17.4	18.1	17.8	17.4	16.6	16.5	16.5
External debt				533	547	556	500	437	399	369	365	341	316	299	263
Real exchange rate				4.6	3.5	2.6	0.9	0.7	1.0	5.5	4.5	1.9	1.3	1.9	2.7
Score															
Price stability				0	1	3	4	4	4	4	5	5	5	5	5
Budget discipline				5	5	4	4	5	5	5	4	5	5	4	4
National savings				2	2	2	2	2	2	3	2	2	2	2	2
External debt				0	0	0	0	0	1	1	1	2	2	2	3
Real exchange rate				5	5	5	5	5	5	4	5	5	5	5	5
Macro indicator				2.4	2.6	2.8	3.2	3.2	3.4	3.4	3.4	3.6	3.6	3.6	3.8

Reliance on trade taxes	10.3	10.4	12.6	11.7	11.7	10.8	10.0	11.3	12.9	12.8	11.6	n.a.	n.a.	n.a.	n.a.
Previous 3-year average				11.1	11.57	12.0	11.4	10.8	10.7	11.4	12.3	12.4	12.2	11.6	n.a.
Score															
Market-oriented				2.0	2.0	2.0	2.5	3.0	3.0	3.5	3.5	3.5	3.5	3.5	3.5
Reliance on trade taxes				3.0	3.0	3.0	3.0	3.0	3.0	3.0	3.0	3.0	3.0	3.0	3.0
Market indicator				2.5	2.5	2.5	2.75	3.0	3.0	3.25	3.25	3.25	3.25	3.25	3.25
HDI	0.64	0.71	0.69	0.72	0.73	0.73	0.74	0.74	0.74	0.75	0.75	0.75	0.76	n.a.	n.a.
Indicator score	2.5	3.0	2.5	3.0	3.0	3.0	3.0	3.0	3.0	3.0	3.5	3.5	3.5	3.5	3.5
FH political rights	3.0	3.0	6.0	5.0	5.0	5.0	4.0	5.0	5.0	5.0	3.0	1.0	2.0	2.0	2.0
Indicator score	3.5	3.5	1.0	2.0	2.0	2.0	3.0	2.0	2.0	2.0	3.0	5.0	4.0	4.0	4.0
FH civil liberties	4.0	5.0	5.0	5.0	4.0	4.0	3.0	4.0	4.0	4.0	3.0	3.0	3.0	3.0	3.0
Indicator score	3.0	2.0	2.0	2.0	3.0	3.0	3.5	3.0	3.0	3.0	3.5	3.5	3.5	3.5	3.5
FH score	3.25	2.75	1.5	2	2.5	2.5	3.25	2.5	2.5	2.5	3.5	4.25	3.75	3.75	3.75
Political sustainability indicator	2.875	2.875	2	2.5	2.75	2.75	3.125	2.75	2.75	2.75	3.5	3.88	3.63	3.63	3.63
Readiness indicator				**2.47**	**2.62**	**2.68**	**2.96**	**2.98**	**3.05**	**3.13**	**3.38**	**3.58**	**3.49**	**3.49**	**3.56**

Note: See table 3.5 for units of measurement.

FH = Freedom House
HDI = Human Development Index
n.a. = not available

Sources: ECLAC (2005), IMF's *International Financial Statistics*, UNDP (2004), Freedom House (2005), and authors' calculations.

Table 3.8 Ecuador's readiness, 1991–2005

Indicator	1991	1992	1993	1994	1995	1996	1997	1998	1999	2000	2001	2002	2003	2004	2005
Price stability	49.0	60.2	31.0	25.3	22.8	25.6	30.7	43.4	60.7	91.0	22.4	9.4	6.1	2.0	n.a.
Budget discipline	-0.6	-1.2	-0.1	0.5	-1.0	-2.7	-2.1	-4.8	-3.9	1.5	0.4	0.6	1.2	n.a.	n.a.
National savings	16.1	19.5	16.4	14.1	14.6	16.6	16.6	15.9	20.5	25.4	22.4	22.8	25.0	26.4	n.a.
External debt	376	344	361	316	268	260	250	328	305	227	255	265	234	196	n.a.
Real exchange rate	77.1	77	68.4	66.1	66.7	68.2	66.2	65.1	89.2	100	70.9	62.8	61.2	63.6	n.a.
Averages/standard deviation, previous three years															
Price stability				46.73	38.83	26.37	24.57	26.37	33.23	44.93	65.03	58.03	40.93	12.63	5.83
Budget discipline				-0.63	-0.27	-0.20	-1.07	-1.93	-3.20	-3.60	-2.40	-0.67	0.83	0.73	0.90
National savings				17.33	16.67	15.03	15.10	15.93	16.37	17.67	20.60	22.77	23.53	23.40	24.73
External debt				360	341	315	281	259	279	294	287	262	249	251	232
Real exchange rate				4.99	5.75	1.19	1.08	1.04	1.57	13.61	17.87	14.71	19.56	5.20	1.22
Score															
Price stability				0	1.0	2.0	3.0	2.0	2.0	1.0	0	0	1.0	4.0	4.0
Budget discipline				5.0	5.0	5.0	5.0	5.0	4.0	3.0	4.0	5.0	5.0	5.0	5.0
National savings				2.0	2.0	2.0	2.0	2.0	2.0	2.0	3.0	3.0	3.0	3.0	4.0
External debt				1.0	2.0	2.0	3.0	3.0	3.0	2.0	3.0	3.0	3.0	3.0	3.0
Real exchange rate				5.0	4.0	5.0	5.0	5.0	5.0	5.0	2.0	3.0	2.0	4.0	5.0
Macro indicator				2.6	2.8	3.2	3.6	3.4	3.2	3.0	2.4	2.8	2.8	3.8	4.2

Reliance on trade taxes	14.3	11.6	10.7	12.8	15.1	13.6	13.1	19.3	13.3	10.5	9.7	9.2	n.a.	n.a	n.a.
Previous 3-year average				12.2	11.7	12.9	13.8	13.9	15.4	15.3	14.4	11.2	9.8	9.4	9.2
Score															
Market-oriented															
Reliance on trade taxes				3.0	3.0	3.0	3.0	2.5	2.5	2.5	2.5	2.5	2.5	2.5	2.5
Market indicator				3.0	3.0	3.0	2.75	2.75	2.25	2.25	2.75	2.75	3.25	3.25	3.25
HDI	0.72	0.78	0.76	0.78	0.72	0.72	0.75	0.72	0.72	0.73	0.73	0.74	0.76	n.a.	n.a.
Indicator score	3.0	3.5	3.5	3.5	3.0	3.0	3.0	3.0	3.0	3.0	3.0	3.0	3.0	3.0	3.0
FH political rights	2.0	2.0	2.0	2.0	2.0	2.0	2.0	3.0	2.0	2.0	3.0	3.0	3.0	3.0	3.0
Indicator score	4.0	4.0	4.0	4.0	4.0	4.0	4.0	3.5	4.0	4.0	3.5	3.5	3.5	3.5	3.5
FH civil liberties	2.0	3.0	3.0	3.0	3.0	3.0	4.0	3.0	3.0	3.0	3.0	3.0	3.0	3.0	3.0
Indicator score	4.0	3.5	3.5	3.5	3.5	3.5	3.0	3.5	3.5	3.5	3.5	3.5	3.5	3.5	3.5
FH score	4.0	3.75	3.75	3.75	3.75	3.75	3.5	3.5	3.75	3.75	3.5	3.5	3.5	3.5	3.5
Political sustainability indicator	3.5	3.625	3.625	3.625	3.375	3.375	3.25	3.25	3.375	3.375	3.25	3.25	3.25	3.25	3.25
Readiness indicator				**2.47**	**2.62**	**2.68**	**2.96**	**2.98**	**3.05**	**3.13**	**3.38**	**3.58**	**3.49**	**3.49**	**3.56**

Note: See table 3.5 for units of measurement.

FH = Freedom House
HDI = Human Development Index
n.a. = not available

Sources: ECLAC (2005), IMF's *International Financial Statistics*, UNDP (2004), Freedom House (2005), and authors' calculations.

Table 3.9   Bolivia's readiness, 1991–2005

Indicator	1991	1992	1993	1994	1995	1996	1997	1998	1999	2000	2001	2002	2003	2004	2005
Price stability	14.5	10.5	9.3	8.5	12.6	7.9	6.7	4.4	3.1	3.4	0.9	2.4	3.9	4.9	n.a.
Budget discipline	-4.2	-4.4	-6.1	-3.0	-1.8	-1.9	-3.3	-4.7	-3.5	-3.7	-6.9	-9.0	-7.9	n.a.	n.a.
National savings	8.6	5.6	5.7	10.7	10.9	11	12.9	12.1	12.9	13.0	10.8	10.6	11.6	13.6	n.a.
External debt	391	490	422	311	367	333	299	343	349	303	290	276	269	202	n.a.
Real exchange rate	93.1	97.2	103.1	109.0	110.8	106.0	103.8	100.0	99.1	100.0	101.4	99.2	108.3	115.5	n.a.
Averages/standard deviation, previous three years															
Price stability				11.43	9.43	10.13	9.67	9.07	6.33	4.73	3.63	2.47	2.23	2.40	3.73
Budget discipline				-4.90	-4.50	-3.63	-2.23	-2.33	-3.30	-3.83	-3.97	-4.70	-6.53	-7.93	-8.45
National savings				6.63	7.33	9.10	10.87	11.60	12.00	12.63	12.67	12.23	11.47	11.00	11.93
External debt				434	407	367	337	333	325	330	332	314	290	278	249
Real exchange rate				5.03	5.90	4.03	2.42	3.58	3.04	2.49	0.52	1.16	1.11	4.75	8.17
Score															
Price stability				4.0	4.0	4.0	4.0	4.0	4.0	5.0	5.0	5.0	5.0	5.0	5.0
Budget discipline				3.0	3.0	3.0	4.0	4.0	3.0	3.0	3.0	3.0	1.0	1.0	0
National savings				1.0	1.0	1.0	1.0	2.0	2.0	2.0	2.0	2.0	1.0	1.0	1.0
External debt				0	1.0	1.0	2.0	2.0	2.0	2.0	2.0	2.0	2.0	3.0	3.0
Real exchange rate				4.0	4.0	5.0	5.0	5.0	5.0	5.0	5.0	5.0	5.0	5.0	4.0
Macro indicator				2.4	2.6	2.8	3.2	3.2	3.4	3.4	3.4	3.4	2.8	3.0	2.6

Reliance on trade taxes	6.0	7.0	6.2	6.7	6.7	6.7	5.9	6.7	6.8	6.0	7.0	6.1	6.1	4.9	4.4	n.a.
Previous 3-year average					6.4	6.6	6.5	6.4	6.4	6.4	6.5	6.6	6.3	6.4	5.7	5.2
Score																
Market-oriented					4.0	4.0	4.0	4.5	4.5	4.5	4.5	4.5	4.5	4.0	4.0	4.0
Reliance on trade taxes					4.0	4.0	4.0	4.0	4.0	4.0	4.0	4.0	4.0	4.0	4.0	4.0
Market indicator					4.0	4.0	4.0	4.25	4.25	4.25	4.25	4.25	4.25	4.0	4.0	4.0
HDI	0.53	0.59	0.58	0.59	0.59	0.63	0.63	0.65	0.64	0.65	0.65	0.67	0.68	0.69	n.a.	n.a.
Indicator score	1.0	1.5	1.5	1.5	1.5	2.0	2.0	2.5	2.0	2.0	2.5	2.5	2.5	2.5	2.5	2.5
FH political rights	2.0	2.0	2.0	2.0	2.0	2.0	2.0	2.0	1.0	1.0	1.0	1.0	1.0	2.0	3.0	3.0
Indicator score	4.0	4.0	4.0	4.0	4.0	4.0	4.0	4.0	5.0	5.0	5.0	5.0	5.0	4.0	3.5	3.5
FH civil liberties	3.0	3.0	3.0	3.0	3.0	3.0	4.0	3.0	3.0	3.0	3.0	3.0	3.0	3.0	3.0	3.0
Indicator score	3.5	3.5	3.5	3.5	3.5	3.5	3.0	3.5	3.5	3.5	3.5	3.5	3.5	3.5	3.5	3.5
FH score	3.75	3.75	3.75	3.75	3.75	3.75	3.5	3.75	4.25	4.25	4.25	4.25	4.25	3.75	3.5	3.5
Political sustainability																
indicator	2.375	2.625	2.625	2.625	2.625	2.875	2.75	3.125	3.125	3.125	3.375	3.375	3.375	3.125	3.0	3.0
Readiness indicator					**3.01**	**3.16**	**3.18**	**3.53**	**3.53**	**3.59**	**3.68**	**3.68**	**3.68**	**3.31**	**3.33**	**3.20**

Note: See table 3.5 for units of measurement.

FH = Freedom House
HDI = Human Development Index
n.a. = not available

Sources: ECLAC (2005), IMF's *International Financial Statistics*, UNDP (2004), Freedom House (2005), and authors' calculations.

political sustainability indicator. The Freedom House indicators report a significant decline in political rights in Bolivia. In October 2003, popular protests forced the resignation of Bolivia's president, Gonzalo Sánchez de Lozada, who had been only narrowly elected the year before. He was replaced by his vice president, Carlos Mesa, who subsequently was forced out in 2005.[24] The protests were led by the "Movement to Socialism" and associated coca growers' unions, led by Evo Morales, the runner-up in a close 2002 presidential election who subsequently scored a clear-cut victory in 2005.

Since taking office in January 2006, Morales has nationalized energy production, and his political overtures to Venezuelan President Hugo Chávez and Cuban President Fidel Castro have deepened anxiety about Bolivia's economic future. While his actions regarding access to and the pricing of natural gas exports will yield a financial bonus for Bolivia, the nationalization of energy resources has raised concern about the management of the Bolivian economy and may well portend a further weakening of its readiness score.

In summary, 10 years ago, Colombia was the clear frontrunner in readiness for a free trade agreement, but today that is no longer the case. While Colombia has come through a turbulent decade without a huge decline in readiness, it has not moved up its readiness score to the levels of current US FTA partners such as Mexico and Chile.[25] As is often the case, the political and economic domestic reforms that are essential to development are also required to leverage the benefits of a free trade agreement with the United States. While the indicators show that Colombia needs to increase gross savings and further reduce its external debt, promoting reforms that strengthen the political sustainability indicator will make the most important contribution to raising Colombia's readiness score.

---

24. See "Water, Oil, and the Mob—Bolivia," *The Economist*, January 22, 2005, 35.

25. In 2001 Mexico's readiness score was 4.11 and Chile's was 4.30 (Schott 2001).

4

Potential Benefits of a US-Colombia FTA

DEAN A. DeROSA and JOHN P. GILBERT

This chapter uses empirical and applied methods of economic analysis to examine the potential quantitative impact of a US-Colombia FTA on bilateral trade, economic welfare, and other major variables for each of the two countries. Empirical analysis involves application of the so-called gravity model, which investigates the determinants of aggregate trade between countries over time, while applied methods involve a point-in-time, static application of a prominent applied general equilibrium (AGE) model of world trade and economic activity known as the Global Trade Analysis Project (GTAP) model.

At the outset, it should be understood that the economic prospects of the United States and Colombia under a bilateral FTA are not easily assessed with precision because of the numerous factors underlying the two nations' economic and political relations vis-à-vis not only one another but also other prominent trading partners in the Andean region (Bolivia, Ecuador, Peru, and Venezuela), the greater Western Hemisphere (Brazil, Canada, Chile, and Mexico), and the global economy (European Union, Japan, and other emerging-market countries). Given the GTAP model's extensive coverage of economic variables, the applied analysis presented here does, however, succeed in providing a fairly in-depth view of the potential impact of the proposed FTA.

Dean A. DeRosa is a visiting fellow at the Institute and principal economist at ADR International Ltd. John P. Gilbert is associate professor of economics in the Department of Economics, Utah State University, Logan, Utah.

As will be seen, the magnitude of the economic impact simulated by the GTAP model is much smaller than that implied by the findings of the complementary gravity model analysis. This may be because of the empirical rather than applied nature of the gravity model. Indeed, in using pooled, cross-sectional data and in relying upon statistical rather than applied methodology, the gravity model analysis may partly capture added expansion of trade motivated by increased foreign direct investment under FTAs not captured by simulations of the GTAP model. Also, a priori specification of behavioral and technical relationships in the GTAP model is subject to a number of questions, including, in particular, whether there is greater substitutability between similar traded goods from different countries in the real world than is assumed in the model, in which case greater changes in trade flows and accommodating domestic production would occur. In addition, with greater substitutability between similar traded goods, greater trade diversion—that is, substitution of high-cost imports from the FTA partner country for lower-cost imports from third countries—might result, implying greater economic costs to the world economy, if not also to Colombia and the United States.[1] Finally, it should be emphasized that the GTAP model analysis considers the economic impact of eliminating tariffs, but not the possible nontariff barriers, that limit trade between the United States and Colombia.

Notwithstanding its possible shortcomings, the GTAP model analysis suggests that the potential benefits to Colombia of the proposed FTA hinge importantly on how widely the United States pursues similar FTAs with other countries. The United States gains from establishing numerous FTAs, gradually covering a substantial proportion of its trade with the world. At the same time, however, the potential gains to Colombia and other US FTA partners decline. Following the so-called competitive liberalization hypothesis, this effect, in combination with possible trade diversion and other adverse effects on the economies of countries excluded from US free trade agreements, might lead to greater support in Colombia, neighboring Andean countries, and countries outside the Andean region for thoroughgoing regional or multilateral trade liberalization under negotiations for a Free Trade Area of the Americas (FTAA) or as part of the Doha Round.[2]

In sum, the empirical and applied quantitative results presented in this chapter offer a useful but still limited view of the prospective economic impact of a US-Colombia FTA. The view is importantly constrained by the

---

1. As a small country, Colombia is more likely to be immune to economic loss from trade diversion than the United States. Indeed, in many if not most sectors, US export capacity might be sufficiently large and internationally competitive to ensure that trade creation rather than trade diversion results widely across sectors for Colombia under a US-Colombia FTA.

2. On the competitive liberalization hypothesis, see Baldwin (1996), Bergsten (1996), and Andrianmananjara (2000).

pre-2000 baseline data used by the gravity model and GTAP model analyses.[3] More importantly, the two quantitative analyses focus solely on the impact of liberalizing merchandise trade. They lack sufficient information and appropriate economic underpinnings to address the possibly more dynamic, and larger, trade and economywide repercussions of liberalizing trade in services and, especially, foreign direct investment.

Gravity Model Analysis to Measure Potential Trade Expansion

The potential for expanded US-Colombia trade may be examined empirically in a rough and ready way, using panel data on aggregate worldwide trade between countries over time and the econometric framework offered by the gravity model of international trade. With the proliferation of preferential trading arrangements over the past decade, and bolstered by recent advances in understanding the bases for the gravity model in economic theory, the model has become a widely used tool for empirical analyses of the consequences for trade of bilateral and regional trading arrangements.[4]

The Gravity Model

The basic gravity model is implemented by statistical regression, using ordinary least squares (OLS) or more advanced techniques for econometric analysis of cross-sectional time series data. It pits bilateral trade flows measured in a common currency (and adjusted for inflation) against the gravitational "mass" of explanatory variables describing the bilateral trading partners, including especially their proximity, combined population, and combined GDP. Most gravity models find that, the greater the combined population and GDP of the two countries and the shorter their distance from one another, the greater is the trade between them. Additional explanatory variables are also frequently important. For instance, trading partners that share a common border or language are typically found to enjoy significantly greater mutual trade.

In gravity model analyses of regional trade agreements (RTAs), a dichotomous (0, 1) explanatory variable is introduced in the regression equation

---

3. Appendix 4B presents an updated analysis using the recently released version of the GTAP model.

4. Greenaway and Milner (2002) provide an excellent introduction to and review of the recent literature on the gravity model and econometric applications of the model for assessing the trade and other effects of preferential trading arrangements among regional trading partners.

for each preferential arrangement among two or more trading partners. If the explanatory variable representing a preferential trading arrangement is positive and significant, then the RTA is judged to expand bilateral trade, with the extent of the trade expansion, usually measured in proportional terms, given by the magnitude of the estimated regression coefficient.[5]

Framework for US-Colombia FTA Analysis

The potential for expansion of US-Colombia trade under the proposed FTA between the two countries is investigated here following the general approach of Frankel (1997) and Choi and Schott (2001), among others, to applying the gravity model to RTAs. The approach consists of representing not only existing but also prospective RTAs in the gravity model regression equation. The potential for greater trade under a prospective free trade agreement may then be assessed by the significance and magnitude of the estimated coefficients of the explanatory variables representing the prospective trade agreements. In addition, the approach takes into account the general openness to trade of prospective FTA partners by including dichotomous explanatory variables representing the trade of the partners with trading partners worldwide. In this way, trade between prospective FTA partners may be judged vis-à-vis their trade with all partners. Where trade between the prospective FTA partners is not significant or is estimated to be substantially less than that of prospective FTA partners with the world at large, a free trade agreement might be expected, broadly speaking, to expand bilateral trade to the same extent (in proportional terms) as estimated by the gravity model for existing RTAs.

The econometric results presented here are based on the particularly extensive set of panel data for world trade between pairs of countries constructed by Rose (2002, 2003). The Rose data cover bilateral merchandise trade between 178 countries from 1948 to 1999 (with gaps, and excluding Taiwan and some centrally planned economies), as compiled from the International Monetary Fund's (IMF) *Directions of Trade Statistics* database. The bilateral trade data are averages of free on board (f.o.b.) export data and cost, insurance, and freight (c.i.f.) import data in dollars, deflated by the US consumer price index. The "core" explanatory variables included in the data set cover distance between trading partners, joint real GDP, and joint real GDP per capita. They also cover a number of country-specific variables, such as landlocked and island status, language, colonizers, and

---

5. Given the typical log-linear specification of the gravity model regression equation, the impact of a free trade agreement on bilateral trade is computed in percentage terms as $100*[EXP(bfta) - 1]$, where $bfta$ is the estimated coefficient for the dichotomous explanatory variable representing the preferential trading agreement and EXP is the natural exponential function operator.

dates of independence. The core explanatory variables are drawn from several standard sources.[6] In all, the basic Rose dataset entails nearly 235,000 observations covering recorded bilateral trade for about 12,000 pairs of countries.

The core explanatory variables are augmented by variables representing past and current preferential trading arrangements. These include an explanatory variable representing the generalized system of preferences (GSP), under which several major industrial countries and other countries extend preferences to less developed countries on a nonreciprocal basis.[7] With respect to RTAs, they also include groups of countries involved in currency unions (Glick and Rose 2002). Most importantly, the augmented explanatory variables include indicators for 12 RTAs around the world, treated individually but also on a combined basis.[8]

Finally, as mentioned previously, to investigate the prospects for expanded US-Colombia trade under a free trade agreement between Colombia and the United States, the data set includes a series of explanatory variables representing mutual trade between the two countries and, separately, bilateral trade between Colombia and the United States, on the one hand, and some prominent individual regional and global trading partners on the other. For Colombia, the bilateral trading partners considered individually, in addition to the United States, are the European Union, Venezuela, Mexico, and Brazil. For the United States, only US bilateral trade with Chile is considered individually, in addition to US bilateral trade with Colombia.

To avoid bias in the coefficient estimates for the specified bilateral trade variables, a series of corresponding "openness" variables are specified. The openness variables indicate trade with the world by either bilateral

6. These include the US Central Intelligence Agency, *World Factbook* database, www.cia.gov (accessed May 22, 2006); IMF, *International Financial Statistics* database, http://ifs.apdi.net (accessed May 22, 2006); Penn World Table Version 6.1 (Heston, Summers, and Aten 2002); and World Bank, *World Development Indicators 2004* database, http://devdata.worldbank.org (accessed February 18, 2005).

7. The GSP programs of major industrial and other countries are monitored by the UN Conference on Trade and Development (UNCTAD), including through a series of manuals describing the individual programs. See www.unctad.org (accessed June 30, 2006).

8. Treatment of the indicators of RTAs on a combined basis enables gravity model estimation of a single coefficient for the impact of preferential trading arrangements on bilateral trade. The Rose dataset includes indicators for the Association of Southeast Asian Nations (ASEAN), European Union, US-Israel FTA, North American Free Trade Agreement, Caribbean Community, Agreement on Trade and Commercial Relations between the Government of Australia and the Government of Papua New Guinea, Australia–New Zealand Closer Economic Relations Trade Agreement, Central American Common Market, South Pacific Regional Trade and Economic Cooperation Agreement, and Southern Cone Common Market. In further support of the present analysis, indicators for the Andean Community, the South Asian Association for Regional Cooperation, and the Bangkok Agreement were added to the Rose dataset.

trading partner, and accordingly the estimated coefficients of these variables suggest the degree to which trade with the world by the specified pairs of trading partners is greater or less than the norm established from estimation of the "core" gravity model.

Estimation of gravity models using cross-sectional time series data presents some problems in econometric methods (Egger 2002, Hsiao 2003). OLS regression can be deemed inadequate or inappropriate because it does not admit possible unobserved effects related to the bilateral pairs of trading countries. Accordingly, analysts frequently turn to so-called fixed-effects or random-effects variants of the gravity model in which the unexplained error component of the regression equation is assumed to incorporate an either fixed or random unobservable element for each bilateral pair of countries in the model. Unfortunately, the simpler and more straightforward of these two variants, the fixed-effects variant, cannot be used because the present analysis specifies several time-invariant explanatory variables, namely, those representing the bilateral trade and openness of Colombia and the United States, which must be dropped from estimation of fixed-effect regression equations.[9] Consequently, the present analysis uses the random-effects variant of the gravity model, which is estimated using generalized least squares (GLS) techniques.[10]

Estimation Results

Table 4.1 presents the gravity model estimation results for the entire sample period, 1948–99, and for two recent subperiods, 1990–99 and 1995–99, which correspond to the resurgence of regionalism during the last decade and the post–Uruguay Round period, respectively. The estimation results are also partitioned according to three broad classes of explanatory variables: "core" gravity model variables, RTAs (considered individually and on a combined basis), and bilateral trade and openness. Finally, the gravity model estimates are presented with and without inclusion of the openness variables corresponding to the specified indicators of bilateral trade.

The bilateral trade variables are central to the present analysis because they focus on the extent of Colombia's trade relations with the United

---

9. In effect, time-invariant variables in the fixed-effects variant of the regression equation are absorbed by the regression constant term, making the separate contribution of the time-invariant variables to the regression results indeterminable.

10. On the application of GLS techniques to random-effects regression models, see Hsiao (2003). Notwithstanding the advantages of the random-effects approach to estimating gravity trade models, an important assumption of the approach, maintained for the estimation results reported here, is that the unobservable random-effects variable is uncorrelated with the observed explanatory variables included in the regression equation. For further discussion, see Hausman (1978), Hausman and Taylor (1981), and Egger (2002).

States and other prominent global and regional trading partners: the European Union, Brazil, Mexico, and Venezuela. For comparison, the bilateral trade variables also focus on the extent of US-Chile trade. The estimated coefficients for these variables would indicate whether bilateral trade of these countries is significantly different from the norms for bilateral trade established by the gravity model's other explanatory variables. Inclusion of the openness variables in the gravity model regression equation provides a more rigorous basis for judging the significance of the US-Colombia trade variable and other specified bilateral trade variables for Colombia and the United States.

The regression results in table 4.1 mirror the widely reported empirical robustness of the gravity model for explaining bilateral trade flows. The model explains 60 to 65 percent of the variation in worldwide trade flows between countries, not only for the entire sample period of 1948–99 but also for the decade of the 1990s and the post–Uruguay Round period of 1995–99.

The core explanatory variables, led by trade distance, joint real GDP, and joint real GDP per capita, predominantly bear the anticipated signs and are generally significant at high levels of probability. Thus, for instance, bilateral trade is often significantly positively related to joint GDP in the partner countries and significantly negatively related to distance between partner countries. Similarly, countries sharing a common border tend to trade significantly more with one another, while landlocked countries tend to trade less than other countries. Notably, nonreciprocal GSP programs add significantly to bilateral trade flows of less developed countries, the beneficiaries of GSP programs. Indeed, the gravity model results in table 4.1 suggest that the magnitude of the positive contribution of GSP to the trade of less developed countries has become substantially greater during the past decade, though this result may reflect the "graduation" of a number of developing countries, leaving access to GSP programs mainly to the least developed countries.

The gravity model estimation results for the RTA variables indicate strong support for the (gross) trade creation effects of several RTAs. In the Western Hemisphere, these include the two most prominent regional arrangements, the North American Free Trade Agreement (NAFTA) and the Southern Cone Common Market (Mercosur). However, they also include the Andean Community (to which Colombia belongs), the Central American Common Market (CACM), and the Caribbean Common Market (Caricom). In Asia, strong support is indicated for the Association of Southeast Asian Nations (ASEAN) Free Trade Area (AFTA), the Australia–New Zealand Closer Economic Relations Trade Agreement (Anzcerta), and the South Pacific Regional Trade and Economic Cooperation Agreement (Sparteca), but notably not for the Bangkok Agreement or the South Asian Preferential Trading Arrangement (SAPTA). Unexpectedly, the gravity model regression results find little support for the EU trading

Table 4.1 Colombia and US trade integration with selected Western Hemisphere countries: Gravity model estimation, 1948–99

Variable	Individual regional trade agreements						Regional trade agreements combined					
	1948–99		1990–99		1995–99		1948–99		1990–99		1995–99	
	Without openness	With openness	Without openness	With openness	Without openness	With openness	Without openness	With openness	Without openness	With openness	Without openness	With openness
Core explanatory variables												
Constant	−20.45***	−20.43***	−17.13***	−17.26***	−15.95***	−16.04***	−20.58***	−20.57***	−16.66***	−16.75***	−15.78***	−15.81***
Distance	−1.32***	−1.27***	−1.29***	−1.24***	−1.21***	−1.18***	−1.31***	−1.26***	−1.33***	−1.28***	−1.22***	−1.19***
GDP	.88***	.84***	1.00***	.98***	.97***	.96***	.88***	.84***	.99***	.97***	.96***	.95***
GDP per capita	.01	.01	−.42***	−.46***	−.44***	−.48***	.01	.01	−.41***	−.45***	−.43***	−.47***
Common language	.27***	.32***	.29***	.37***	.33***	.40**	.27***	.31***	.33***	.41***	.35***	.43***
Common border	.63***	.82***	.95***	1.06***	1.07***	1.15***	.66***	.86***	.90***	1.02***	1.03***	1.12***
Landlocked	−.53***	−.53***	−.70***	−.69***	−.72***	−.71***	−.53***	−.53***	−.70***	−.70***	−.73***	−.71***
Island	.20***	.37***	.09*	.33***	.09*	.33***	.18***	.35***	.14***	.38***	.11**	.35***
Land area	−.06***	−.02*	−.18***	−.15***	−.18***	−.15***	−.06***	−.02*	−.17***	−.14***	−.17***	−.14***
Com colonizer	.18***	.38***	−.05	.12	.06	.23***	.16**	.36***	−.05	.11	.05	.21***
Colony	.30***	.30***	.50	.50	.44	.43	.32***	.31***	.50	.50	.44	.43
Ever a colony	2.15***	1.40***	1.60***	.96***	1.54***	.98***	2.14***	1.39***	1.61***	.98***	1.51***	.97***
Common country	1.23	1.12	.46	.17	.03	−.23	1.22	1.12	.40	.11	.04	−.23
Currency union	.59***	.60***	.60***	.55***	.40**	.33*	.61***	.61***	.66***	.60***	.40**	.34*
GSP	.31***	.28***	1.44***	1.00***	1.33***	.91***	.31***	.27***	1.46***	1.02***	1.34***	.93***
Regional trade agreements												
European Union	1.05***	1.04***	−.43***	−.45***	1.01**	.08						
US-Israel	.48	.50	2.96	2.38	2.96	2.35						
NAFTA	.86***	.86***	.65	.65	2.35**	2.35**						
Caricom	.38***	.36***	1.39***	1.39***	1.13***	1.15***						
Patcra	−.05	−.03										
Anzcerta	.89**	.87**	5.82***	5.66***	5.69***	5.55***						
CACM	1.88***	1.88***	.88	1.19*	.94	1.22**						
Mercosur	1.02***	1.01***	.26	.26	.56**	.48*						
ASEAN	.64***	.69***	.59***	.63***	.69***	.76***						
Sparteca	.32**	.33**	2.89***	3.34***	2.72***	3.15***						
Andean Community	1.11***	1.11***	1.16*	1.70**	1.40**	1.95***						

	(1)	(2)	(3)	(4)	(5)	(6)	(7)	(8)	(9)	(10)	(11)	(12)
SAPTA	.42***	.42***	.42***	-.01	-.01	-1.64***	-1.51***				.88***	.87***
Bangkok agreement	.87***	.90***	.87***	-.72	-.50	.27	.38			.89***	.88***	.87***
Regional trading arrangements combined								.89***	.89***	.32***	.34***	
Bilateral trade												
Colombia-US	1.78	1.94	1.32	.97	1.32	1.51	.84	1.78	1.96	.88	1.51	.77
Colombia-EU	.32*	-.13	2.13***	1.68***	2.13***	1.08***	1.44***	.37**	-.09	1.18***	1.20***	.86***
Colombia-Venezuela	-2.26	-1.79	-.73	-.91	-.73	-.80	-.79	-2.14	-1.67	.31	-.26	.22
Colombia-Mexico	-.61	-.02	.88	1.27	.88	1.14	1.72	-.61	-.02	1.16	1.13	1.63
Colombia-Brazil	-1.84	-1.44	-.43	-.11	-.43	-.43	.11	-1.87	-1.46	-.16	-.39	.07
US-Chile	2.44	1.50	2.29	1.65	2.29	2.40	1.73	2.44	1.50	1.64	2.39	1.70
Bilateral openness												
Colombia-US	.77***	.77***			.13	.13	-.34*	.77***			.14	-.31*
Colombia-EU	1.22***	1.22***			1.33***	1.33***	1.21***	1.32***			1.22***	1.20***
Colombia-Venezuela	-.86***	-.86***			-.95***	-.95***	-.79***	-.85***			-.91***	-.76***
Colombia-Mexico	-1.31***	-1.31***			-.87***	-.87***	-.60***	-1.32***			-.84***	-.56***
Colombia-Brazil	-.14	-.14			.20	.20	.16	-.14			.21	.16
US-Chile	.50***	.50***			1.29***	1.29***	1.78***	.49***			1.30***	1.77***
R²	.61	.62	.62	.62	.63	.64	.60	.61	.62	.63	.63	.63
Observations	235	235	73	73	38	38	235	235	73	73	38	38
Pairs (thousands)	12	12	11	11	10	10	12	12	11	11	10	10

***, **, * indicate that the coefficients are statistically significant at the 99, 95, and 90 percent levels, respectively.

Anzerta = Australia–New Zealand Closer Economic Relations Trade Agreement
CACM = Central American Common Market
Caricom = Caribbean Community
GSP = generalized system of preferences
Mercosur = Southern Cone Common Market
NAFTA = North American Free Trade Agreement
Patcra = Agreement on Trade and Commercial Relations between the Government of Australia and the Government of Papua New Guinea
SAPTA = South Asian Preferential Trading Arrangement
Sparteca = South Pacific Regional Trade and Economic Cooperation Agreement

Notes: Regressand is log real trade. Distance, GDP, GDP per capita, and land area are measured in log terms. Estimated year effects are not reported.

Source: Authors' calculations based on generalized least squares estimation of the gravity model with random effects and using an augmented version of the dataset provided by Rose (2002, 2003).

arrangement during 1990, especially when the substantial openness of the European Union is explicitly taken into account by the Colombia-EU openness variable. Similarly, the US-Israel FTA is not found to expand US bilateral trade with Israel. Though a positive coefficient is estimated for the US-Israel FTA variable, the estimated coefficient is not statistically different from zero.

When the individual RTA variables are combined to form a single RTA variable, the gravity model results remain robust, and the coefficient of the aggregate RTA variable is estimated to be positive and highly significant across the three periods considered. The coefficient estimate for the aggregate RTA variable, however, is appreciably lower for the decade of the 1990s (0.32 to 0.34) than for either the 1948–99 period (0.89) or the post-Uruguay Round period of 1995–99 (0.87 to 0.88), apparently reflecting the negative coefficient estimated for the EU trading arrangement over the 1990s (–0.43 to –0.45). Despite this curious result, the coefficient estimates for the single RTA variable imply that, on average, successful RTAs expand the mutual trade of RTA members by between 38 percent (based on 1990s estimates) and 140 percent (based on post–Uruguay Round estimates).

Finally, the gravity model estimation results for the bilateral trade and openness variables bear directly on the potential for expanding US-Colombia trade under a bilateral free trade agreement. Across the estimation periods and across the alternative specifications of the RTA variables in table 4.1, the bilateral trade variables in the gravity model are uniformly insignificant, except in the case of Colombia's trade with the European Union. Even when the general openness of EU trade (if not also Colombian trade) is taken into account, the estimation results find that Colombia's trade with the European Union is greater than expected for bilateral trade in the estimated gravity model. With respect to US-Colombia trade, the results indicate that Colombia's bilateral trade with the United States is neither significantly above nor significantly below the gravity model norms for bilateral trade, including when the openness of US-Colombia trade with the world is taken into account.

The marginal insignificance of US-Colombia trade in the present gravity model estimation results implies appreciable potential for expansion of trade between the United States and Colombia under an FTA. Grist for expanded US-Colombia trade would be found in reciprocal trade preferences exchanged between the two countries under the free trade agreement. Indeed, the negative coefficients estimated for the openness variables related to Colombia's trade with Mexico, Venezuela, and, marginally, the United States during the post–Uruguay Round period suggest that reduced protection in Colombia, if not also the United States, should be expected to expand trade between the two countries.

More precisely, the gravity model estimation results for the single RTA variable suggest that if a free trade agreement between Colombia and the United States were successfully negotiated, US-Colombia trade might be expanded by between 38 and 140 percent. Such magnitudes, as noted by Rose (2003), may be somewhat larger than generally found in the literature on AGE models and other applied economic models, but they do imply substantial, and statistically robust, positive impacts of a US-Colombia FTA on bilateral trade.

GTAP Model Analysis to Measure Potential Welfare Gains

This section draws on the results of simulations of the GTAP model of world trade and economic activity to provide more in-depth quantitative analysis of the potential economic impact of a US-Colombia free trade agreement, covering not only aggregate trade between the two nations but also trade and production by major sectors, primary factor incomes, and, especially, economic welfare in the two countries and potential spillover effects on neighboring Andean, Mercosur, and other third countries.[11]

The GTAP Model

The GTAP model is a multisector, multicountry applied economic model based on general equilibrium theory, developed with the objective of being a practical tool for policy analysis (Hertel 1997, Dimaranan and McDougall 2002). Like other AGE models, the GTAP model rigorously enforces economywide resource and expenditure constraints. It assumes perfect competition in goods and factor markets and constant returns to scale in production. Bilateral trade is handled via the so-called Armington (1969) assumption, which treats similar goods imported from different countries as imperfect substitutes. Production is modeled using nested constant elasticity of substitution functions, with intermediate goods used in fixed proportions. Representative household demand uses a nonhomothetic function that takes into account changes in demand structures as incomes rise.

The GTAP model is publicly available and has been widely applied to issues in international trade and economic development, including, recently, US bilateral free trade agreements (DeRosa and Gilbert 2004). It is particularly well suited to analyzing bilateral trade agreements and RTAs. By linking markets for traded goods between countries, the model captures relevant feedback and flow-through effects associated with changes in trade policy undertaken in two or more countries simultaneously, in-

---

11. The analysis in this section uses 1997 data from the GTAP5 database. In the technical appendix to this book, John Gilbert provides more extensive details of the present analysis. The GTAP6 database, which is updated to 2001, recently became available. Appendix 4B to this chapter by Scott Bradford presents a less detailed overview of the US-Colombia FTA using the more recent data.

cluding potential second-best consequences of discriminatory free trade agreements (Panagariya 2000). Against these significant advantages, the GTAP model and similar other AGE models are highly data-intensive and subject to uncertainties of specification, experimental design, and choice of parameter values. Accordingly, AGE simulation results should be evaluated carefully.[12]

Experimental Design

The GTAP model database (version 5.4) identifies 78 regions and 57 sectors. As a practical matter, however, it is necessary to aggregate the data to a higher level. The simulations for the present analysis use an aggregation of 30 regions and 23 sectors, presented in table 4.2.

Following DeRosa and Gilbert (2004), the regional aggregation is chosen to reflect individual partners in prospective free trade agreements with the United States that can be identified in the GTAP model database. In the Western Hemisphere, these partners include Colombia and the other Andean Community members, the Central American Free Trade Agreement–Dominican Republic (CAFTA-DR) countries, Panama, and of course NAFTA partners Canada and Mexico and Chile, US FTA partners since 1994 and 2003, respectively. Other countries and regions are selected primarily on the basis of the extent of their trading relations with the United States and Colombia (China, the European Union, Japan, and the Mercosur countries).[13]

The sectoral aggregation, which is also presented in table 4.2, highlights important commodities in the bilateral trade (exports plus imports) of the United States and Colombia. It is also intended to identify the most critical commodities and manufactures of both countries in their trade with the world.[14]

The basic simulation design also follows DeRosa and Gilbert (2004), with some extensions to account for overlapping free trade agreements in the Americas. In the main analysis, the proposed FTA between the United States and Colombia is simulated independently of the existence of other

---

12. For recent surveys of the application of AGE models to regional trade negotiations, see Scollay and Gilbert (2000, 2001) Gilbert and Wahl (2002), and Robinson and Thierfelder (2002). For a recent examination of unilateral economic reform in Colombia and other countries in Latin America, see Gilbert (2003).

13. Other countries included in the regional aggregation, such as those in the Southern African Customs Union (SACU) and ASEAN countries, are included on the basis of their potential as US FTA partners outside of the Western Hemisphere.

14. Services trade is an increasingly important part of the US-Colombia trading relationship, although it is still outweighed by commodity and manufactures trade by a ratio of approximately 8 to 1. Unfortunately, the current GTAP database does not contain data on services protection, and hence only indirect effects of trade reform can be captured.

Table 4.2   Regional and sectoral aggregates in the GTAP model analysis

Regional aggregation	Sectoral aggregation	Detailed categories
Argentina	Grains	Paddy rice
Australia		Wheat
Botswana		Cereal grains nec
Brazil	Vegetables and fruits	Vegetables, fruit, nuts
Canada	Other crops	Oilseeds
Central America and Caribbean		Sugar cane, sugar beet
Chile		Plant-based fibers
China		Crops nec
Colombia	Other agriculture	Bovine cattle, sheep and goats, horses
European Union		Animal products nec
Indonesia		Raw milk
Japan		Wool, silkworm cocoons
Korea	Forestry and fisheries	Forestry
Malaysia		Fishing
Mexico	Coal	Coal
Morocco	Oil and gas	Oil
New Zealand		Gas
Peru		Minerals nec
Philippines	Food products	Bovine cattle, sheep and goat meat products
Rest of Andean Community		Meat products
Rest of Southern African Customs Union		Vegetable oils and fats
Rest of South America		Dairy products
Rest of world		Processed rice
Singapore		Sugar
Sri Lanka		Food products nec
Taiwan		Beverages and tobacco products
Thailand	Textiles	Textiles
Uruguay	Wearing apparel	Wearing apparel
United States		Leather products
Venezuela	Lumber	Wood products
	Pulp and paper	Paper products, publishing
	Petroleum and coal products	Petroleum, coal products
	Chemicals	Chemical, rubber, plastic products
	Nonmetallic minerals	Mineral products nec
	Metals	Ferrous metals
		Metals nec

(table continues next page)

Table 4.2   Regional and sectoral aggregates in the GTAP model analysis
         (continued)

Regional aggregation	Sectoral aggregation	Detailed categories
	Fabricated metal products	Metal products
	Motor vehicles	Motor vehicles and parts
	Other transportation equipment	Transport equipment nec
	Electronic equipment	Electronic equipment
	Machinery	Machinery and equipment nec
	Other manufactures	Manufactures nec
	Services	Electricity
		Gas manufacture, distribution
		Water
		Construction
		Trade
		Transport nec
		Water transport
		Air transport
		Communication
		Financial services nec
		Insurance
		Business services nec
		Recreational and other services
		Ownership of dwellings

GTAP = Global Trade Analysis Project
nec = not elsewhere classified

potential agreements, and the simulation results thus reflect the impact of the proposed FTA in isolation. However, a US-all partners FTA experiment is also considered, in which the proposed US-Colombia FTA is implemented simultaneously, with other proposed US FTAs expected to be in force by 2005.[15] In all cases, the arrangements are implemented on a "clean" basis, meaning that all import tariffs are reduced to zero in the participating economies on a preferential basis. All other tariffs (i.e., those applied to imports from nonparticipating economies) are left in place. The tariffs used are those in place in the current base year of the GTAP model (1997).[16] Summary measures of the tariff estimates in the database are pre-

---

15. Based on the current list of USTR notifications to Congress and the availability of data in the current GTAP model, the list of agreements in the all-partners scenario is: US-Andean, US-Australia, CAFTA-DR, US-Chile, US-Morocco, US-SACU, US-Singapore, and US-Thailand.

16. GTAP protection data are derived from the Organization for Economic Cooperation and Development's Agricultural Market Access Database (AMAD) for agricultural trade and UNCTAD's Trade Analysis and Information System (TRAINS) database for other merchan-

Table 4.3 Unadjusted initial tariff rates (weighted average, percent)

| Sector | United States | | | Colombia | | |
	Overall	Colombia	Remaining Andean Community	Overall	United States	Remaining Andean Community
Grains	1.52	0	0	11.86	11.86	12.22
Vegetables and fruits	4.69	4.69	4.69	14.07	14.09	14.08
Other crops	21.23	21.51	21.35	9.97	10.14	10.07
Other agriculture	.84	.57	.63	8.01	7.98	7.93
Forestry and fisheries	.31	.20	.68	12.43	7.76	18.23
Coal	0	0	0	0	0	0
Oil and gas	.25	.40	.40	5.44	5.32	5.12
Food products	11.13	20.04	13.52	18.18	18.11	18.24
Textiles	8.92	12.48	12.03	16.83	15.90	17.62
Wearing apparel	12.08	13.89	16.81	18.52	19.48	18.53
Lumber	.82	1.96	1.96	16.53	16.91	15.38
Pulp and paper	.34	.98	1.09	10.82	12.64	15.61
Petroleum and coal products	1.64	2.45	2.32	10.17	10.23	10.25
Chemical	2.67	4.71	5.02	8.35	8.27	11.12
Nonmetallic minerals	4.41	2.37	2.76	14.17	13.97	14.19
Metals	1.61	2.06	1.64	8.88	11.89	7.63
Fabricated metal products	2.70	2.88	3.36	14.07	14.15	14.06
Motor vehicles	1.26	1.17	1.20	25.65	14.76	32.85
Other transportation equipment	1.30	2.22	2.01	6.18	3.08	11.11
Electronic equipment	1.03	2.03	3.22	6.48	5.85	11.32
Machinery	1.86	2.69	3.55	9.41	9.39	13.32
Other manufactures	1.59	.97	5.37	16.83	16.73	19.54

Source: Initial data from the GTAP5.4 database (Dimaranan and McDougall 2002). Estimates from simulation results.

sented in table 4.3 as trade-weighted averages. It should be noted that the GTAP model database does not presently incorporate data on services protection. Hence, the simulations should be interpreted as representing the potential effect of trade liberalization in merchandise goods only. In the experiment with all US FTAs, the bilateral free trade agreements are implemented simultaneously with the United States only. That is, prefer-

dise trade. In the case of agriculture, applied rates are used where available instead of most favored nation bound rates. US Department of Agriculture estimates are used in the case of rice to Japan, Korea, and the Philippines. In the case of other merchandise, the rates are generally most favored nation bound rates. Tariffs are specified on a bilateral basis, with the differences reflecting the differences in the composition of trade at the disaggregate level. Tariff preferences for NAFTA, EU–European Free Trade Association, Anzcerta, and SACU are included in the database. Other preferences are not. For full details, see Dimaranan and McDougall (2002).

ential trade liberalization among all countries in the Andean region and other highlighted areas is not considered.[17]

Only a limited number of existing preferential agreements are accounted for in the protection data in the current GTAP model. For the present analysis, an attempt is made to account for a number of important preferential trading arrangements that provide a backdrop to the proposed US-Colombia FTA. The method used is to estimate the impact of the preferential trading arrangements (including in the Andean Community) by simulation, producing a new equilibrium dataset in which the arrangements are present.[18] The set of US FTA experiments described above is then repeated, using this new equilibrium as the baseline. This experimental design avoids potentially attributing effects to a US-Colombia FTA that might not occur, given, for example, free trade within the Andean Community.

The simulations of the GTAP model are run on a comparative statics basis. Factor market closure in the model allows full mobility of capital and labor (skilled and unskilled) across domestic activities. Hence, the implicit time period is the long run (typically this closure is regarded as corresponding to a 10- to 12-year adjustment period). However, the adjustment path is not directly modeled. Land is treated as imperfectly mobile across agricultural activities, while natural resources are assumed to be specific factors. The parameters that govern the degree of substitutability between imports and domestic goods and among similar imports from various sources in the model are the default values in the GTAP model database. They range in value from 2 to 5 and from 4 to 10, respectively.

US-Colombia Free Trade Agreement Scenario Results

Tables 4.4 through 4.9 show the effects of the proposed US-Colombia FTA in isolation, as simulated using the GTAP model. Table 4.4 reports the simulated results for several key economywide variables. The first two columns present results for the United States, the next two for Colombia. The first column allocated to each economy presents the initial values, in millions of 1997 dollars, for the relevant economic variable. The subsequent column presents the simulated change in that variable under the FTA. Export and import changes are given as percentages, evaluated at

---

17. A benchmarking exercise, as detailed in the technical appendix to this book, considers simulated reform to multilateral trade. Under this scenario, all economies in the model are assumed to eliminate all tariffs on a most favored nation basis.

18. This method has been used to eliminate the effect of the following existing and proposed agreements: EU-Chile FTA, EU-Mexico FTA, EU-Mercosur FTA, CAFTA-DR, Mercosur, Andean Community, and Chile-Andean FTA.

Table 4.4 Changes in key economywide variables:
GTAP model results for US-Colombia FTA

Variable	United States		Colombia	
	Initial value (millions of 1997 dollars)	US-Colombia FTA	Initial value (millions of 1997 dollars)	US-Colombia FTA
Total import value				
(percent change)	1,022,879.3	.16	17,848.90	8.61
From partner	5,542.3	37.22	5,851.50	44.06
From rest of world	1,017,337.0	−.04	11,997.40	−8.67
Total export value				
(percent change)	852,807.6	.17	15,306.90	8.61
To partner	5,584.1	43.50	5,159.80	37.44
To rest of world	847,223.5	−.11	10,147.10	−6.04
Tariff revenue				
(dollar change)	25,089.0	−545.90	1,696.20	−676.50
From partner	391.5	−391.50	510.60	−510.60
From rest of world	24,697.5	−154.40	1,185.60	−165.90
Welfare as percent of GDP	7,945,411.00	0	94,561.20	.43
Total equivalent variation				
(millions of dollars)		227.30		403.20
Allocative efficiency		17.10		67.70
Terms of trade		210.20		335.50

GTAP = Global Trade Analysis Project

Source: Initial data from the GTAP5.4 database (Dimaranan and McDougall 2002). Estimates from simulation results.

world prices. Tariff revenue and equivalent variation (EV) estimates are presented as changes in millions of 1997 dollars.

The proposed US-Colombia FTA is expected to result in a significant increase in total trade between the two countries. The total value of bilateral exports from Colombia to the United States increases by an estimated 37 percent, while the value of bilateral exports from the United States to Colombia increases by an estimated 44 percent. In the case of the United States, the increase in Colombian imports does not come at the expense of a significant drop in nonpartner trade, but in the case of Colombia there is a decrease in imports from third countries of approximately 9 percent.

Tariff revenue changes are presented both in terms of the total revenue change and the changes in revenue obtained from partner and nonpartner sources. These figures give a direct indication of the revenue consequences

Table 4.5 Changes in sectoral pattern of production: GTAP model results for US-Colombia FTA

| | United States | | Colombia | |
| | Initial value (millions of 1997 dollars) | US-Colombia FTA (percent change in volume) | Initial value (millions of 1997 dollars) | US-Colombia FTA (percent change in volume) |
Sector				
Grains	53,900.0	.14	960.3	−6.83
Vegetables and fruits	34,953.2	.01	4,132.0	−1.33
Other crops	50,922.8	−.56	4,163.1	9.07
Other agriculture	109,960.0	.01	5,811.0	.23
Forestry and fisheries	15,370.8	−.01	995.9	−.23
Coal	32,701.1	.00	962.6	−.63
Oil and gas	83,149.9	−.02	5,252.1	−.72
Food products	556,329.6	.01	20,954.9	.49
Textiles	111,569.7	.06	2,160.1	2.30
Wearing apparel	102,131.5	−.05	3,710.4	12.76
Lumber	176,993.5	0	1,047.6	−1.76
Pulp and paper	310,167.5	.01	3,300.7	−1.65
Petroleum and coal products	165,142.6	.01	2,343.4	−.27
Chemical	573,930.6	.04	8,244.8	−2.40
Nonmetallic minerals	94,685.0	.04	2,035.0	−2.99
Metals	201,119.0	.02	1,425.7	−4.75
Fabricated metal products	224,697.7	.03	1,248.0	−5.57
Motor vehicles	366,300.8	.08	1,580.0	−8.04
Other transportation equipment	158,054.6	−.06	293.9	−3.24
Electronic equipment	290,664.6	−.03	429.1	−8.59
Machinery	633,468.4	.03	2,462.1	−8.05
Other manufactures	46,886.9	.07	1,113.6	−3.87
Services	9,958,251.0	0	94,734.9	−.24

GTAP = Global Trade Analysis Project

Source: Initial data from the GTAP5.4 database (Dimaranan and McDougall 2002). Estimates from simulation results.

of the proposed FTA. The breakdown into two components extends the approach of Fukase and Martin (2001) for examining trade diversion consequences of preferential trading arrangements. The loss in tariff revenue from the partner reflects the elimination of tariffs on goods imported from the partner. The change in the nonpartner revenue indicates the implications of reductions in the volume of trade flows not being liberalized and

Table 4.6 Changes in sectoral pattern of exports: GTAP model results for US-Colombia FTA

Sector	United States Initial value (millions of 1997 dollars)		United States US-Colombia FTA (percent change in value)		Colombia Initial value (millions of 1997 dollars)		Colombia US-Colombia FTA (percent change in value)	
	Total	To Colombia	Total	To Colombia	Total	To United States	Total	To United States
Grains	10,924.9	234.6	.67	37.56	1.3	0.2	–7.87	–6.67
Vegetables and fruits	5,053.1	15.9	.21	83.48	522.5	169.0	–4.79	8.39
Other crops	13,610.7	92.9	.69	48.87	2,739.7	1,020.9	21.64	84.71
Other agriculture	2,939.6	9.3	.02	55.20	40.5	11.2	–12.54	–11.81
Forestry and fisheries	2,648.2	1.1	–.06	52.83	10.5	3.9	–5.14	–3.60
Coal	3,388.4	0	0	0	838.5	80.4	1.53	1.59
Oil and gas	3,032.3	6.7	–.03	28.27	2,644.7	2,125.6	–11.81	–11.50
Food products	30,674.1	188.9	.11	100.23	925.2	255.5	27.81	118.39
Textiles	11,484.6	118.6	.70	79.14	299.2	46.3	12.25	79.59
Wearing apparel	9,126.5	96.9	1.91	194.49	585.5	329.7	124.38	222.11
Lumber	9,473.4	24.4	.13	103.60	30.5	7.4	4.53	13.65
Pulp and paper	19,912.9	142.4	.23	42.90	230.7	26.6	1.73	4.92
Petroleum and coal products	6,383.0	23.4	.09	41.84	215.2	122.7	46.80	52.53
Chemical	84,186.3	1,015.3	.24	26.06	1,143.6	125.3	1.73	18.58
Nonmetallic minerals	11,920.5	76.8	.41	84.74	183.5	52.8	2.25	12.53
Metals	20,523.8	90.1	.19	73.32	294.5	90.4	1.35	9.48
Fabricated metal products	13,714.1	103.2	.43	74.11	109.7	13.5	2.56	18.11
Motor vehicles	56,832.5	200.2	.63	219.93	96.1	2.9	14.20	30.82
Other transportation equipment	45,807.6	240.7	–.12	22.22	14.6	0.8	7.89	29.76
Electronic equipment	109,331.5	756.6	0	17.46	13.6	2.3	3.99	13.72
Machinery	160,560.8	1,382.6	.20	37.60	340.0	12.4	3.24	19.13
Other manufactures	11,322.0	69.3	.42	94.23	186.7	86.3	6.43	9.52
Services	210,090.1	696.4	–.10	3.12	3,794.9	698.0	–2.52	–2.68

GTAP = Global Trade Analysis Project

Source: Initial data from the GTAP5.4 database (Dimaranan and McDougall 2002). Estimates from simulation results.

Table 4.7 Changes in regional pattern of exports: GTAP model results for US-Colombia FTA

Country/region	Initial value (millions of 1997 dollars)			US-Colombia FTA (percent change in value)		
	Total	To United States	To Colombia	Total	To United States	To Colombia
Australia	70,568.6	7,770.0	84.4	-.01	-.03	-3.97
Botswana	2,912.2	86.1	0.7	-.02	-.06	2.99
China	292,747.5	75,785.2	215.7	-.03	-.15	-7.14
European Union	2,360,091.5	221,163.9	4,030.1	-.02	.01	-7.21
Japan	490,466.4	127,323.8	1,200.1	-.01	.07	-13.34
Korea	149,305.6	25,365.0	383.5	-.03	.01	-15.73
Morocco	8,789.0	763.8	5.7	-.02	-.09	.71
New Zealand	17,027.0	2,066.9	27.8	-.02	-.22	-3.70
Rest of Southern African Customs Union	34,388.6	3,567.7	45.7	-.01	-.04	-5.36
Sri Lanka	4,781.2	1,779.3	7.4	-.05	-.40	-1.08
Taiwan	136,412.9	35,280.6	178.6	-.02	.00	-11.34
Rest of world	835,098.5	100,689.7	1,013.1	-.02	-.13	-5.39
Argentina	28,565.5	2,504.1	186.9	-.05	-.44	-9.40
Brazil	57,882.7	10,302.5	527.0	-.05	-.45	-12.03
Central America and Caribbean	39,264.9	16,076.4	148.3	-.05	-.49	-6.72
Chile	18,801.1	2,627.0	231.9	-.06	-.18	-7.70
Colombia	15,306.9	5,159.8		8.61	37.44	
Peru	7,829.8	1,925.9	159.2	-.13	-.51	-7.51

Uruguay	3,989.8	423.3	20.5	−.04	−.13	−3.95
Venezuela	23,515.0	12,644.9	1,377.9	−.23	.24	−9.31
Rest of Andean Community	6,946.2	2,492.8	429.6	−.28	−.11	−10.17
Rest of South America	4,436.6	465.1	7.9	−.02	−.10	−4.81
Indonesia	56,891.9	10,537.8	40.6	−.05	−.47	−6.75
Malaysia	95,089.8	18,817.8	64.6	−.01	−.01	−1.75
Philippines	40,995.1	11,849.6	51.0	−.02	−.12	1.06
Singapore	125,733.8	22,395.5	117.7	−.02	0	1.23
Thailand	70,705.3	14,566.9	59.8	−.02	−.16	−1.76
Total ASEAN	389,415.9	78,167.6	333.7	−.02	−.11	−.88
Canada	230,960.7	168,165.2	339.8	−.01	−.01	−7.66
United States	852,807.6		5,584.1	.17		43.50
Mexico	115,222.0	86,409.2	575.1	−.03	.01	−10.95
Total NAFTA	1,198,990.2	254,574.4	6,499.0	.12	0	36.01
Total world	6,197,533.7	989,005.8	17,114.4	.03	.16	8.39

ASEAN = Association of Southeast Asian Nations
GTAP = Global Trade Analysis Project
NAFTA = North American Free Trade Agreement

Source: Initial data from the GTAP5.4 database (Dimaranan and McDougall 2002). Estimates from simulation results.

Table 4.8 **Changes in net welfare by region: GTAP model results for US-Colombia FTA** (millions of 1997 dollars)

| Country/region | Initial GDP | US-Colombia FTA | | |
		Total benefits	Allocative efficiency	Terms of trade
Australia	392,832.2	−6.9	−0.9	−6.0
Botswana	4,774.8	−0.1	0	−0.1
China	994,719.3	−50.2	−22.0	−28.3
European Union	7,957,874.0	−159.1	−21.6	−137.5
Japan	4,255,576.5	−34.8	1.5	−36.4
Korea	445,523.8	−24.1	−7.9	−16.2
Morocco	34,946.6	−0.5	−0.2	−0.3
New Zealand	65,078.6	−3.0	−0.3	−2.7
Rest of Southern African Customs Union	139,040.8	−1.8	−0.4	−1.4
Sri Lanka	15,592.4	−3.7	−1.5	−2.2
Taiwan	299,662.4	−9.6	−1.0	−8.6
Rest of world	3,195,647.3	−77.6	−26.8	−50.8
Argentina	325,978.2	−13.4	−4.1	−9.4
Brazil	789,792.2	−53.4	−27.9	−25.5
Central America and Caribbean	94,073.2	−54.6	−19.5	−35.0
Chile	76,151.1	−8.9	−2.0	−6.9
Colombia	94,561.2	403.2	67.7	335.5
Peru	64,919.8	−12.6	−4.4	−8.2
Uruguay	19,060.2	−0.4	0	−0.3
Venezuela	83,736.4	−37.2	−0.3	−37.0
Rest of Andean Community	27,248.1	−29.8	−9.2	−20.7
Rest of South America	10,605.8	0	−0.1	0.1
Indonesia	208,823.4	−13.5	−2.0	−11.6
Malaysia	106,086.1	−1.9	−0.8	−1.1
Philippines	78,356.6	−7.0	−3.7	−3.3
Singapore	79,791.7	1.4	−0.7	2.1
Thailand	157,789.5	−10.2	−1.9	−8.3
Total ASEAN	630,847.1	−31.2	−9.1	−22.1
Canada	631,155.3	−52.5	−2.5	−50.0
United States	7,945,411.0	227.3	17.1	210.2
Mexico	388,840.3	−40.5	2.0	−42.5
Total NAFTA	8,965,406.7	134.3	16.6	117.7
Total world	28,983,648.3	−75.4		

ASEAN = Association of Southeast Asian Nations
GTAP = Global Trade Analysis Project
NAFTA = North American Free Trade Agreement

Source: Initial data from the GTAP5.4 database (Dimaranan and McDougall 2002). Estimates from simulation results.

Table 4.9 Changes in real returns to factors of production: GTAP model results for US-Colombia FTA

Factor	United States	Colombia
Land	−.23	13.24
Unskilled labor	.01	.91
Skilled labor	.01	.55
Capital	.01	.68
Natural resources	−.07	−4.19

GTAP = Global Trade Analysis Project

is an indicator of trade diversion.[19] In the case of a US-Colombia FTA, the latter effect is negative for both countries.

The EV measure is the basic indicator of changes in economic welfare. It represents the change in income at constant prices that is equivalent to the proposed change. To give an indication of the significance of the dollar measure relative to total economic activity, the EV is also presented as a percentage of the base year GDP. The dollar measure is further decomposed into allocative efficiency and terms of trade effects, following the procedure developed by Huff and Hertel (1996). These indicators are a numerical implementation of Harberger's (1971) fundamental equation of applied welfare economics. In essence, allocative efficiency effects measure the economic implications of reallocation of resources across activities (consumption, production, and trade). The greater the distortions in the economy, the greater the potential allocative efficiency effects of policy reform (both direct and indirect, or second-best). Terms of trade effects, on the other hand, measure the implications of changes in the prices faced by the economy in international trade. The larger the economy, the greater the expected terms of trade consequences of policy reform. Negative terms of trade consequences of an FTA for third countries are another indicator of trade diversion, since the changes in trade prices reflect the reduction of imports by members from nonmember sources. Strong positive terms of trade effects for FTA members can reflect both an improvement vis-à-vis nonmembers and the effects of improved access to partner markets (preferential access).

The results indicate that the proposed US-Colombia FTA would result in small welfare benefits for both partners, although the result for Colom-

---

19. Fukase and Martin (2001) identify a third component, the increase in revenues associated with increased trade volumes of liberalized imports. This effect is not present in this study because of the assumption that liberalization is complete (i.e., the post-FTA preferential tariffs are zero).

bia is more significant in both absolute and relative terms ($403 million corresponds to roughly 0.4 percent of GDP).[20]

In addition to the overall effects on the economy, the proposed FTA typically will have differential impacts by sector, an understanding of which is critical to grasping the potential domestic political economy implications of the reform. The simulated sectoral impacts of the proposed US-Colombia FTA are presented in table 4.5 in terms of the percentage change in output volume relative to the 1997 base year.[21] In table 4.5 (and the subsequent tables discussed here), it is important to keep in mind that very large percentage changes may indicate significant structural responses in the economies in question. In some cases, however, large percentage changes can be misleading, as they principally reflect extremely small initial levels of economic activity.[22] In these cases, a large percentage change may disguise an insignificant change in economic activity.

For the United States, a US-Colombia FTA would have only a minor effect on the production structure of the economy, with "other crops" being the most affected sector. Colombia, being the smaller partner, would likely face much larger structural adjustment issues. The results indicate that most manufacturing sectors would decline, with heavy manufactures most affected (although from a relatively small base). Increases in output of other crops, textile and wearing apparel, and food products (a small increase, but from a large base) would absorb jobs lost in other sectors. This is not unexpected, as small economies are generally likely to specialize in a relatively small number of goods.

Table 4.6 presents the estimated sectoral implications of a US-Colombia FTA in terms of the percentage change in the value of exports (evaluated at world prices) relative to the baseline. Both the percentage change in total export value and the percentage change in the value of exports to the FTA partner are presented in the scenarios. Table 4.6 gives indications of which sectors are likely to gain or lose from preferential market access. While overall US exports are unlikely to be greatly affected by the proposed US-Colombia FTA, there is significant bilateral expansion in some trade categories: motor vehicles, lumber, wearing apparel, and food products. For Colombia, the overall effects are more significant, as expected, given the small size of the Colombian economy and the importance of the US market. The largest export increases are in wearing apparel, petroleum prod-

---

20. It is worth noting that the assumed values of the Armington price elasticities of import demand have an important influence here. In general, higher Armington elasticities lead to greater allocative efficiency effects and a smaller terms-of-trade effect for a given volume of trade.

21. In GTAP, as in almost all AGE models, initial prices are normalized to unity, implying that value measures at the initial point are also volume measures.

22. This is especially likely to be the case when examining bilateral trade figures by sector, where the initial values are often very small.

ucts, other crops, and food products. Export declines are seen in grains, other agriculture, and oil and gas.

Table 4.7 considers the regional aspect of changes in the pattern of exports. The specific variables considered are the percentage change in the value of total exports to all countries and the percentage change in the value of exports to Colombia and the United States (evaluated at world prices). This table provides another means of evaluating the potential trade diversion effects of preferential trade reform by direct observation of changes in the regional trade pattern. For the United States, other economies in South and Central America appear to be the main economies from which trade is diverted under a US-Colombia FTA, with imports from Argentina, Brazil, the Caribbean, and Peru all falling by around 0.5 percent. Given efforts to integrate these regions into the proposed FTAA, a US-Colombia FTA might create some positive tensions, namely, nudging the FTAA negotiations forward. For Colombia, US exports seem to replace those of a wide variety of countries, with the economies of Northeast Asia (Japan, Korea, and Taiwan) and Brazil most affected. Again, this latter result could create positive forces of competitive liberalization in favor of completing the FTAA negotiations.

Table 4.8 illustrates how the proposed US-Colombia FTA could affect economic welfare in third countries and thus provides further indications of the possible welfare consequences of trade diversion and creation. As in table 4.4, the simulation results are the total equivalent variation in welfare, in millions of 1997 dollars, decomposed into allocative efficiency and terms of trade components. The proposed US-Colombia FTA causes a small net welfare loss for the world. Also, it hurts the United States' NAFTA partners, Canada and Mexico, because they lose preferential access as the US trade regime is liberalized further. Although this resembles a trade diversion effect, it may really reflect a positive impact on NAFTA, namely, replacement of imports from a relatively inefficient original partner with imports from a more efficient new trading partner. This pattern of economic adjustment is sometimes termed preference dilution. A similar result holds for the members of the Andean Community. Other countries that are significantly and negatively affected by the proposed agreement are those in the European Union and Japan.

Finally, table 4.9 presents the effects of trade policy reform simulated by the GTAP model on real factor returns in percentage change terms. Examining the changes in factor returns for the five primary factors of production identified in the GTAP model is a way of gaining insights into the distributional consequences of the proposed FTA. Because the ability to move into alternative economic activities is an important mechanism in mitigating the shocks associated with trade reform on factor incomes, the largest changes tend to be observed in those factors with limited mobility (i.e., natural resources and land). In the United States, only very small changes in factor returns are indicated, again reflecting the relatively small size of US-Colombia trade in relation to the total US economy. For Colombia, the effects are much larger, with all factors except natural resources estimated to benefit from reform. Increased returns to land in Colombia are especially large, estimated at 13.2 percent.

Effects Assuming Multiple US Free Trade Agreements and Preexisting Preferential Trading Arrangements

Because the United States has recently negotiated several bilateral free trade agreements and is in the process of negotiating several more, it is important to consider how the impact of the proposed US-Colombia FTA might be affected by the other US trade agreements. Following DeRosa and Gilbert (2004), this possibility is addressed by considering a "US–all partners FTA" scenario in which the other recently approved or proposed US FTAs are simulated simultaneously with the proposed US-Colombia FTA. The simulation results are summarized in table 4.10 and fully presented in chapter appendix tables 4A.1 through 4A.5 following the same format as tables 4.5 through 4.9.

When the entire set of prospective US FTAs is taken into account, the annual economic benefits to the United States of pursuing bilateral free trade agreements, measured in terms of equivalent variation, become substantially larger, rising to around $4 billion from just $200 million. For the potential US FTA partners, however, the benefits of preferential access to the US market are appreciably eroded as more countries forge free trade agreements with the United States. Thus, the annual benefits to Colombia, while remaining positive, fall from approximately $403 million (0.4 percent of GDP) to $203 million (0.2 percent of GDP). The estimated welfare impact is $134 million for Peru, –$151 million for Venezuela, and $110 million for the rest of the Andean Community. The case of Venezuela is interesting in that a welfare loss is estimated. However, sensitivity analysis indicates that the negative welfare result for Venezuela is not significantly different from zero. Also, importantly, reflecting the cumulative negative consequences of trade diversion, world economic welfare declines by $1 billion under the multiple US FTAs scenario (appendix table 4A.4), compared with a decline of $75 million under the US-Colombia FTA scenario (table 4.8).

Finally, table 4.11 summarizes the economywide results of the GTAP model simulations starting from a baseline that incorporates the presence of preexisting US and other FTAs that, as mentioned at the outset, might influence the effects of the proposed US-Colombia FTA, but for which preferential tariff and other relevant information are not included in the current database of the GTAP model.[23]

---

23. See the technical appendix to this book for complete tabulations of the GTAP simulation results when preexisting bilateral and regional preferential trading arrangements are more fully taken into account in GTAP model.

Table 4.10 Changes in key economywide variables: GTAP model results for US–all partners FTA

Variable	United States	Australia	Botswana	Chile	Colombia	Morocco	Peru	Venezuela	Rest of Andean Community	CAFTA-DR	Singapore	Thailand	Rest of SACU
Import value (percent change)	1.96	1.20	-.97	2.24	6.77	3.74	6.75	5.40	5.16	16.80	.17	4.43	2.40
From partner(s)	23.73	15.73	33.46	43.64	40.13	92.80	55.15	49.10	47.33	63.70	-.78	60.32	43.42
From rest of world	-.25	-2.60	-2.40	-9.59	-9.51	-5.17	-9.13	-20.15	-8.43	-5.13	.35	-4.44	-3.60
Export value (percent change)	2.18	.89	-.95	1.71	6.91	4.26	6.43	1.58	4.25	13.07	.13	2.89	1.65
To partner(s)	35.14	12.35	.55	16.67	34.02	19.09	38.96	4.99	22.88	58.38	6.07	32.14	17.75
To rest of world	-1.61	-.53	-1.00	-.71	-6.87	2.85	-4.18	-2.39	-6.18	-18.34	-1.15	-4.70	-.22
Tariff revenue (dollar change)	-2,811.20	-555.50	-7.00	-617.50	-677.70	-291.20	-359.50	-1,188.50	-246.60	-1,639.40	-30.30	-1,494.90	-455.20
From partner(s)	-2,232.80	-435.40	-2.10	-442.40	-510.60	-115.30	-281.60	-720.00	-183.50	-2,331.10	-25.30	-826.30	-233.70
From rest of world	-578.40	-120.10	-4.90	-175.10	-167.10	-175.90	-77.90	-468.50	-63.10	691.70	-5.00	-668.60	-221.50
Welfare as a percent of GDP	.05	-.01	-.07	-.14	.21	-.27	.21	-.18	.40	3.44	.29	.55	-.06
Total equivalent variation (millions of dollars)	4,009.00	-52.20	-3.20	-104.70	202.50	-94.70	134.50	-151.00	109.50	3,232.40	235.10	875.60	-86.20
Allocative efficiency	580.60	-42.20	.10	-92.10	7.10	-23.80	78.40	-128.50	17.20	1,379.80	8.70	4.00	-54.00
Terms of trade	3,428.40	-10.00	-3.30	-12.70	195.50	-70.90	56.10	-22.50	92.30	1,852.70	226.30	871.60	-32.10

CAFTA-DR = Central American Free Trade Agreement–Dominican Republic
GTAP = Global Trade Analysis Project
SACU = Southern African Customs Union

Table 4.11   Changes in key economywide variables (refined): GTAP model results for US-Colombia FTA

Variable	United States		Colombia	
	Initial value (millions of 1997 dollars)	US-Colombia FTA	Initial value (millions of 1997 dollars)	US-Colombia FTA
Total import value (percent change)	1,022,879.3	0.15	17,848.9	7.07
From partner	5,542.3	36.73	5,851.5	40.33
From rest of world	1,017,337.0	−0.10	11,997.4	−5.66
Total export value (percent change)	852,807.6	0.16	15,306.9	7.08
To partner	5,584.1	39.74	5,159.8	36.93
To rest of world	847,223.5	−0.10	10,147.1	−5.62
Tariff revenue (dollar change)	24,849.1	−529.70	1,130.4	−557.40
From partner	380.1	−380.10	483.9	−483.90
From rest of world	24,469.0	−149.60	646.5	−73.50
Welfare as percent of GDP	7,945,411.0	0	94,561.2	0.51
Total equivalent variation (millions of dollars)		186.60		480.30
Allocative efficiency		10.30		132.50
Terms of trade		176.30		347.80

GTAP = Global Trade Analysis Project

Note: This table summarizes the economywide results of the GTAP model simulations starting from a baseline that incorporates the presence of preexisting US and other FTAs that might influence the effects of the proposed US-Colombia FTA, but for which preferential tariff and other relevant information are not included in the current database of the GTAP model.

Source: Initial data from the GTAP5.4 database (Dimaranan and McDougall 2002). Estimates from simulation results.

The "refined" simulation results indicate slightly larger welfare gains to Colombia and slightly smaller welfare gains to the United States under the proposed US-Colombia FTA (comparing table 4.4 with table 4.11). When the several proposed US FTAs are implemented simultaneously, the net welfare gains are slightly smaller for both Colombia and the United States (comparing table 4.10 with table 4.11). Though not reported in table 4.11, the negative effect of the proposed US-Colombia FTA on the other economies of the Andean Community is somewhat worse than before. This occurs because the starting point of the simulations takes into account preferential access to the Colombian market under the Andean

Community. Thus, the degree of preferential access is diminished when Colombia extends preferential tariffs to the United States under the proposed agreement. This follows from the preference dilution effect discussed previously. Nonetheless, the net welfare effect on the Andean partners remains small, and, as before, it is reversed for the Andean countries except Venezuela when the other prospective US FTA partners simultaneously implement free trade agreements with the United States. Finally, the broad pattern of anticipated sectoral changes is unchanged, but the magnitude of the changes is somewhat subdued when preexisting bilateral and regional trading arrangements are more fully taken into account in the GTAP model.

Appendix 4A

Table 4A.1   Changes in sectoral pattern of production: GTAP model results for US–all partners FTA
(percent change in volume)

Sector	United States	Australia	Botswana	Chile	Colombia	Morocco	Peru	Venezuela	Rest of Andean Community	CAFTA-DR	Singapore	Thailand	Rest of SACU
Grains	.10	.10	.31	.08	1.13	.66	.49	.21	.38	1.03	.16	.19	1.04
Vegetables and fruits	.03	.01	.12	.07	.24	.03	.10	.02	.56	.92	.26	.38	.12
Other crops	.30	.03	.12	1.24	.87	.29	.49	.50	.95	1.01	.14	.47	.20
Other agriculture	.09	.07	.03	.06	.11	.13	.12	.04	.30	.48	.22	.10	.13
Forestry and fisheries	.05	.02	.05	.04	.05	.06	.02	.02	.08	.49	.03	.14	.01
Coal	.02	.02	.03	.02	.14	.06	.16	.09	.06	.38	.01	.16	.02
Oil and gas	.03	.05	.17	.08	.17	.19	.43	.09	.13	.80	.06	.23	.09
Food products	.13	.22	.17	.09	.17	.85	.16	.09	.61	.30	.15	.20	.24
Textiles	.51	.16	.11	.08	.84	1.48	.58	.09	.15	5.24	2.24	2.45	.43
Wearing apparel	.78	.21	2.16	.06	3.24	.91	1.93	.05	.20	12.98	11.23	5.04	3.31
Lumber	.03	.02	.26	.07	.40	.19	.10	.34	.38	2.38	.04	.80	.10
Pulp and paper	.01	.02	.08	.11	.27	.10	.14	.05	.32	1.07	.11	.14	.03
Petroleum and coal products	.05	.01	.17	.19	.07	.07	.02	.26	.09	.81	.01	.13	.03
Chemical	.05	.07	.04	.16	.38	.11	.18	.12	.15	.95	.06	.32	.07
Nonmetallic minerals	.06	.09	.17	.15	.50	.12	.23	.31	.25	2.43	.23	.44	.05
Metals	.04	.12	1.41	.17	.58	.37	1.23	.40	.26	3.98	.25	.70	.28
Fabricated metal products	.09	.04	1.66	.23	.92	.13	.20	.25	.16	2.11	.22	1.09	.05
Motor vehicles	.34	.43	4.24	.78	2.13	.34	.76	2.53	1.76	3.19	.45	1.20	.75
Other transportation equipment	.29	.17	1.17	1.92	.33	.73	.59	.40	1.19	3.26	.12	.58	.28
Electronic equipment	.22	.11	.89	1.40	1.16	.48	.87	.25	.56	1.47	.07	.64	.14
Machinery	.06	.15	.22	.98	1.35	.17	.87	.59	.69	2.96	.04	.24	.08
Other manufactures	.04	.05	.57	.36	.59	.13	.31	.44	.90	2.69	.15	.21	.27
Services	.01	.01	.08	.02	.05	.04	.04	.03	.06	.56	.03	.19	.03

CAFTA-DR = Central American Free Trade Agreement–Dominican Republic; GTAP = Global Trade Analysis Project; SACU = Southern African Customs Union

	United States				Colombia			
	Initial value (millions of 1997 dollars)		US–all partners FTA (percent change in value)		Initial value (millions of 1997 dollars)		US–all partners FTA (percent change in value)	
Sector	Total	To Colombia	Total	To Colombia	Total	To United States	Total	To United States
Grains	10,924.9	234.6	17.89	55.04	1.3	0.2	5.38	–30.00
Vegetables and fruits	5,053.1	15.9	17.72	104.40	522.5	169.0	18.66	37.86
Other crops	13,610.7	92.9	11.83	58.61	2,739.7	1,020.9	27.35	90.23
Other agriculture	2,939.6	9.3	6.89	69.03	40.5	11.2	4.96	–2.14
Forestry and fisheries	2,648.2	1.1	16.25	32.73	10.5	3.9	15.52	26.41
Coal	3,388.4	0	24.19	0	838.5	80.4	25.09	0
Oil and gas	3,032.3	6.7	9.97	50.00	2,644.7	2,125.6	–4.36	–6.35
Food products	30,674.1	188.9	17.55	103.29	925.2	255.5	46.88	112.23
Textiles	11,484.6	118.6	19.32	75.72	299.2	46.3	45.14	78.32
Wearing apparel	9,126.5	96.9	39.51	201.19	585.5	329.7	132.29	184.16
Lumber	9,473.4	24.4	12.42	106.19	30.5	7.4	42.98	21.62
Pulp and paper	19,912.9	142.4	7.52	49.63	230.7	26.6	24.55	10.98
Petroleum and coal products	6,383.0	23.4	6.84	35.81	215.2	122.7	55.26	62.99
Chemical	84,186.3	1,015.3	5.46	30.56	1,143.6	125.3	23.28	21.36
Nonmetallic minerals	11,920.5	76.8	11.06	83.92	183.5	52.8	43.07	36.17
Metals	20,523.8	90.1	4.90	73.77	294.5	90.4	11.26	11.12
Fabricated metal products	13,714.1	103.2	8.10	67.93	109.7	13.5	47.25	25.26
Motor vehicles	56,832.5	200.2	5.74	9.34	96.1	2.9	231.73	46.90
Other transportation equipment	45,847.6	240.7	.85	20.30	14.6	0.8	72.53	51.25
Electronic equipment	109,331.5	756.6	1.17	18.89	13.6	2.3	16.03	9.57
Machinery	160,560.8	1,382.6	2.98	39.03	340.0	12.4	55.12	20.48
Other manufactures	11,322.0	69.3	6.15	96.58	186.7	86.3	14.55	7.98
Services	210,090.1	696.4	–.07	3.68	3,794.9	698.0	–3.57	–3.84

GTAP = Global Trade Analysis Project

Source: Initial data from the GTAP5.4 database (Dimaranan and McDougall 2002). Estimates from simulation results.

Table 4A.3   Changes in regional pattern of exports: GTAP model results for US–all partners FTA

Country/region	Initial value (millions of 1997 dollars)			US–all partners FTA (percent change in value)		
	Total	To United States	To Colombia	Total	To United States	To Colombia
Australia	70,568.6	7,770.0	84.4	7.93	16.27	−2.09
Botswana	2,912.2	86.1	0.7	4.33	1.85	0
China	292,747.5	75,785.2	215.7	8.79	8.88	−.37
European Union	2,360,091.5	221,163.9	4,030.1	2.31	1.32	−8.03
Japan	490,466.4	127,323.8	1,200.1	3.16	3.34	−26.16
Korea	149,305.6	25,365.0	383.5	3.06	1.91	−39.09
Morocco	8,789.0	763.8	5.7	10.79	22.03	2.98
New Zealand	17,027.0	2,066.9	27.8	5.95	4.81	−5.94
Rest of Southern African Customs Union	34,388.6	3,567.7	45.7	7.48	21.65	−8.16
Sri Lanka	4,781.2	1,779.3	7.4	3.68	−2.24	5.68
Taiwan	136,412.9	35,280.6	178.6	4.54	2.31	−11.85
Rest of world	835,098.5	100,689.7	1,013.1	4.09	2.65	−5.74
Argentina	28,565.5	2,504.1	186.9	43.50	−27.10	−31.67
Brazil	57,882.7	10,302.5	527.0	26.33	−0.48	−19.85
Central America and Caribbean	39,264.9	16,076.4	148.3	19.94	62.82	−21.52
Chile	18,801.1	2,627.0	231.9	12.92	21.58	82.59

Colombia	15,306.9	5,159.8	0	20.75	39.76	0
Peru	7,829.8	1,925.9	159.2	15.48	44.83	50.11
Uruguay	3,989.8	423.3	20.5	28.56	-39.61	-40.63
Venezuela	23,515.0	12,644.9	1,377.9	13.24	9.04	99.85
Rest of Andean Community	6,946.2	2,492.8	429.6	19.98	23.71	128.67
Rest of South America	4,436.6	465.1	7.9	3.86	2.47	-1.77
Indonesia	56,891.9	10,537.8	40.6	5.78	.48	-4.26
Malaysia	95,089.8	18,817.8	64.6	3.24	1.45	-.50
Philippines	40,995.1	11,849.6	51.0	1.51	0	2.35
Singapore	125,733.8	22,395.5	117.7	2.39	6.97	.98
Thailand	70,705.3	14,566.9	59.8	6.36	36.42	-6.69
Total Association of Southeast Asian Nations	389,415.9	78,167.6	333.7	3.72	9.20	-1.11
Canada	230,960.7	168,165.2	339.8	2.05	1.48	-8.20
United States	852,807.6	0	5,584.1	4.57	0	38.52
Mexico	115,222.0	86,409.2	575.1	3.32	2.06	-12.03
Total North American Free Trade Agreement	1,198,990.2	254,574.4	6,499.0	3.96	1.71	31.61
Total world	6,197,533.7	989,005.8	17,114.4	4.21	4.66	18.54

GTAP = Global Trade Analysis Project

Source: Initial data from the GTAP5.4 database (Dimaranan and McDougall 2002). Estimates from simulation results.

Table 4A.4 Changes in net welfare by region: GTAP model results for US–all partners FTA (millions of 1997 dollars)

| Country/region | Initial GDP | US–all partners FTA | | |
		Total benefits	Allocative efficiency	Terms of trade
Australia	392,832.2	−52.2	−42.2	−10.0
Botswana	4,774.8	−3.2	0.1	−3.3
China	994,719.3	−1,251.5	−512.1	−739.4
European Union	7,957,874.0	−2,442.9	−615.6	−1,827.3
Japan	4,255,576.5	−1,256.1	−301.2	−954.9
Korea	445,523.8	−394.3	−120.3	−274.0
Morocco	34,946.6	−94.7	−23.8	−70.9
New Zealand	65,078.6	−55.7	−7.5	−48.2
Rest of Southern African Customs Union	139,040.8	−86.2	−54.0	−32.1
Sri Lanka	15,592.4	−64.0	−27.2	−36.7
Taiwan	299,662.4	−213.5	−17.6	−196.0
Rest of world	3,195,647.3	−1,179.8	−476.0	−703.8
Argentina	325,978.2	−178.1	−60.7	−117.4
Brazil	789,792.2	−589.8	−318.8	−270.9
Central America and Caribbean	94,073.2	3,232.4	1,379.8	1,852.7
Chile	76,151.1	−104.7	−92.1	−12.7
Colombia	94,561.2	202.5	7.1	195.5
Peru	64,919.8	134.5	78.4	56.1
Uruguay	19,060.2	−10.2	−3.7	−6.5
Venezuela	83,736.4	−151.0	−128.5	−22.5
Rest of Andean Community	27,248.1	109.5	17.2	92.3
Rest of South America	10,605.8	−13.1	−5.6	−7.5
Indonesia	208,823.4	−196.7	−48.6	−148.1
Malaysia	106,086.1	−118.9	−27.3	−91.5
Philippines	78,356.6	−148.4	−78.0	−70.5
Singapore	79,791.7	235.1	8.7	226.3
Thailand	157,789.5	875.6	4.0	871.6
Total Association of Southeast Asian Nations	630,847.1	646.7	−141.1	787.8
Canada	631,155.3	−667.3	−54.2	−613.1
United States	7,945,411.0	4,009.0	580.6	3,428.4
Mexico	388,840.3	−534.4	−7.7	−526.7
Total North American Free Trade Agreement	8,965,406.7	2,807.2	518.6	2,288.6
Total world	28,983,648.3	−1,008.1		

GTAP = Global Trade Analysis Project

Source: Initial data from the GTAP5.4 database (Dimaranan and McDougall 2002). Estimates from simulation results.

Table 4A.5 Changes in real returns to factors of production: GTAP model results for US–all partners FTA

Factor	United States	Australia	Botswana	Chile	Colombia	Morocco	Peru	Venezuela	Rest of Andean Community	CAFTA-DR	Singapore	Thailand	Rest of SACU
Land	1.08	.90	–1.63	5.92	12.87	–3.99	6.15	.91	8.99	–5.05	1.36	–2.99	–1.84
Unskilled labor	.13	.13	–.27	.46	.64	.85	.72	.86	1.64	7.84	.46	1.97	.38
Skilled labor	.12	.12	–.21	.35	.31	.89	.55	.98	1.37	7.87	.36	1.64	.37
Capital	.13	.12	.18	.40	.44	.83	.51	1.08	1.05	9.17	.34	1.81	.34
Natural resources	–.90	–.25	2.35	1.77	–1.51	3.81	–1.02	3.01	–2.70	–18.71	–1.41	–5.22	.75

CAFTA-DR = Central American Free Trade Agreement–Dominican Republic
GTAP = Global Trade Analysis Project
SACU = Southern African Customs Union

Appendix 4B
General Equilibrium Analysis of a US-Colombia
Free Trade Agreement

SCOTT BRADFORD

This appendix uses a multisector, global applied general equilibrium (AGE) model to simulate the broad economic effects of a US-Colombia free trade agreement. Unlike approaches that examine different sectors in isolation, AGE models use equations and detailed data to take account of key intranational and international relationships among producers and consumers. This allows such models to provide better estimates of how trade reforms will affect production, consumption, trade, prices, employment, and overall welfare in each region.

The model for this appendix has 22 sectors, five factors of production (unskilled labor, skilled labor, capital, land, and natural resources), and four regions (Colombia, the United States, Peru, and the rest of the world). The economic structure is standard:[1] perfect competition, constant returns to scale, and fully employed factors that can move freely across sectors but not across international boundaries.[2] The model also assumes, as is standard, that the amounts of the four factors besides capital are fixed. Two assumptions are made concerning the capital stock in each region, with each assumption leading to different simulation results. Assumption one is that the amount of capital is fixed, as with the other four factors. This assumption gives what one might call medium-term results—the economic effects after factors have adjusted across sectors. Assumption two is that the capital stock is allowed to increase through investment after trade opening. This gives what one might call long-term results—the economic effects after both factor movement and capital stock growth.

The model uses the most recent version of the state-of-the-art Global Trade Analysis Project (GTAP) database: GTAP6. Constructing such datasets is a huge undertaking, so the data have a lag of a few years. The GTAP6 data, released in 2005, are from 2001. These data do not include estimates for services trade barriers, which are probably large. Reform of services and a related boost to foreign direct investment almost always add to the gains from trade opening, so the estimates presented here will probably understate the likely gains from the FTA.

Scott Bradford is a visiting fellow at the Institute and associate professor in the Department of Economics, Brigham Young University.

1. The basic structure of the model is the same as that used in Bradford and Lawrence (2004) and Bradford, Greico, and Hufbauer (2005).

2. Land and natural resources are restricted to the agriculture and other primary products sectors.

Table 4B.1   Changes in equivalent variation

Country	Medium term: Capital stock fixed	Long term: Capital grows
Colombia		
Billions of US dollars	−.063	.550
Percent of GDP	−.060	.520
United States		
Billions of US dollars	.347	.706
Percent of GDP	0	.010
Peru		
Billions of US dollars	−.003	−.010
Percent of GDP	0	−.010
Rest of the world		
Billions of US dollars	−.377	−.614
Percent of GDP	0	0

A simple scenario is run to paint a broad-brushed picture of the potential effects of a US-Colombia FTA: complete free trade between the United States and Colombia. This allows for seeing the overall stakes involved in this endeavor. As described above, medium- and long-term results are computed. The adjustment path is not explicitly modeled. The simulations simply report the prediction for the new equilibrium after all adjustment has occurred. No effort is made to try to take account of possible spillover effects from other US and Colombian FTAs.

Table 4B.1 shows the overall welfare results, in billions of US dollars and as a percentage of GDP. The table reports the change in equivalent variation (EV) for each region, net of losses to people whom trade opening would hurt.[3] These numbers do not take account of the adjustment costs that many would have to bear as they move from one sector to another. Other analyses of such costs indicate that they could range from 10 to 30 percent of the net gains reported here.

The results imply that, in the medium term, Colombia would actually lose a small amount, on net, from an FTA with the United States: $63 million, or about 0.06 percent of GDP. It appears that the losses from trade diversion—sourcing more imports from the United States, which would not be the low-cost supplier—outweigh the benefits from trade creation induced by the lower barriers. In the longer run, however, after investment

---

3. Equivalent variation is the amount of money one would need to give the region (without any change in policy) to make it just as well off as it would be after the trade opening. A negative value for EV means that the region is hurt by the opening and that one would need to take money away to put it at the same welfare level as it would be after the trade opening.

Table 4B.2 Percent change in real factor prices, Colombia

Factor	Medium term: Capital stock fixed	Long term: Capital grows
Unskilled labor	.6	1.2
Skilled labor	.5	.9
Capital	.5	−.7
Land	−.3	.4
Natural resources	−.3	.3

increases the capital stock, Colombia does gain a substantial amount: $550 million each year, or about a 0.5 percent permanent boost to GDP.

The US effects are much smaller, for two main reasons. First, the US economy is more than 100 times bigger than the Colombian economy, so a US-Colombia FTA has a much smaller impact on the United States. Second, the United States has lower initial barriers, so that it does not reap as much in the way of internal efficiency gains. The modeling indicates that a US-Colombia FTA would not have a significant impact on Peru's overall welfare or on the rest of the world.

This model can provide a rough indication of the distributional effects of the FTA. Table 4B.2 shows the changes in real factor prices in Colombia caused by the FTA. (The factor price impacts in the other regions are tiny.) The changes are quite small. This stems mainly from the fact that Colombia's initial tariffs are fairly uniform across all sectors, so that no one factor gets greatly disproportionate protection under the current regime.[4] This contrasts with East Asian countries such as Japan and Korea, which heavily protect agriculture but not manufacturing, so that trade opening there would greatly hurt land and natural resources, while helping other factors. Under a US-Colombia FTA, land and natural resources would suffer small losses in the medium term, indicating that protection is slightly biased toward agriculture and other raw products. In the long run, only capital is hurt. This makes sense, since the capital stock expands, but the amounts of the other factors do not.

Table 4B.3 provides a more nuanced look at adjustment and the distribution of gains and losses. In the medium term, wheat, other primary products, and meat sectors in Colombia would shrink. While wheat output would decrease significantly in percentage terms, it has a very small initial output. The light manufacturing sectors—textiles, clothing, and leather—would expand substantially, while most of the heavier manufacturing sectors would shrink. Interestingly, motor vehicles and other trans-

---

4. See table 4B.4 for the initial tariff rates that each country imposes on the other.

Table 4B.3 Percent change in output

Sector	Share of output Colombia	Share of output United States	Medium term Colombia	Medium term United States	Long term Colombia	Long term United States
Paddy rice	.0028	.0001	0	.2	.7	.1
Wheat	.0010	.0004	−15.1	.7	−14.6	.7
Vegetables and fruits	.0208	.0015	0	0	.5	−.1
Other primary products	.1060	.0168	−.6	.1	0	0
Beef	.0137	.0048	−.4	0	.4	0
Other meat	.0136	.0039	−1.4	.1	−.7	0
Dairy	.0110	.0047	.1	0	1.3	0
Processed rice	.0042	.0001	.1	.1	.9	0
Other food products	.0576	.0280	.5	0	1.4	0
Textiles	.0098	.0081	7.7	1	8.6	.1
Wearing apparel	.0133	.0061	23.3	0	24.0	−.1
Leather products	.0040	.0009	3.2	0	3.2	0
Chemical, rubber, and plastic products	.0433	.0399	−.8	0	.6	0
Iron, steel, and nonferrous metals	.0131	.0141	−.7	0	−.1	0
Motor vehicles	.0064	.0260	2.0	0	2.3	0
Other transport	.0017	.0108	2.7	0	3.0	0
Electronic equipment	.0020	.0196	−7.7	0	−7.4	0
Other machinery and equipment	.0093	.0439	−4.0	0	−3.9	0
Other manufactured goods	.0658	.0694	−1.0	0	−.4	0
Trade and transport services	.1849	.1741	−.2	0	.4	0
Business services	.0828	.2133	0	0	.7	0
Other services	.3331	.3137	−.1	0	.2	0

port would expand, although these are tiny sectors in Colombia. Thus, the FTA would, in general, cause resources to move from heavier manufacturing in Colombia to lighter manufacturing, in which the country has a comparative advantage relative to the United States. This occurs despite the fact that Colombia has higher protection in light manufacturing. The United States has initial barriers that are skewed even more toward these sectors, which overrides Colombia's smaller preferences toward them (as shown in table 4B.4).

The medium- and long-term scenarios tell very similar stories concerning the differential effect of the FTA across sectors in Colombia. The major difference between the two is that overall output is higher in the longer term, so that expansions are larger and contractions are smaller or become positive. The modeling indicates that the FTA would have negligible out-

Table 4B.4 Initial tariff rates in the model (percent)

Sector	Colombia	United States
Paddy rice	10.5	0
Wheat	12.5	0
Vegetables and fruits	13.9	0
Other primary products	13.0	.3
Beef	16.2	2.7
Other meat	19.8	0
Dairy	18.3	20.2
Processed rice	20.0	0
Other food products	16.2	7.1
Textiles	16.4	9.1
Wearing apparel	20.0	12.1
Leather products	15.7	4.8
Chemical, rubber, and plastic products	8.1	2.3
Iron, steel, and nonferrous metals	11.0	0
Motor vehicles	14.5	0
Other transport	2.3	0
Electronic equipment	5.8	0
Other machinery and equipment	9.2	0
Other manufactured goods	13.8	.6
Trade and transport services	0	0
Business services	0	0
Other services	0	0

put effects in percentage terms in the United States, since its economy dwarfs that of Colombia.

Overall, an FTA would induce structural change in the Colombian economy. In particular, there would be shifts in employment across sectors. Such potential changes would spur political opposition from those who would lose their jobs. Table 4B.5 presents estimates of the number of jobs that would be gained or lost on net in the individual sectors in the medium-term scenario. These numbers are based on a guesstimate of 15 million low-skilled workers in Colombia. According to the International Labor Organization, there are about 18 million workers in Colombia, of which about 85 percent are not highly skilled. Overall, agriculture, heavier manufacturing, and services would shed lower-skilled jobs. Adding up just the negative numbers shows that about 63,000 low-skilled workers would be displaced. All of these, however, would get hired in the expanding sectors. The great majority of the hiring would occur in lighter manufacturing: textiles, clothing, and leather. These medium-run scenarios show that total employment would not change much. As trade economists repeatedly emphasize, trade opening does not have a significant impact on total employment; rather, trade opening causes sectoral shifts in employment that make the economy more efficient.

Table 4B.5 Change in nonskilled employment in Colombia, medium-term scenario

Sector	Initial employment	Change
Paddy rice	65,190	–196
Wheat	23,055	–3,527
Vegetables and fruits	482,205	–1,447
Other primary products	1,689,810	–15,208
Beef	142,020	–568
Other meat	143,430	–2,008
Dairy	65,235	60
Processed rice	41,535	22
Other food products	475,260	1,925
Textiles	112,995	8,698
Wearing apparel	210,195	48,833
Leather products	71,070	2,265
Chemical, rubber, and plastic products	330,390	–2,964
Iron, steel, and nonferrous metals	157,710	–1,249
Motor vehicles	49,185	986
Other transport	13,350	358
Electronic equipment	27,030	–2,100
Other machinery and equipment	134,220	–5,469
Other manufactured goods	625,650	–6,989
Trade and transport services	4,340,085	–9,418
Business services	1,029,960	–1,524
Other services	4,770,435	–10,447

5

Agriculture

TIM JOSLING

Agriculture has been a highly contentious issue in the US-Colombia trade talks. The United States is a major supplier of temperate zone agricultural products to Colombia, but trade barriers still exist and local producers have objected to any significant improvement in market access. Colombian farm groups argue that US exports are assisted by a variety of subsidies associated with domestic farm programs.[1] US agricultural interests, however, generally support the free trade agreement, as it will open markets for US produce. It will also guard against loss of competitiveness in Colombian markets relative to suppliers from the Southern Cone Common Market (Mercosur) and, in the future, the European Union.

Under existing trade preferences, Colombian farm products already have relatively unencumbered access to the US market and, as they are mostly tropical products, they pose little direct threat to US producers. However, better access for sugar and sugar-related products has been firmly resisted by US farm interests.[2] So the staging of tariff cuts, the de-

Tim Josling is a senior fellow at the Institute for International Studies, Stanford University.

1. At an early FTA negotiating session in Atlanta in June 2004, US officials proposed free access for US farm products, but this met with the complaint that US farmers benefited from disproportional subsidies. Reductions in those subsidies in the context of the World Trade Organization (WTO) Doha Round will not come quickly enough to significantly impact this issue. The asymmetry in the ability to assist farmers in times of weak markets will continue to be a major source of contention among the parties.

2. The increased importation of cut flowers from Colombia also caused trade friction with the United States over the past decade, but these issues have largely been settled by agreements with the industry.

sign of safeguards, and the possible exemptions for certain agricultural products are likely to be important issues in the political acceptability of the FTA in both Colombia and the United States.[3]

Colombia enjoys a wide range of agroclimatic zones, from the Caribbean and Pacific coastal regions to the uplands of the Andes. Tropical products such as bananas and sugar cane dominate the coastal areas and coffee is the main crop in the highlands. But some parts of Colombia are favorable for growing temperate zone crops, such as wheat and barley, and for raising cattle. Rice is also cultivated widely in Colombia, and some has been exported to neighboring countries in recent years. Large plantations dominate the export crops, except for coffee. But the most sensitive import-competing crops are those grown on small farms, such as maize and beans. In some cases, the alternative crops that such farmers could grow would be narcotics to feed the supply to rich countries, making the issue of pressure on small farmers very sensitive. Adding to the political sensitivity is the fact that agriculture has generally grown more slowly than the rest of the economy in the decade since the adoption of more open economic policies, and poor infrastructure and ongoing security problems have held back the rural economy. The ultimate acceptability of the agricultural provisions in an FTA will depend on how the different parts of the Colombian agricultural sector perceive the costs of more pressure from imports and the benefits of more secure export markets.

Bilateral Agricultural Trade Flows Between the United States and Colombia

Colombia sold $1.436 billion of agricultural goods to the United States in 2005, mainly traditional tropical exports of coffee, bananas, and sugar, along with nontraditional products such as cut flowers, lobster, and shrimp (table 5.1).[4] The value of bilateral trade fluctuates with world prices, particularly for tropical goods such as coffee, but the US market remains a major outlet for Colombia's agricultural exports. The United States sold $677 million of agricultural products to Colombia in 2005, mainly corn, wheat, and other temperate-zone staples, cotton for the production of textiles, poultry, and other livestock products (table 5.2). US sales of agricultural goods to Colombia are small in relation to total ex-

---

3. The inclusion of Peru and Ecuador in the talks, along with the later incorporation of Bolivia, complicates the process of addressing specific agricultural concerns but does not markedly change the nature of the problems. Peru has a more liberal trade regime and does not apply the Andean price band, and Ecuador has a narrower range of local products, focused more on tropical commodities.

4. Exports of tuna were valued at $8.9 million in 1999 but have declined sharply since canned tuna was excluded from preferential access to the US market under the Andean Trade Preference Act.

Table 5.1 Exports of agricultural products from Colombia to the United States, 2000–2005 (millions of dollars)

Product	2000	2001	2002	2003	2004	2005
Nursery products	349.0	306.4	293.4	347.5	421.2	424.7
Raw coffee	381.9	258.5	276.5	322.6	348.8	553.0
Bananas	219.7	184.6	186.5	164.4	165.0	195.8
Roasted coffee	69.3	59.6	51.8	51.5	56.8	75.2
Raw sugar	26.8	17.43	29.9	39.0	35.4	34.5
Shrimp	32.8	31.5	25.7	17.0	22.1	22.7
Processed fruits and vegetables	10.8	13.9	10.8	14.7	15.3	20.7
Lobster	7.0	8.0	10.6	9.1	8.7	7.2
Cocoa paste	2.3	5.0	2.3	4.7	6.9	6.3
Tobacco	1.2	1.5	1.7	4.3	3.5	1.7
Spices	0.5	0.7	3.1	3.7	4.9	5.1
Tropical oils	0.4	0.5	0.9	2.2	2.3	2.4
Total agriculture	1,187.6	925.9	929.5	1,030.9	1,162.0	1,436.5

Source: US Department of Agriculture, Foreign Agricultural Service, Bulk, Intermediate, and Consumer-Oriented (BICO) Import Commodity Aggregations, www.fas.usda.gov/ustrade/ (accessed May 22, 2006).

ports of farm commodities, though Colombia is among the largest buyers in South America of these US products.

In addition to these trade flows, there are other links between the agriculture and food sectors of Colombia and the United States. Foreign direct investment by US firms in Colombian food processing industries had reached $217 million by the end of 2002, some of it in enterprises that sell to US markets. And illegal crops, grown or transshipped, add significantly to the (unrecorded) receipts from Colombian exports. But these crops also impose high security costs on the exporting country and on the law enforcement agencies and consumers in the importing country.

Colombia's Agricultural Trade Regime

Colombia has generally low tariffs, including those for agricultural goods, and applied tariffs are well below bound levels. But trade impediments remain. Along with some other Andean Community members, Colombia has implemented a price-triggered safeguard system for sensitive agricultural commodities (wheat, corn, sorghum, rice, barley, milk, and poultry products).[5] The Andean price band system allows for additional duties when import prices fall below the average of the past five years, and

---

5. In addition to the 13 main products, duties for some 120 "related" products are also tied to the price band system.

**Table 5.2   Exports of agricultural products from the United States
to Colombia, 2000–2005** (millions of dollars)

Product	2000	2001	2002	2003	2004	2005
Coarse grains	156.6	150.4	182.0	172.0	210.7	228.1
Wheat	69.0	68.7	97.8	108.0	106.4	125.6
Cotton	26.2	30.7	35.1	47.1	57.4	52.4
Soybeans	19.2	28.9	41.1	30.9	34.1	41.7
Feeds and fodders	19.3	34.4	27.4	24.1	19.7	27.6
Animal fats	6.3	10.2	12.5	12.7	13.9	10.3
Poultry meat	10.2	12.0	7.6	10.3	4.2	9.6
Soybean meal	12.3	9.7	11.4	111.3	43.7	57.0
Fresh fruits	6.5	6.3	5.2	6.4	6.6	11.6
Red meats	6.4	6.0	6.2	4.8	3.7	5.8
Live animals	2.6	2.9	4.2	4.5	2.5	3.9
Processed fruits and vegetables	3.8	4.7	4.6	3.7	2.2	2.3
Total agriculture	420.1	452.2	520.1	511.8	592.7	676.6

Source: US Department of Agriculture, Foreign Agricultural Service, Bulk, Intermediate, and Consumer-Oriented (BICO) Import Commodity Aggregations, www.fas.usda.gov/ustrade/ (accessed May 22, 2006).

this can lead to significant (and unpredictable) import barriers.[6] The price band system is an element of an Andean Common Agricultural Policy, though unlike its European namesake, this policy does not involve significant common support programs.[7]

As a member of the Andean Community, Colombia enjoys relatively free reciprocal access to the markets of Ecuador, Venezuela, Bolivia, and Peru for agricultural as well as other goods.[8] Most agricultural trade affected by this agreement is between Colombia and Venezuela and Colombia and Ecuador, though some Bolivian products also enter Colombia. In addition to the Andean FTA, Colombia has entered into FTAs with Mexico and Venezuela (the G-3) and with Chile. The recent signing of an FTA with Mercosur offers the prospect of opening up trade with most countries of South America. Trade relations in agriculture with Mercosur (most of which is covered in the bilateral agreement) could become important in

---

6. The price band system does have its advocates. Economist Joseph Stiglitz has argued that the abolition of the price band, specifically for rice and corn, would harm small farmers, who would turn to the production of illegal crops. He praised the system as a sensible way to defend against fluctuating eternal prices. The adoption of a special safeguard mechanism in the WTO is a part of the July 2004 framework agreement and is intended to replace such national schemes.

7. The common agricultural policy includes the Andean agricultural health system as well as the price band system.

8. See Josling (1997) for more details on the agricultural policies of the Andean Community.

the future, though for Colombian farmers this raises similar problems, as would increased access to US products. Colombia has a nonreciprocal trade agreement with the Caribbean Community that has led to a modest increase in imports from that region. Colombia enjoys preferential access of a nonreciprocal nature into the European Union under an enhanced generalized system of preferences (GSP), particularly designed to encourage diversification away from narcotics.[9] Discussions with the European Union about converting this program into a reciprocal free trade agreement currently are on hold.

US Trade Preferences and Colombian Agriculture

Many agricultural products (and horticultural exports such as cut flowers) have benefited from tariff-free access under the Andean Trade Preference Act (ATPA). However, as indicated above, this preference system will need to be renewed in 2006. Colombia has a strong incentive to lock in this access to avoid the uncertainties of unilateral preferences. The recent extension of this program through the Andean Trade Promotion and Drug Eradication Act (ATPDEA) of 2002 expanded somewhat the range of goods that were afforded duty-free treatment, but this did not increase market access for agricultural goods. Imports of some agricultural products are restricted (mainly sugar) under existing tariff-rate quotas (TRQs), and Colombia would clearly benefit from an expansion of these quotas.

The key to the benefits of easier access into the US market for Colombia lies in the relationship that the United States has with competitive suppliers of tropical and other products. In this respect, the recently negotiated Central American Free Trade Agreement–Dominican Republic (CAFTA-DR) could be significant for Colombia and the other Andean countries. Competing suppliers in Central America will have enhanced access to the US market. Though tariffs on tropical beverages are typically low in the United States (and other industrial countries), tropical fruits often compete with temperate zone products that are protected by tariffs.

Agricultural Framework for the US-Colombia Free Trade Agreement

The key to an acceptable agreement for Colombia was to find an appropriate staging of its own tariff cuts and to design suitable safeguards. For the United States, the main focus was on ensuring expanded access to Colombian markets while protecting a few sensitive sectors from additional competition. The skill of the negotiators was fully engaged to de-

---

9. The Andean GSP allows preferential access for most Colombian exports, including coffee, flowers, tuna, and leather goods.

vise arrangements that allow for steady trade expansion rather than encumber the trade relationship with a web of product-specific deals that allows little room for such growth. The agricultural arrangements contained in the North American Free Trade Agreement (NAFTA), and more recently in the Chile and Australian FTAs and CAFTA-DR, reflected similar sensitivities and gave an indication of possible solutions to those problems.[10] The main agricultural provisions of these four agreements are summarized in table 5.3.[11] Their similarities and differences with the US-Colombia FTA are discussed below.

Staging Tariff Cuts and Tariff Rate Quotas

The US-Mexico part of NAFTA created a convenient device for dealing with sensitive sectors by establishing a mutual commitment to an eventual duty-free market but allowing for different timetables for the most sensitive products.[12] Tariff elimination "stages" reflect domestic sensitivities without allowing for exceptions for particular sectors. The Chile FTA and CAFTA-DR followed this practice, with slightly modified timetables for achieving free trade.[13] In some cases, the tariff cuts themselves have been delayed, with the result that the agreement is backloaded.

A major part of the negotiating effort in the US-Colombia FTA revolved around "offers" of tariff elimination schedules and timetables. The United States was keen to keep transition periods to a minimum on market access into Colombia. Long transition periods are a useful political device, but significant liberalization of market access in the WTO could make some of the more extended bilateral tariff reduction schedules look less than ambitious.[14]

The outcome of the negotiations confirmed the intention to move to tariff-free trade in agricultural goods between the United States and Colombia (subject to one exception, noted below). Colombia agreed to grant immediate duty-free access to those commodities where imports were well-established: high-quality beef, cotton, wheat, soybeans and meal,

---

10. The detailed agricultural provisions in the US FTAs with Israel and Morocco are somewhat less directly applicable, and the US FTAs with Jordan and Singapore have less agricultural content.

11. A number of other provisions, such as those on intellectual property protection and on general safeguards, have relevance to agriculture. For brevity, only the specific agricultural aspects are included in table 5.3.

12. This procedure differs from the alternatives of omitting sensitive sectors (as in the US-Canada FTA) or of setting more modest tariff reduction targets (as is used in the WTO).

13. The US FTA with Australia reverted to the older formulation in the case of sugar (no increased access or tariff cuts) and dairy products (TRQs but no preferential tariffs).

14. It may be useful in such cases to "rebase" the preferential tariff by taking into account the reduction in most favored nation tariff levels since the start of the FTA.

Table 5.3 Comparison of agricultural components of US FTAs

Component	North American Free Trade Agreement	Chile Free Trade Agreement	Central American Free Trade Agreement–Dominican Republic	Australia Free Trade Agreement
Tariff cuts	Some tariffs eliminated; others reduced over 5, 10, and 15 years	Some tariffs eliminated; others reduced over 4, 8, 10, and 12 years; some cuts delayed for 2 and 4 years	Some tariffs eliminated; others reduced over 5, 10, and 15 years; other cuts delayed for 6 to 10 years; duty free after 15 or 20 years	Most tariffs eliminated; others reduced over 4, 10, and 18 years
Tariff-rate quotas (TRQs)	Introduced during transition period for sensitive products	No use of TRQs introduced	TRQs for sensitive products in Annex 3.3. Rules on administration of TRQs (in addition to GATT Article XIII)	TRQs for avocados, cotton, peanuts, tobacco, beef, and dairy products into the United States expanded. Above-quota duties for beef phased out over 18-year period. Current sugar TRQs not increased: no cuts in above-quota tariff
Agricultural safeguards	TRQs allowed as special safeguard for horticultural crops (Annex 703.3)	Additional duties linked to price trigger (Article 3.18) for goods listed in Annex 3.18. Total duties not to exceed most favored nation rate. Safeguard not operative after 12 years, or when zero-duty stage reached	Additional duties linked to trigger quantities (Article 3.14) for products listed in Annex 3.14. Total duties not to exceed most favored nation rate. Safeguard not operative when zero-duty stage reached	Additional customs duties linked to price trigger for horticultural products (Annex 3-A Section A) and to quantity triggers for beef (Annex 3-A section B): price triggers used for beef in 19th year of agreement (Annex 3-A section C). Safeguard not operative when zero-duty stage reached
Other safeguards	Safeguards (Chapter 8A): Snapback to previous year's tariff on bilateral trade or most favored nation tariff	Trade Remedies (Chapter 8): GATT 1994 Article XIX safeguards	Trade Remedies (Chapter 8): GATT 1994 Article XIX safeguards	Chapter 9 (safeguards): GATT 1994 Article XIX safeguards

(table continues next page)

121

Table 5.3 Comparison of agricultural components of US FTAs *(continued)*

Component	North American Free Trade Agreement	Chile Free Trade Agreement	Central American Free Trade Agreement–Dominican Republic	Australia Free Trade Agreement
Export subsidies	Agreement to avoid use of export subsidies on bilateral trade unless third countries subsidized exports to NAFTA markets. Agreement to work together for elimination in the GATT	Agreement to avoid use of export subsidies on bilateral trade unless third countries subsidized exports to Chile or the United States. Agreement to work together for elimination in the WTO	Agreement to avoid use of export subsidies on bilateral trade unless third countries subsidized exports to CAFTA-DR markets. Agreement to work together for elimination in the WTO	Agreement to avoid use of export subsidies on bilateral trade unless third countries subsidized exports to Australia. Agreement to work together for elimination in the WTO
Domestic support	Agreement to work together in GATT for the reduction of domestic support levels and shift to less trade-distorting instruments	Agreement to work together in WTO for the reduction of domestic support levels and shift to less trade-distorting instruments	Agreement to work together in WTO for the reduction of domestic support levels and shift to less trade-distorting instruments	Agreement to work together in WTO for the reduction of domestic support levels and shift to less trade-distorting instruments
Sanitary and phytosanitary (SPS) measures	Precursor of WTO SPS Agreement (Chapter 7B)	Affirm commitment to SPS Agreement	Affirm commitment to SPS Agreement	Work to resolve trade conflicts over SPS barriers
Institutions	Committee on Agricultural Trade; Working Group on Agricultural Subsidies; Advisory Committee on Private Commerce Disputes regarding Agricultural Goods	Working Group on Agricultural Trade; Committee on Sanitary and Phytosanitary Matters	Committee on Agricultural Trade; Agricultural Review Commission; Committee on Sanitary and Phytosanitary Matters	Committee on Agriculture; Standing Technical Working Group on Animal and Plant Health Measures

GATT = General Agreement on Tariffs and Trade
WTO = World Trade Organization

Source: Based on the text of the agreements available on the Web site of the Office of the US Trade Representative.

apples, pears, peaches, cherries, and certain processed goods.[15] More sensitive commodities such as pork are to enter Colombia tariff-free after five years, and most remaining products will be tariff-free by the end of a 15-year transition period.

The products for which a transition regime proved most difficult to agree were rice, chicken leg-quarters, corn, and dairy products.[16] For these commodities, Colombia was able to negotiate TRQs that expanded over the transition period and acted as a safeguard for domestic producers. The combination of an increase in the quantity allowed and a reduction in the above-quota tariff effectively removes the TRQ over a period of years. A TRQ for poultry of 26,000 tons, which will be phased out over 18 years, was agreed upon as a way to protect Colombian producers.[17] A TRQ for corn of 2 million tons will be phased out over 12 years, and a TRQ for dairy products of 9,000 tons will be in operation for 15 years.

In the case of rice, an additional complication hampered negotiations. Colombia sought to be able to maintain a "performance requirement" that would have tied imports of rice to purchases of the domestic product.[18] However, US officials consider such a requirement to be contrary to the WTO (they are currently challenging a similar policy by Turkey) and were not prepared to accept this condition. In the end, the provision was dropped as part of a last-minute deal. As a result, a duty-free TRQ for rice of 75,000 tons (well above current export levels) was agreed upon, with the above-quota tariff of 80 percent being phased out over 19 years.

The United States also had concerns about Colombian exports. Though most exports of agricultural products already enter duty-free under the terms of the ATPDEA, sugar has remained subject to quotas. Sugar was a sensitive issue, as it was in NAFTA, CAFTA-DR, and US-Australia FTA negotiations. Sugar was included in the US-Mexico bilateral part of NAFTA, but has caused friction ever since. Sugar was excluded from the market access provisions of the Australia FTA, but CAFTA-DR producers got some small quota increases.

Currently, Colombia has a sugar quota of 25,000 tons, but requested a considerable increase (originally put at 350,000 tons). An increase in sugar exports was seen as a necessary condition for agreement in Colombia, but the US sugar industry has become wary of the erosion of its own market by bilateral deals. In the end, a substantial increase in the TRQ was agreed upon: an additional amount of 50,000 tons of sugar was to be added to the

---

15. These processed goods include frozen french fries and cookies.

16. Imports of high-fructose corn syrup into Colombia were also contentious, as these imports affect the sugar market.

17. Chicken leg-quarters, an export item resulting from the preference of US consumers for breast meat, have caused problems for domestic poultry producers in the region for many years. The United States rejected a Colombian request for a built-in review of the poultry quota after nine years with an option of stopping the TRQ expansion.

18. A similar condition was raised in the agreement with El Salvador.

existing TRQ upon signing, and this amount would increase by 1.5 percent a year. However, in contrast to all other farm products, there would be no reduction of the above-quota tariff. Thus the prospect of Colombia eventually having free access to the US sugar market has (for now) been denied.[19]

Safeguards and Other Contingent Arrangements

The willingness to open up sensitive areas to imports depends on the comfort level afforded by safeguards against import surges and world price declines. An argument can be made that agricultural goods warrant a special safeguard, triggered by price declines or by import quantities, that is easily applied, requires little investigation of costs or subsidy levels, and does not necessitate compensation for exporters. But these safeguards are not without their critics in the exporting countries. The most contentious agricultural issue between Colombia and the United States (with respect to legal trade) is the operation of the Andean price band system, a price-triggered safeguard which the United States has singled out for criticism in the US Trade Representative's annual reports on foreign trade barriers as being nontransparent and subject to protectionist manipulation (USTR 2004a). A similar issue was a point of contention in the FTA talks with Chile. The Chilean system was challenged by Argentina and was found to be inconsistent with the WTO in certain respects, and the FTA instituted a safeguard system (on bilateral trade) designed to replace it.[20]

Despite the problems that the WTO panel found with the similarity between a variable levy and the duties generated by a price band, the concept of a price trigger has some merit. Price changes are clearly the most disruptive aspect of open markets to import-competing industries. Import volumes can change for a variety of reasons, including domestic shortages or demand shifts, and stemming imports by additional duties may be harming consumers with little benefit to competitive producers. But price-triggered safeguards, so long as they are temporary, may be useful as a complement to the general safeguard and other trade remedies and to the provision of agricultural safeguards in the WTO.

A price-triggered safeguard was incorporated in the US-Chile FTA to deal specifically with sensitive agricultural imports.[21] The agricultural

---

19. An additional provision has been included, as it was in the CAFTA-DR, that would allow the United States to unilaterally decide to compensate Colombian sugar producers rather than import their sugar.

20. The WTO Dispute Settlement Panel found that the Chilean price band scheme was inconsistent with Article 4.2 of the Agreement on Agriculture that outlaws variable levies (WT/DS207/R, May 3, 2002). The Appellate Body agreed with the panel in this respect, while modifying other parts of the report (WT/DS207/AB/R, September 23, 2002).

21. The US-Australia FTA has similar provisions for a price-based safeguard but includes a quantity-based trigger as well for certain products.

safeguard measure contains a specific mechanism for imposing additional import duties on a list of goods (specified in an annex to the agreement) if the unit price of the good enters the party's markets at a level below a set trigger price (also in the annex). The additional duties are limited so as not to be higher than the prevailing most favored nation rate or the most favored nation rate in force when the agreement went into effect.

A safeguard for agricultural goods was also incorporated into the CAFTA-DR, but this is quantity-triggered. In the first years of the agreement, the safeguard allows the duty to revert back to most favored nation levels if there is an import surge (relative to quantities entered in the schedule).[22] The special agricultural safeguard cannot be used in conjunction with the general safeguard included in each agreement, and it is limited to the transition period identified in the respective agreements.

As with the staging of tariff cuts, much of the negotiation of the agricultural part of the agreement with Colombia and the other Andean countries revolved around choosing the nature of the agricultural safeguard and the commodities to include. The safeguards incorporated in the agreement include a provision that links the quantity of imports with the size of the TRQ. Colombia can increase duties if imports exceed 120 percent of the TRQ volume. But this provision expires at the end of the transition period for each sensitive product.

Subsidies

Beginning with the NAFTA text, the agricultural chapter of each free trade agreement has included exhortative language on the parties working together in the General Agreement on Tariffs and Trade (GATT) and the WTO toward the elimination of export subsidies and the reduction of trade-distorting domestic support.[23] Going beyond such encouraging sentiments has not been easy. Any mutual reduction of subsidies on bilateral trade would give rise to difficulties of implementation (identifying which subsidies apply to such trade): An agreement to reduce such subsidies more generally gives rise to the "free rider" problem, as nonparties would gain without reducing their own subsidies. Where the subsidies are given on exports, some attempt has been made to restrict such practices on bilateral trade, but the United States has insisted on being able to counter European Union and other nonparty subsidies in partner markets.[24] For

---

22. The safeguard quantities are only specified for the Central American countries.

23. The NAFTA text, predating the final Uruguay Round Agreement on Agriculture, was more explicit in laying out the "common" view on subsidies but contained no more substantive obligations.

24. The US-Canada FTA did in fact include an agreement to avoid export subsidies on bilateral trade, but this was not included in the US-Mexico part of NAFTA.

domestic subsidies, the consistent position of the United States has been that no progress can be made on such reductions outside the WTO negotiations. Negotiating partners tend to see this issue somewhat differently. They have argued that the asymmetry between the high level of domestic support in the United States and the much lower levels in their countries makes it difficult to open up their markets.

As a result of these tensions and the reality of the lack of bargaining power by countries such as Colombia in the area of US domestic farm programs, it should be no surprise that the US-Colombia FTA does not address the question of subsidies. The likelihood of any substantive agreement on domestic and export subsidies outside the WTO is remote.

Sanitary and Phytosanitary Measures

Somewhat more progress has been made recently at a bilateral level to reduce trade barriers that arise from differences in sanitary and phytosanitary measures. Many of these barriers are the result of differences in regulatory practices and in the lack of adequate testing and certification facilities in developing countries.[25] FTAs with the United States tend to include renewed commitments to the principles and practices of the WTO Agreement on the Application of Sanitary and Phytosanitary Measures. The US-Colombia FTA is no exception. But, in addition, the United States has agreed to help Colombian exporters to meet US standards. The United States rejected Colombian suggestions that there should be any differentiation of standards to take into account administrative constraints in Colombia, but it agreed to work to resolve issues of food inspection involving imports of beef, pork, and poultry. Though not all trade problems involving sanitary and phytosanitary issues are likely to be resolved in bilateral consultations, the establishment of institutional links between regulatory agencies can be a practical advantage.

Institutions

In keeping with the practice in other free trade agreements, an agricultural committee will be set up in conjunction with the US-Colombia FTA. A precursor of this committee is the US-Colombia Consultative Committee on Agriculture that was set up in April 2003 to improve communication and coordination in areas such as food safety and research. Such institutions can be a useful way of channeling issues that might otherwise result in disputes. But so far these bilateral and regional institutions have

---

25. See Josling, Roberts, and Orden (2004) for a discussion of the benefits of greater coordination of sanitary and phytosanitary policies to expand trade without sacrificing health and safety standards.

played no role in policy development and have yet to find a constructive role in deepening integration among the parties involved.

Impact on Multilateral and Regional Negotiations

There is little doubt that the FTAs between the United States and the Central American and Andean countries are negotiated with an eye toward the bigger "fish" in the Latin American pond. Specifically, Brazil and Argentina would constitute more significant prizes in the "competitive liberalization" contest.[26] Concessions in the bilateral agreements with smaller economies are limited by the need not to create precedents for future negotiations, and novel devices can be seen in the light of experimentation with solutions for larger problems. This is particularly true in agriculture, where it is critical to search for ways to integrate the North and South American markets without encountering opposition that blocks all progress. Thus, the impact of the US-Colombia FTA on the Free Trade Area of the Americas (FTAA) and its treatment of agriculture are of interest. Mechanisms used for sequencing the opening of market access have been further refined in the talks.[27] Of course, whether "competitive liberalization" extends to competing with Mercosur and the European Union to give better access to Colombian exports remains to be seen.

The impact on the WTO negotiations of a US-Colombia FTA is also somewhat indirect and speculative and probably not significant. There is the possibility that Colombia and the other Andean countries might have been encouraged to support the US position more vigorously as a result of the bilateral ties, but this impact has not been noticeable during the negotiations.[28] But the impact of a possible WTO agreement in the context of the Doha Development Agenda on bilateral agreements is of more interest.[29] Agreement to end export subsidies would relieve the bilateral

---

26. This is consistent with the message of Schott (2004) that, for the United States, it may be better to seek agreements with the more significant markets.

27. One example of this is the provision in the US-Colombia FTA for joint export trading companies that would bid for the TRQ licenses and share the rents from the quotas equally between the two countries. In the absence of such a device, it is not clear whether the importer or the exporter will gain from the quota license.

28. Colombia is a member of the Cairns Group and supported the G-20 position at the WTO Ministerial Conference in Cancún in 2003. In many respects, Colombia has a more open view of agricultural trade relations than does the United States, with its concern about competition from Brazil and other low-cost suppliers.

29. For a discussion on the merits of various aspects of the agricultural talks, see Josling and Hathaway (2004). A framework agreement for the Doha Round was agreed upon on August 1, 2004, but the "modalities" for the agricultural talks were yet to be agreed upon as of May 2006 (WTO 2004).

and regional FTAs from the need to juggle the desire to eliminate subsidies within the region with the reality of subsidies granted by nonparties. Similarly, substantive restrictions on domestic support in the WTO round would reduce the tensions associated with US farm programs. Market access improvement in the WTO reduces the danger of trade diversion in regional trading arrangements and makes the task of selling preferential access to import-competing interests somewhat easier. The anticipated introduction of a special safeguard mechanism for agriculture in the WTO, for use by developing countries, will further reduce the need for bilateral safeguards of this nature.

Conclusions

The main gains to Colombia in agricultural trade are likely to be more secure and preferential market access to the US market. Colombia will regain parity with Mexico in that regard, with the exception of sugar, where exports to the United States will continue to be limited by quota. US agricultural exports stand to gain a small but not insignificant preference in the Colombian market for temperate-zone agricultural produce, particularly by regaining parity with other regional suppliers and beating the European Union to preferential access. Gains in the rice market are also significant for US farmers. However, the long time periods for phasing out tariffs for sensitive products and safeguard provisions that will replace the current price band system will temper the impact on trade flows.

The impact on agricultural trade needs to be seen in the context of the many other changes that will take place over the phase-in period for improved market access. The Doha Round of WTO negotiations, if successfully concluded, will have finally set a date for the elimination of export subsidies (2013) and have negotiated further restrictions on domestic support. These changes will relieve some of the pressures that may build up in bilateral trade relations. Market access may have been significantly improved through cuts in most favored nation tariffs, and a new safeguard system may be in place for agricultural goods in the WTO. The European Union may well have negotiated free trade areas with the Caribbean countries and possibly with Central American countries. Colombia may negotiate such an agreement as well, giving that country secure access to markets on both sides of the Atlantic. The Free Trade Area of the Americas could be a reality within a few years, rendering many of the bilateral and regional preferences of little practical value. In short, the US-Colombia free trade agreement could have a brief, if positive, period of relevance to the expansion of agricultural trade.

6

Labor Standards

KIMBERLY ANN ELLIOTT

Beginning with the Trade Act of 1974, the US Congress included language on worker rights as an objective in legislation authorizing international trade negotiations. US negotiators never succeeded in getting the issue on the multilateral trade agenda in the General Agreement on Tariffs and Trade (GATT) or World Trade Organization (WTO). But "taking steps" to improve implementation of "internationally-recognized worker rights" was made a condition of unilateral US trade preference programs in 1984.[1] And worker rights became a divisive and partisan issue in the free trade negotiations with Mexico in the early 1990s.

In the years following approval of the North American Free Trade Agreement (NAFTA) in 1993, US policymakers debated vigorously whether and how to incorporate labor (and environmental) standards in trade agreements. In the 1990s, the Clinton administration and congressional Democrats, supported by labor unions and human rights organizations, generally favored including standards in trade agreements. The Republican party and business community representatives generally opposed it. These differences remained unresolved when George W. Bush took office in 2001.

In August 2002, a carefully crafted compromise on labor (and environmental) standards permitted congressional approval of new Trade Promotion Authority that defines what Congress wants to see in trade agreements and commits the body to vote them up or down, without amendment (as

Kimberly Ann Elliott is a senior fellow jointly at the Institute for International Economics and the Center for Global Development.

1. See Section 502(b)(7)g Title V of the Trade Act of 1974, as amended by the Tariff and Trade Act of 1984.

long as the president follows certain procedures). In the past, the principal negotiating objectives included in trade legislation were generally regarded as advisory but not necessarily binding and, until the 2002 Trade Act, the language on worker rights was not pursued vigorously. But increasing partisanship in the Congress and the hard-fought battle over the 2002 act—the House sent the initial bill to the Senate by one vote and ultimately approved the final amended bill by just a three-vote margin—have contributed to the prominent role that labor standards now play in congressional trade politics.

While the six US bilateral trade agreements ratified from 2001 to 2005 include a labor chapter that closely mimics the Trade Act's language, these provisions were regarded by Democrats as unacceptably weak in the case of the agreement with Central America and the Dominican Republic (referred to as CAFTA-DR). The implementing legislation for this agreement passed the House in late July 2005 by just two votes. While there are important differences between Colombia and Central America, there are enough similarities, including perceptions of serious worker rights problems, that the trade agreement with Colombia is drawing opposition from similar sources.

Core Labor Standards and Development

Developing countries often resist including labor standards in trade agreements because they fear they will be misused for protectionist purposes.[2] In 1998, in part to fend off pressures to incorporate labor standards in WTO rules, members of the International Labor Organization (ILO) approved a "Declaration on Fundamental Rights and Principles at Work" that identified certain labor standards that should be respected and promoted by all countries, regardless of their level of development or whether they have ratified the associated legal conventions. The follow-up mechanism for promoting these "core standards" emphasized transparency and cooperation and warned against using them as an excuse for trade protection.

The core standards (with the associated ILO convention numbers in parentheses) are freedom of association and the right to organize and bargain collectively (87, 98); abolition of forced labor (29, 105); elimination of child labor, beginning with its worst forms (138, 182); and nondiscrimination in employment (100, 111). These standards are also often called "framework" or "enabling" standards because they support an environment in which workers are able to negotiate with management about other conditions of work, including wages, hours, and health and safety conditions.

Despite arguments frequently heard to the contrary, the global application of these standards does not force developing countries to adopt

---

2. See Elliott and Freeman (2003, chapter 1) for a more detailed discussion of labor standards and globalization.

developed-country standards. Rather, these standards relate to freedom of choice for workers and are an essential element of well-functioning markets and strong democracies. Even the legally binding ILO conventions that define the core standards in some detail leave substantial room for national differences (for example, in designing industrial relations institutions). Moreover, there is broad acceptance of the legitimacy of three of the four standards—ending forced labor, child labor (as the ILO defines it), and discrimination.[3]

The fourth standard—freedom of association and the right to collective bargaining—is more controversial. Governments and employers often resist this standard because freedom to form unions and negotiate over working conditions increases the power of workers relative to managers and the state. In Colombia and other countries where political violence is a problem, unions are often suspected of being sympathetic to or allied with leftist guerrilla movements. This politicizes freedom of association in ways that can be extremely difficult to overcome even when peace finally comes, as in parts of Central America today.

Some skeptics do not necessarily oppose freedom of association in principle but regard unions in developing countries as elitist, corrupt, and rent-seeking institutions that reduce a country's growth prospects. But where unions fit that image, politicians and firms are also typically elitist, corrupt, and rent-seeking, because they are all operating in an environment without transparency, accountability, or competition. Even under these conditions, however, unions are sometimes a force for democracy and the protection of property rights in opposition to corrupt regimes. Since the late 1990s, for instance, Zimbabwe's trade unions have been the main opposition to the Mugabe dictatorship and its land seizures. Unions were also a leading force in the campaign against apartheid in South Africa, and the Solidarity trade union was a major force in toppling the communist leadership in Poland in the 1980s. Where unions are elitist and corrupt, the solution is the same as for firms and politicians: exposure to competition and democratic reforms to ensure accountability to members. Since increased competition and the rule of law are central goals of proponents of free trade, their goals and those of proponents of labor standards are in fact consistent and mutually reinforcing.

Nevertheless, US negotiators have been unsuccessful in convincing developing countries to accept even a study group on worker rights at the WTO, and there is to date no labor text in the draft agreement for a Free Trade Area of the Americas (FTAA). The only success in incorporating labor standards in trade agreements to date has been in bilateral negotia-

---

3. The ILO definition of child labor does not encompass all economic activity but only work that endangers the health of children or interferes with their ability to go to school (up to a minimum age of 15 or 16). In 1999, the ILO further delineated priorities in this area by adopting a new convention calling for immediate action against the "worst forms of child labor."

tions with much smaller trading partners, where the United States has overwhelming leverage in setting the terms of the negotiation.

Evolution of Labor Standards in US Trade Agreements

The labor chapter template developed in recent FTAs requires only that the parties to them enforce their own national labor laws, with no requirement that those laws be consistent with ILO core labor standards. This modest standard did not pose a barrier to ratification by the US Congress of agreements with Singapore, Chile, Morocco, or Bahrain (at least not after the latter submitted a letter promising to continue working with the ILO to ensure that its laws are consistent with international standards). But critics argued that the standard was not sufficient for CAFTA-DR because both the laws and enforcement in those countries were too weak, especially with respect to freedom of association and collective bargaining rights.

Similar complaints that the "enforce-your-own-laws" standard is not adequate have been raised with respect to the agreement with Colombia.[4] This section reviews how labor standards have been incorporated in past US trade agreements. What the debate over CAFTA-DR says about prospects for a US-Colombia deal will be examined subsequently.

In general, the labor chapters in recent FTAs exhort signatories to ensure that their laws are consistent with ILO core standards, but they only provide for cooperative activities and no sanctions to promote that particular provision. Moreover, the national labor laws that can be challenged under the enforce-your-own-laws standard are based on a 20-year-old unilateral US definition rather than the international consensus reflected in the ILO declaration. The US definition of "internationally recognized worker rights" excludes nondiscrimination in employment and includes "acceptable conditions of work" with respect to wages, hours, and health and safety, which the ILO consensus does not address.[5] Finally, the recent US trade agreements limit enforcement when disputes arise to the use of "monetary assessments" rather than the trade sanctions traditionally used in commercial disputes.

In contrast with the original NAFTA model, which addressed labor standards in a side agreement with a separate dispute settlement mecha-

---

4. Similar concerns with respect to the agreement with Peru have been raised by Congressman Sander Levin (D-MI), a member of the House Ways and Means Trade Subcommittee. His remarks are available at www.house.gov (accessed April 6, 2006).

5. Neither US nor Colombian negotiators revealed it publicly, but according to a letter to US Trade Representative Robert Portman from Human Rights Watch, Andean negotiators proposed including nondiscrimination in the definition of labor laws covered by the agreement. US negotiators declined to do so. See www.hrw.org (accessed September 6, 2005).

nism, recent agreements include a labor chapter in the main text.[6] The North American Agreement on Labor Cooperation (NAALC) used essentially the same enforce-your-own laws standard, but the agreements that have followed creation of the trade promotion authority (TPA) eliminate that agreement's three-tiered treatment of labor standards, under which penalties can be applied as a last resort only for child labor and technical standards relating to minimum wages and occupational health and safety.[7] Under NAFTA, allegations regarding forced labor, discrimination issues, and migrant labor can be the subject of a formal expert committee investigation, but there are no penalties if violations are confirmed. And allegations of violations of freedom of association and the right to organize and bargain collectively are limited to consultations and cannot even be examined by expert panels. The more recent agreements are a step forward in removing this tiered approach to standards, but they also take a step back by ignoring discrimination entirely.

Another difference between the more recent FTAs and the NAALC relates to the dispute settlement mechanism. The dispute resolution process in the new FTAs is largely the same as that used for commercial disputes and is, in theory, more streamlined than that in the NAALC. For those standards subject to formal dispute adjudication, the NAFTA side agreement requires lengthy consultations and expert review before reaching the enforcement phase, a point not reached in any case to date.

The NAALC and the more recent agreements are similar, however, in restricting the enforcement mechanism to the use of monetary assessments rather that trade sanctions. Both agreements permit the revocation of tariff reductions if the fines are not paid, but only to the extent necessary to collect the fine. The value of the fines is capped in all the agreements and the revenues are supposed to be returned to the defendant country and devoted to remedying the problem identified as a violation. Fines are also an enforcement option in commercial disputes, but the revenues remain in the complaining country. Implicitly, therefore, the assumption is that violations of labor standards are a problem of capacity, while commercial disputes arise from failures of political will. It is not clear how returning the fine revenue to a government that lacks the political will to enforce its laws will help, or what else might be done in such a case.

Regardless of whether the post–2002 Trade Act agreements are improvements relative to the NAALC, critics view them as a step back from the US-Jordan FTA ratified in the fall of 2001. That agreement not only included labor in the main text, subject to the same dispute settlement procedures

---

6. See Charnovitz (2004) for a more detailed comparison of labor standards in various international trade agreements.

7. See Hufbauer and Schott (2005, chapter 2) for a more detailed description and assessment of the NAFTA side agreement.

as the rest of the agreement, but it also made no distinction with respect to remedies.[8] Moreover, the language calling on the parties to "strive to ensure" that domestic laws are consistent with international norms and that they not be weakened to encourage trade or investment is not explicitly excluded from dispute settlement as it is in the other agreements. Proponents of the "Jordan standard" argue that, while it would be difficult, this leaves an opening to challenge departures from the core standards.

Overall, however, the labor standards language in all these agreements, including the FTA with Jordan, is so filled with caveats that it seems unlikely any dispute will get as far as considering sanctions. The only "shall" in these agreements refers to the obligation of the party to "not fail to effectively enforce its laws" on a sustained basis in a way that affects trade. But other paragraphs in that section preserve the discretion of governments to adopt, modify, and enforce labor laws and regulations so that a party will be in compliance with its labor obligations under the agreement if, as stated in section 4(b) of Article 6, "a course of action or inaction [in enforcing labor laws] reflects a reasonable exercise of such discretion, or results from a bona fide decision regarding the allocation of resources."

The key criticism of this approach is the failure to include adherence to core labor standards as an enforceable obligation of these agreements. But, in fact, the gap between developing-country labor laws and the core ILO conventions is often not that great on paper, at least in countries that are nominally democratic. There is a problem with perverse incentives, however, since a standard based on enforcing one's own laws gives countries a reason not to improve existing laws, and the failure to authorize sanctions for weakening or waiving one's labor laws to promote trade or investment sends the wrong signal. But even where effective labor law enforcement is the primary problem, as in Colombia and many other countries, it is not clear that the US government would enforce the labor chapters in these agreements vigorously enough to provide a meaningful incentive to improve labor conditions.

Status of and Policies Toward Labor Standards in Colombia

Colombia has ratified 60 ILO conventions and all eight of the core conventions. By contrast, the United States has ratified just 14 conventions and only two of the core conventions, one on forced labor and the recent convention on the worst forms of child labor. ILO expert analysis also suggests that Colombia's labor laws are not far from international norms.

---

8. However, US Trade Representative Robert Zoellick exchanged letters with Jordan's ambassador to the United States in which each stated that they did not anticipate using trade sanctions to enforce the agreement's labor rights provisions.

Table 6.1 Labor standards in Colombia in comparative perspective, 2000–2002

Country/region	Percent of children aged 10–14 in the labor force, 2002	Adult illiteracy rate, 2000 (percent)	Difference in female/male illiteracy rates, 2000 (percent)	Union membership as percent of nonagricultural labor force[a]	Gross national income per capita, 2002 (in dollars; Atlas method)
Colombia	6.0[b]	8.4	0	7.0	1,880
Latin America and Caribbean	8.0	11.6	1.8	15.9	3,560
Middle East and North Africa	4.0	35.2	20.7	20.7[d]	2,000
East Asia and Pacific[c]	6.0	14.5	8.4	10.1[e]	900
Sub-Saharan Africa	28.0	38.5	15.7	13.8	470
South Asia	14.0	45.2	22.5	5.1	450
Addendum:					
Ecuador	4.0	8.4	3.3	9.8	1,400
Peru	2.0	10.1	9.4	7.5	2,320
Bolivia	10.0	14.6	12.8	16.4	870

a. Data are most recent available from late 1980s and mid-1990s; regional averages are unweighted.
b. According to the US State Department's *Human Rights Report,* the Colombian National Department of Statistics reports that 15 percent of children were employed, but the age range is not specified.
c. Excludes developed countries and South Korea and Taiwan.
d. Egypt, Jordan, and Morocco only; most of the undemocratic oil-exporting regimes restrict or ban unions.
e. Excludes China's misleading 55 percent; includes Indonesia, Malaysia, the Philippines, and Thailand.

Source: World Bank, *World Development Indicators* database.

But ratification of conventions does not ensure compliance, and nearly two decades of critical scrutiny by the Committee on Freedom of Association point to significant problems with union rights, especially the high level of violence against trade union organizers and members.[9]

Table 6.1 presents basic data on various labor standards in Colombia and also shows averages for Latin America and other developing regions

---

9. The ILO's Committee of Experts on the Application of Conventions and Recommendations reviews member country reports on the application of ratified conventions and identifies discrepancies between national law and practice and convention provisions. These "observations" are available in the ILO's Application of International Labor Standards (APPLIS) database (www.ilo.org). Because of the importance of freedom of association in the ILO framework, the special Committee on Freedom of Association was created several decades ago to hear complaints that a government is violating these core rights. For this standard only, a country need not have ratified the associated conventions (87, 98) in order to have its practices scrutinized.

for comparison. These data must be interpreted carefully because of cross-country differences in definitions and weaknesses in data collection. To the extent that the data at least reflect broad patterns across countries, however, they suggest that Colombia is not doing badly on child labor for a country at its income level and is doing better than most developing countries in reducing illiteracy and ensuring that women are not left behind. Recent analysis by the Colombian National Department of Planning found relatively modest gender-based wage gaps: 8 percent for the lowest (less than high school) and 10 percent for the highest (college degree or higher) educated workers. There was virtually no gap between men and women with moderate levels of education (high school degree or some college or postsecondary technical training) (Angel-Urdinola and Wodon 2003).

The 2004 human rights report by the US State Department finds child labor mainly in the informal sector, including on small family farms. There are no data on forced labor, but the 2004 report of the Committee of Experts on the Application of Conventions and Recommendations lists Colombia as one of 28 "cases of progress" because of changes to its penal laws that bring them into compliance with Convention No. 29 on forced labor in prisons.

With respect to the legal basis for freedom of association, the ILO's Conference Committee on the Application of Conventions and Recommendations noted in 2001 that 10 of 13 discrepancies between Colombian law and ILO conventions had been addressed in a legal reform adopted the previous year. The remaining three discrepancies all relate to the right to strike, mainly in the public sector. Although it is not explicitly mentioned in either Convention 87 or 98, ILO experts have concluded that the right to strike is essential to effective exercise of the right to collective bargaining. But the experts also note that this right is more conditioned than others related to freedom of association, and the precise definition of the conditions under which it can be restricted remains one of the more controversial areas of international labor law. For example, representatives of the ILO Employers' Group noted in a discussion of Colombia's situation at the 2004 International Labor Conference that their group disagrees with the Committee of Experts' interpretation of Convention 87 as covering the right to strike.

Another controversial area relates to the public sector, where the ILO recognizes that the need to provide "essential" public services may override the right of some public sector workers to strike. But the experts are constantly battling with member governments over the scope of essential services. The Colombian government has come under repeated criticism, as have other governments with state-owned petroleum sectors, for defining activities related to the production and processing of petroleum as essential and therefore restricting the right to strike.

Table 6.2 Murders of trade unionists in Colombia, 1998–2004

Year	Government figures		ICFTU	ICFTU global total
	Total	Teachers		
1998	n.a.	n.a.	98	123
1999	n.a.	n.a.	69	140
2000	155	69	135	209
2001	205	82	185	223
2002	196	97	184	213
2003	101	54	90	129
2004	89	47	n.a.	n.a.

ICFTU = International Confederation of Free Trade Unions

n.a. = not available

Sources: International Labor Organization, *Report to the Governing Body of the Committee on Freedom of Association*, November 2004; International Confederation of Free Trade Unions, *Annual Survey of Trade Union Rights*, various issues; Embassy of Colombia, Washington.

More broadly, while cross-country data on union membership is particularly difficult to interpret because of differences in how it is collected and reported, Colombia appears to be below other Latin American countries in the proportion of workers organized in unions (table 6.1). The table reports figures for the proportion of union members in the nonagricultural labor force because it is available for more countries. The figure for union members as a share of formal sector wage earners in Colombia is more than two times higher (17 percent), but the pattern across countries is similar and, whichever measure of union density is used, Colombia has among the lowest ratios in Latin America. Moreover, ILO data show that trade union density dropped by more than a third from 1985 to 1995, though this is actually a smaller decline than in many other countries in the region (ILO 1997).

The most serious problem in Colombia, and the one that garners the most attention, is the high level of violence against trade union organizers and members. The International Confederation of Free Trade Unions (ICFTU) reports that of the more than 1,000 trade union members murdered worldwide from 1998 through 2003, 70 percent were Colombian. Disaggregated data from the Colombian government shows that many of the murdered unionists were teachers and many others worked in other public services (table 6.2). Thus, in contrast to Central America, where problems organizing in export processing zones attracted much attention, the most serious problems in Colombia are primarily in the public sector and not linked to trade.

The level of concern over the violence against trade union members is reflected in the fact that Colombia has been the subject of repeated ILO investigations and discussions. The Colombian government has responded to ILO criticisms with labor law reforms and other programs to protect unionists, but the scrutiny continues. As an indication of the seriousness with which the ILO regards the problem, an Article 26 complaint—a procedure reserved for the gravest violations—was accepted for formal investigation in 1998. When serious problems are confirmed, an Article 26 investigation can lead to appointment of a Commission of Inquiry, which, if it upholds the findings of serious and unremediated violations, can recommend that the ILO Governing Body take action against the recalcitrant member. To date, the ILO has appointed a "direct contacts mission" and a special envoy from the director-general to work with Colombia to improve its performance, but it has repeatedly declined to create a Commission of Inquiry.

Opponents of pursuing a more aggressive stance against Colombia note that this case fits the pattern of others where allegations of egregious violations are rooted in political and ideological conflict. In the 1970s, when the human rights situation deteriorated in a number of Latin American countries, often under military governments, Argentina, Bolivia, Chile, and Uruguay were all the subject of Article 26 investigations involving conventions 87 and 98.[10] ILO attention to Colombia increased as the conflict there worsened in the late 1980s and when, according to the Freedom House ratings, it slipped from being a "free" to only a "partly free" nation.

In such cases, protecting freedom of association ultimately depends on a resolution of the broader conflict in which the violence against union organizers is embedded. But even then, recent experiences in El Salvador and Guatemala illustrate the difficulty in getting employers and government officials to view unions as legitimate social actors in the economic sphere if they are perceived, rightly or wrongly, as having supported leftist, antigovernment factions during civil conflict. Critics argue that these attitudes contribute to a climate of impunity in which the perpetrators are not punished and the violence against legitimate unionists continues.

In Colombia, officials note that the number of unionists murdered declined by roughly half in 2003, and by another 10 percent in 2004 (table 6.2). They also argue that most of the murders of union members are for political reasons and are not tied to their union activities. Officials point to the election of a former union leader as mayor of Bogotá and of a for-

---

10. Peru has actually been the most frequent target of freedom of association complaints in the region over the past decade or so. Most of the charges involve issues related to anti-union discrimination and restrictions on collect bargaining or the right to strike, and without the levels of violence seen in Colombia.

mer labor minister and union confederation leader as a provincial governor as evidence that there is more political space for union activists in Colombia than in Central America.[11]

At the ILO's 92nd International Labor Conference in June 2004, worker representatives from various countries welcomed the decline in murders but lamented that the numbers are still much too high. Some also argued that the decline has more to do with a ceasefire declared by paramilitaries in 2002 than action by the government.[12] The worker representative from the United States also noted that the culture of impunity remains a problem, citing an admission from Colombia's own National Prosecutorial Unit on Human Rights that only 5 of 3,000 murders of trade unionists between August 1986 and April 2002 had resulted in convictions. Finally, the worker representative from Chile pointed to cases where threats and acts of violence had allegedly been used to interfere with the exercising of union rights by workers. Worker representatives at the 2005 ILO Conference also noted the overall low and declining union density rate in Colombia and attributed it to government hostility to unions.

The administration of President Alvaro Uribe argues that its efforts to protect unionists and other groups targeted by guerrillas and paramilitaries have had an impact. Government figures reported to the ILO Committee on Freedom of Association show that expenditures for protection of vulnerable groups increased from roughly 4 billion pesos (around $2 million) a year over 1999–2000 to 37 billion pesos in 2003 ($13 million), with 5 billion pesos of that from the US Agency for International Development. The figures also show that more than half the total was spent on protection for trade unions and that, since 1999, nearly 4,500 individuals affiliated with unions received some protection, compared with 3,000 from nongovernmental organizations, 2,300 local government officials, and more than 300 journalists.[13]

In addition, the Uribe government argues that it is addressing the climate of impunity through systematic reform of the criminal justice system. The Colombian legislature passed a bill in June 2004 intended to speed up trials, in part by replacing the requirement for every part of the proceeding to be in writing, with provisions for oral hearings. The reforms are being implemented in four major cities and will be extended to the rest of the country by 2008. With $80 million in assistance from the US Department of Justice, Colombia is also developing a human rights unit under the attorney general and training thousands of prosecutors, police

---

11. See BBC News online, January 1, 2004, www.bbc.co.uk; and Colombia Week online, September 6, 2004, www.colombiaweek.org.

12. See Report of the Conference Committee on the Application of Conventions and Recommendations to the 92nd International Labor Conference, June 2004.

13. See Report of the Committee on Freedom of Association to the ILO Governing Body, November 2004.

investigators, and judges to improve the capacity for prosecuting human rights cases.

While choosing not to appoint a commission of inquiry, the ILO did create a special program of technical assistance for Colombia, including training for judges on international labor standards. Responding to an invitation from the Colombian government representative at the 2005 ILO Conference, the ILO also agreed that a tripartite delegation, composed of the chair of the Committee on Freedom of Association and spokespersons for employers' and workers' groups, should visit Colombia and report back on the law and practice relating to freedom of association, as well as on the technical cooperation program.

Progress is being made in reducing levels of violence in general and against trade union members. But the levels remain high, and regardless of the reasons why unionists are targeted, there can be no question that high levels of violence create a climate of fear that interferes with the ability of workers to fully exercise their association and bargaining rights. This problem will no doubt be an issue in the congressional debate over ratifying the US-Colombia FTA.

Similarities and Differences with CAFTA-DR

More than a year after the February 2004 notification to Congress that a trade agreement with Central America and the Dominican Republic had been reached, CAFTA-DR was finally ratified by a two-vote margin in the US House of Representatives. The 10-vote margin in the US Senate was also the closest in decades. What, if anything, does this portend for congressional approval of the agreement with Colombia?

The content of the agreement with Colombia (as well as the one with Peru) suggests that the principal lesson US negotiators took from the CAFTA-DR experience was the need to minimize opposition from sensitive constituencies that are disproportionately represented by Republicans in Congress. US negotiators insisted on, and Colombian negotiators accepted, only minor increases in access for Colombian sugar and apparel exports, in the latter case because of strict rules of origin requiring the use of local or US inputs. The labor chapter, however, is quite similar to those in previous agreements, including CAFTA-DR. At the time of this writing, and in contrast to CAFTA-DR, there was no accompanying statement or side letter to the US-Colombia FTA specifying funds that might be allocated for capacity-building on labor rights in Colombia, nor were there any specifics on projects that might be undertaken.

As an indication of how tight the vote on the US-Colombia FTA might be in the current environment, table 6.3 shows the vote tallies in the US House of Representatives for recent trade legislation. While substantial

Table 6.3   Recent trade votes in the US House of Representatives

Legislation and date of passage	Final vote totals	Party distribution in that session of Congress		Democrats voting in favor
Trade Act of 2002, August 2002	215 to 212	221	Republicans	25
		212	Democrats	
		2	Independents	
US-Singapore FTA, July 2003	272 to 155	229	Republicans	75
		204	Democrats	
		1	Independent	
US-Chile FTA, July 2003	270 to 156	229	Republicans	75
		204	Democrats	
		1	Independent	
US-Morocco FTA, July 2004	323 to 99	229	Republicans	120
		204	Democrats	
		1	Independent	
CAFTA-DR, August 2005	217 to 215	231	Republicans	15
		202	Democrats	
		1	Independent	

CAFTA-DR = Central American Free Trade Agreement–Dominican Republic

numbers of Democrats voted for the Singapore and Chile FTAs and a majority voted for the Morocco trade agreement, only 25 voted for the Trade Act of 2002, and it passed in the House by three votes. Although the Republican party tripled the size of its majority in the last two elections, the margin is still relatively narrow, and the House vote on CAFTA-DR was even narrower than the final vote on trade promotion authority, with only 15 Democrats voting in favor.

The dilemma for the Republican majority, and what gives the Democrats leverage on the labor issue, is that a handful of isolationists refuse to vote for trade agreements under almost any circumstances, and other Republicans representing sugar, textile, and other sensitive import-competing constituencies find it difficult to vote for agreements that increase access for those products. Thus, a certain number of minority party votes are needed and Democrats have made labor standards a litmus test for trade agreements they will support. On the first three trade votes after the 2002 Trade Act, labor standards was not an issue—Singapore is a high-wage country and Chile and Morocco both passed labor law reforms prior to completion of negotiations. With respect to Central America and Colombia, however, violations of at least some of the core labor standards are both frequent and serious, and many Democrats argue that the language used in the other agreements is not strong enough in these and similar cases.[14]

In the case of CAFTA-DR, US Trade Representative Robert Portman made a belated effort to address concerns about labor standards raised by Senator Jeff Bingaman (D-NM) just before the Senate Finance Committee vote on CAFTA-DR implementing legislation in July 2005. As a result of discussions between Portman and Bingaman, the Bush administration agreed to support several years of US funding for capacity-building on the enforcement of labor standards, provide funding for the ILO to monitor labor conditions in the region, and seek multilateral and bilateral funding for adjustment programs for Central American farmers displaced as a result of liberalization. The deal appears to have brought on board few if any Democrats, other than Bingaman, in either the House or Senate. A similar agreement with Colombia, albeit with different priorities and monitoring provisions given differences in the situation there, could be helpful and more credible if it is not done at the last moment.

But the Central American countries and Colombia also differ in important ways, and the administration's approach to both agreements suggests that additional efforts on labor standards will only be undertaken if needed to gain ratification of the Colombia FTA. As shown in table 6.4, more than 50 percent of Central American and Dominican Republic exports are in the most import-sensitive sectors, while only 10 percent of Colombia's exports are in these categories. However, Colombia's sugar exports are sharply restricted by the US tariff-rate quota. Colombia is actually a larger global sugar exporter than any of the Central American countries except Guatemala and would be expected to sharply increase exports to the US market if the quota were eliminated. Given the strident opposition of the sugar industry to CAFTA-DR, it is not surprising that US negotiators offered only modest increases in the amount of sugar that Colombia can export under the agreement and that they refused to phase out the overquota tariff. US negotiators also forced Colombia to accept stringent rules of origin on its textile and apparel exports, providing even less flexibility to source fabrics from third countries than was provided in CAFTA-DR. Those concessions by Colombia should make it easier to get the needed votes.

In addition, the source of the worker rights problems in Colombia could also affect the tenor of a congressional debate. The anti-union violence there is mostly against teachers and others in public service, sectors that are generally not related to trade. By contrast, allegations of core labor violations are widespread in many of the apparel export processing zones in Central America. There were labor disputes in Colombia in the petroleum and banana sectors in 2004, which are major exports to the US mar-

---

14. In the first half of 2006, leading House Democrats raised questions about the adequacy of the labor provisions following the signing of agreements with Oman and Peru.

Table 6.4 Exports of sensitive products to the United States, 2004
(millions of dollars)

	Sugar	Textiles and apparel	Total exports to United States	Sugar and textiles as share of total (percent)
CAFTA-DR	258	9,753	17,663	56.7
Colombia	69	644	7,361	9.7

CAFTA-DR = Central American Free Trade Agreement–Dominican Republic

Source: US International Trade Commission trade database, docs.lib.duke.edu/maps/guides/usitc. html (accessed May 22, 2006).

ket, and restrictions on strikes in the publicly owned petroleum sector have been the subject of repeated criticism by the ILO.[15] But these products currently enter the US market under low or no tariffs and do not trigger allegations of unfair competition with US workers. Moreover, both labor disputes in 2004 were settled on terms regarded as favorable by international union federations.[16]

Conclusions

The near defeat of CAFTA-DR illustrates the continuing divisions over trade and worker rights issues in the United States and highlights the political sensitivities that could make the congressional debate over an FTA with Colombia nearly as contentious. Were it not for the high levels of violence against union members and leaders in Colombia, the debate over a US-Colombia agreement might look more like that over Chile, because Colombia's exports are more diversified than Central America's and less concentrated in sensitive sectors, and because worker rights problems are more concentrated in the public sector than in export processing zones. The decline in murders shown in table 6.2 demonstrates important progress in reducing the level of violence against union members. But, to be persuasive, this must be accompanied by continued and even accelerated judicial reforms and punishment of the perpetrators, which would address the climate of impunity and ensure that the improvement is not temporary.

---

15. The ILO takes a restrictive approach to defining "essential public services" in which it is acceptable to limit the right to strike in the public sector. It is often at odds with governments, including Colombia's, over this issue.

16. International Federation of Chemical, Energy, Mine, and General Workers' Unions, "Colombia Oil Strike Ends in Victory: Government Will Not Privatise State-Owned Ecopetrol," *ICEM Update,* May 29, 2004; International Union of Food, Agricultural, Hotel, Restaurant, Catering, Tobacco and Allied Workers' Associations, "Colombia Banana Strike Ends in Union Victory," *IUF News,* June 14, 2004.

Concerns about labor standards in Colombia could also be ameliorated by adapting the Environmental Cooperation Agreement announced in the spring of 2005 by US, Central American, and Dominican Republic officials, and by including provisions for funding capacity-building similar to those agreed upon with Senator Bingaman for CAFTA-DR. This cooperation agreement, a version of which was also adopted in the recent agreements with Colombia and Peru, calls for the creation of benchmarks for measuring improvements in environmental standards, independent monitoring of progress, and the setting of priorities for technical cooperation in meeting these goals. These agreements could have served as a template for similar agreements on labor issues, but that has not been done in any of these recent FTAs. Such agreements on the labor side could also provide a framework for institutionalizing funding commitments, monitoring, and cooperation priorities as outlined in the ad hoc agreement with Senator Bingaman for Central America.[17]

As of late spring 2006, however, the Bush administration had made no announcements regarding plans or funding for capacity-building on labor issues in Colombia. Moreover, the labor chapter text in the Colombia FTA appears slightly weaker than what was included in CAFTA-DR. It does not require identification of a special roster of labor experts for disputes under that chapter, though the dispute settlement chapter does call for some of those on the regular roster to have expertise in the labor area. Neither does the article on capacity-building include the language in the CAFTA-DR text that speaks of "endeavoring to strengthen each party's institutional capacity to fulfill the common goals of the Agreement." The annex on cooperation and capacity-building is also less detailed than the one in CAFTA-DR.

It is possible that concrete plans for cooperation to improve labor standards in Colombia will emerge at a later date. USTR Portman reached out to Democrats to address their concerns over inadequate labor laws in Bahrain and Oman, as well as in Central America, and his successor, Susan Schwab, may well do so when the Colombian agreement is submitted to Congress. But any such efforts will be less credible and persuasive if they are seen simply as bribes to buy Democratic votes. And, since opposition from the sugar and textile constituencies has been more muted than during the debate over CAFTA-DR, the administration may conclude that outreach to Democrats is optional, especially since the deal with Senator Bingaman attracted few if any additional Democratic votes in favor of that earlier agreement.

---

17. President George W. Bush's proposed budget for fiscal 2007, as in previous years, calls for eliminating all funding for technical assistance programs by the Department of Labor's International Affairs Bureau, arguing that these activities duplicate similar programs in the State Department and US Agency for International Development. The CAFTA-DR deal negotiated with Senator Bingaman does not reverse the broader decision ending specific budget support for promotion of labor standards in general.

7

Intellectual Property Rights

KEITH E. MASKUS

On February 27, 2006, the governments of the United States and Colombia announced that they had reached agreement on the text of a free trade agreement (FTA).[1] As in other recent bilateral trade accords negotiated by the United States, standards for protecting intellectual property rights (IPRs) were controversial in the negotiation of the agreement. Indeed, as one publication noted, particular IPR demands made by the United States regarding protection of confidential test data and extension of patent protection had been "largely responsible" for the stalled broader negotiations between the United States and Colombia, Ecuador, and Peru.[2] Negotiators from the three Andean countries were concerned that such requirements would significantly restrain their governments' ability to manage health costs and public health crises. As discussed below, there were and are numerous other sources of controversy, including, inter alia, the scope of exclusive rights for plant varieties, the exhaustion of exclusive rights, and rules for preventing the circumvention of technological devices protecting digital copyrights.

Keith E. Maskus is professor and chair of economics at the University of Colorado, Boulder.

1. This agreement is virtually identical to an earlier one announced by the United States and Peru and, in fact, these agreements jointly establish a three-way accord among the nations involved.

2. See "Intellectual Property Protection Dogs Regional Trade Deals," *Bridges*, January 2005. By other accounts, agriculture was also an area in which negotiations were significantly delayed (see chapter 5).

In the negotiating text, released on May 8, 2006, by the US Trade Representative (USTR), Colombia committed itself to strengthening several areas of intellectual property protection, some of which mirror US practices. The pressure to impose strong standards comes from a sharply articulated US negotiating agenda for bilateral FTAs. A central objective of US trade policy is to strengthen IPR regimes in partner countries to levels that are at least similar to, if not more protective than, the systems already in place in the United States. Through the bilateral route, the United States is capable of pushing international standards well beyond those required in the World Trade Organization's Agreement on Trade-Related Aspects of Intellectual Property Rights (WTO TRIPS). US negotiators have had considerable success in this regard in reaching agreements with Chile, Morocco, Bahrain, Jordan, Singapore, and Vietnam, as well as with signatories to the Central American Free Trade Agreement–Dominican Republic (CAFTA-DR). The objective is also paramount in draft language covering the prospective Free Trade Area of the Americas (FTAA). Each of these agreements embodies various examples of so-called TRIPS-plus protection for intellectual property.

For its part, Colombia faced a delicate task during the IPR negotiations. Its negotiators seemed aware that some aspects of the TRIPS-plus agenda could be problematic in terms of their country's own development policy, even as they hoped for more certain access for Colombian products into the US market. On an institutional level, some of Colombia's sovereignty over intellectual property rights had been ceded to the Commission of the Andean Community (Bolivia, Colombia, Ecuador, Peru, and Venezuela). Thus, in some dimensions, the country could only agree to provisions that it believed it could persuade the commission to adopt.

This chapter examines various aspects of these complex problems in the context of the negotiated draft of the US-Colombia FTA, starting with a description of the main points in the agreement's chapter 16 covering IPRs. The agreement reflects instances in which the US negotiators achieved substantial increases in Colombia's (and Peru's) standards, but also cases in which those nations' diplomats were able to resist even stronger demands. The chapter then recasts this discussion in terms of the TRIPS-plus IPR agenda of the United States in bilateral trade agreements, before turning to a tentative evaluation of the stronger standards based on their potential economic implications for Colombia's development. Some aspects of these rules may provide long-term benefits, but they could be costly in the short to medium term. Presumably, the Colombian authorities believe that their nation is gaining sufficiently greater access to US markets and technology to justify bearing this cost. Regardless, there remain policy areas where Colombia may wish to complement these new intellectual property standards in order to maximize the scope for longer-term gains.

Negotiated Changes in Intellectual Property Rights

This section compares the preexisting situation of key aspects of intellectual property rights in Colombia with the significant changes required by the FTA. Intellectual property rights are rules governing competition (exclusivity, entry, investment, and unfair activities) in knowledge goods. These rules are qualified by limitations on the scope of exclusive rights arising from economic and social objectives. IPRs cover patents, utility models, industrial designs, trademarks, geographical indications, integrated circuit designs, copyrights and related rights, and rules governing unfair competition and the protection of trade secrets. Plant varieties are protected through a sui generis system discussed below. The use of traditional knowledge in a request for a patent typically requires prior informed consent. Each of these areas is covered by legal regimes that vary widely in their mechanisms and approaches.

As a member of the Andean Community, Colombia's industrial property rules are determined largely by joint decisions of the Commission of the Andean Community. The current harmonized regime was adopted in 2000 in Decision 486, which was designed to make the laws of member states compliant with TRIPS requirements and other conventions, while also recognizing the need for consistency with the Convention on Biodiversity. Individual countries were given control over some procedures, including unfair competition, trade name protection, and applicable procedures in national legislation. The main features of Decision 486, their implementation into existing Colombian policy and the changes in them required by the US-Colombia FTA, are discussed in the sections that follow.[3]

Patents

Decision 486 limits patentable subject matter to the minimum required by TRIPS. Thus, in addition to standard exemptions from patentability, it excludes discoveries (e.g., genetic sequences); any living things found in nature, including natural biological processes, genomes, and germplasm; business methods; and computer programs and software. In contrast, the United States makes all of these items patentable (subject to novelty, inventiveness, and applicability requirements) and is anxious to encourage the Andean countries to follow suit. The Andean Community regime's general exceptions also exclude "second-use patents" from eligibility in

---

3. See Ladas & Parry LLP bulletin, "Andean Community—New Intellectual Property Law," www.ladas.com (accessed May 22, 2006); and International Law Office newsletter, "New Legislation Clamps Down on Copyright Infringement," www.internationallawoffice.com.

Colombia.[4] These are patents issued on a new use of a chemical entity (e.g., pharmaceuticals) that had been patented for a prior use.

The decision also states that patent rights in materials derived from any country's "biological heritage and traditional knowledge" must safeguard and respect that biological and genetic heritage, together with the traditional knowledge of local communities. In effect, this means that individuals seeking patents must meet laws or treaties (such as the Convention on Biodiversity) regarding informed consent, disclosure of the source of genetic materials, and removal and payment formalities. For its part, the United States has not ratified the biodiversity convention, nor does its patent law recognize formalities of this kind. This is a significant difference between the United States and Colombia, and one that raised thorny issues for the FTA negotiations.

Colombia, through Decision 486, places limits on the scope of patent rights that depart considerably from US practice. Colombia recognizes that prior use before patent filing is not infringing activity, nor is experimental use or use for teaching, academic, or scientific research or noncommercial activity. Patents are subject to international exhaustion, meaning that Colombia is open to parallel imports of goods placed legitimately on markets in other countries.[5] Decision 486 imposes an obligation on patent holders to exploit their invention in member countries, but this obligation may be satisfied by imports, which is consistent with TRIPS.[6]

Under the law, it is permissible for the government to issue compulsory licenses, which force transfer of patented technologies to local firms, subject to the provisions of Article 31 of TRIPS. An interesting feature is that such licenses cannot be compelled by an individual Andean Community member if the invention is sufficiently exploited in another member. In this context, the licensing regime anticipates that the Andean Community is effectively a regional grouping with free parallel trade among members. Compulsory licensing may also be ordered in the event that a later patent (or "dependent patent") involving substantial technological progress must have access to rights under a prior patent and the later patentee has not been able to secure a voluntary license.

Under terms of the FTA, Colombia will be required to make a number of important changes in this structure of patent rules, though the country was able to sustain some important limitations on patent scope. In terms of strengthening the regime, Colombia committed to acceding to the Patent

---

4. They are not expressly excluded in the law, but an Andean Community court ruling confirmed that second-use patents are ineligible.

5. This is true as well of goods protected by copyrights and other forms of intellectual property.

6. There remains considerable controversy over the interpretation that TRIPS permits importation to satisfy exploitation requirements, as opposed to domestic production or "working" (International Centre for Trade and Sustainable Development [ITCSD] 2005).

Cooperation Treaty by 2008 and to "make all reasonable efforts" to ratify or accede to the Patent Law Treaty at some point. The Patent Cooperation Treaty is an international agreement under which a potential patent holder can register in multiple countries upon payment of a single fee and can enjoy certain grace periods in exclusivity from the time of initial registration. Use of the Patent Cooperation Treaty tends to reduce administrative costs for patent registration offices and encourage more patenting in member countries. The Patent Law Treaty is more prescriptive regarding examination standards for issuing patents and effectively commits patent offices to recognize a presumption of validity on the part of internationally issued patents. While both agreements should reduce Colombia's administrative costs for patenting, membership in the Patent Law Treaty could diminish the government's discretion in approving international patent applications.

The FTA permits Colombia to retain an exemption for research use of patented information in pharmaceutical products and agricultural chemicals, but only for purposes of meeting marketing approval requirements for generic products, which cannot be sold prior to patent expiration. Nor can such generic products be exported during the patent term except to satisfy marketing approval requirements. In essence, this provision would prevent Colombia from permitting domestic generic pharmaceutical producers to supply the needs of poor countries issuing compulsory import licenses under the TRIPS waiver of August 2003.[7] The main objective for the patent-intensive pharmaceutical companies, however, is to prevent early generic competition in Colombia.

More significantly, the FTA commits Colombia to compensate patent holders by extending the duration of patent rights when there are "unreasonable delays" (defined as a period more than five years from patent application or three years after a request for patent examination) in approving an application. This provision is extended for pharmaceutical products, wherein patent length may be attenuated by delays in marketing approval. For such goods a restoration of patent term is required. This principle is designed to limit the discretion (or abuse) of regulatory authorities in encouraging rapid entry of generic competitors on the Colombian market in favor of full-term patent rights.

While these changes signal benefits for patent holders, Colombian negotiators did successfully resist inclusion of a number of policy objectives sought by the intellectual property industries of the United States.[8] Colombia is not required to extend patent eligibility to new areas, with the

---

7. A side letter to the agreement clarifies that Colombia may, in the event of a declared national emergency, take advantage of this waiver as an importer.

8. For industry preferences, see *The U.S.-Peru Trade Promotion Agreement (TPA): The Intellectual Property Provisions*, Report of the Industry Trade Advisory Committee on Intellectual Property Rights (ITAC-15), February 1, 2006, www.ustr.gov (accessed June 29, 2006). Recall that the Peruvian and Colombian agreements are effectively identical.

exception noted in the following section on confidential test data. Thus, patents need not be required on higher-order (or multicellular) animals, discoveries in genetic sciences, software, and business methods. Next, the agreement does not require so-called second-use patents, under which a new use for an existing patented chemical entity (e.g., a pharmaceutical product) must be patented. The FTA does not change the essentials of the compulsory licensing regulations, leaving them keyed to the conditions required in TRIPS. In addition, the agreement says nothing about Colombia's rules permitting pre-grant opposition to patents, despite US industry's clear preference for eliminating this provision. Finally, no change in the exhaustion regime is required, permitting Colombia to remain open to parallel imports.

Confidential Test Data

Among the most controversial issues in the negotiation of bilateral FTAs has been US insistence on a lengthy period of protection for confidential data, typically developed in expensive clinical trials, submitted to achieve marketing approval or patents in particular countries. Health authorities require such data in order to understand the safety and efficacy of particular drugs and agricultural chemicals. However, it has been the practice in many countries to release these data quickly to potential generic producers in order to permit them to establish bioequivalence of their formulations without going through costly clinical trials. Patent laws do not necessarily prevent such release, and pharmaceutical companies are keen to have a period of exclusive data use rights without facing the generic competition facilitated by it.

While the TRIPS agreement mentions the need for protecting test data from unfair commercial use (Article 39), it does not set out a minimum period during which the data may not be used. For its part, Colombia enacted Decree 2085 in 2002 that phased in data exclusivity and provides five years for pharmaceuticals registered in 2003 or later. In 2003, similar protection was provided in Decree 505 for agricultural chemicals. In this regard, Colombia already met basic US expectations for data protection in pharmaceuticals and agrochemicals.

However, the standard practice for the United States in its bilateral FTAs has been to demand protection periods of ten years for agrochemicals and five years for pharmaceuticals. The FTA adopts exactly this provision, thereby extending the protection period for new agricultural chemical entities. These periods extend also to test information issued for approvals in other countries, meaning that even if such data are publicly available in those countries, the Colombian authorities cannot approve marketing by a rival company on the basis of such data. Moreover, if a patent expires before the end of these periods of exclusive data use, the government cannot approve competitive entry of generic versions. This principle can effectively extend exclusive marketing rights well beyond patent periods.

Plant and Animal Varieties

Colombia currently is a member of the 1978 Union for the Protection of New Plant Varieties (UPOV) and regulates plant varieties through Decision 345 of the Andean Community.[9] As such, it provides sui generis protection for new plant varieties. This protection provides exclusive rights for registrants to sell seeds but preserves a research exemption for the development of competing varieties and also sustains a farmer's privilege under which harvested seeds may be used and exchanged among farmers. Unlike the United States, Colombia does not offer patent protection for new plant varieties.

Under the FTA, Colombia must ratify or accede to the 1991 revision of UPOV, which is considerably more restrictive in its usage rights. Specifically, UPOV 1991 sharply restricts the ability of competing horticultural companies to use protected varieties in their research programs and also limits farmers to keeping harvested seeds for their own use, making it difficult to share or exchange them. Further, the FTA requires Colombia to "undertake all reasonable efforts to make . . . patent protection available" for new plant varieties. This provision is aimed primarily at ensuring that transgenic plants, especially those arising from biotechnological research, will be eligible for patents in Colombia.

Comments by US industry officials clearly anticipate that such patents will become available for new plants, while expressing disappointment that they were not extended to transgenic animals.[10] Overall, these new provisions, especially in conjunction with the strong protection for confidential test data, represent significant victories for international pharmaceutical and life science companies operating in Colombia.

Trademarks and Geographical Indications

By updating protection in these areas to the standards required by TRIPS, Decision 486 established regimes that were largely consistent with the preferences of US negotiators. The rules broaden the definition and protection of well-known trademarks and remove the requirement that, to be eligible, such trademarks must be formally registered and in use. This is a

---

9. UPOV is the acronym for the French name of this international treaty. Colombia's existing law is based on the 1978 Act of UPOV.

10. See *The U.S.-Peru Trade Promotion Agreement (TPA): The Intellectual Property Provisions*, Report of the Industry Trade Advisory Committee on Intellectual Property Rights (ITAC-15), February 1, 2006. www.ustr.gov (accessed June 29, 2006).

significant departure from prior rules, based on European traditions of civil law, that registration formalities and local use were necessary for protection. Decision 486 also permits objection to the registration and use of a domain name that might cause confusion as regards well-known names, though in general there are registration formalities in Colombia for domain names to be protected as industrial property. There is also an expanded definition of trademark dilution through exploitation of confusingly similar trademarks in closely related goods and services.

Decision 486 established further that misleading use of names or trademarks that contain an indication of origin for alcoholic beverages is not permitted. This provision extends to geographical indications, which are terms signifying that some quality characteristic of a good is related to the physical location of production. In Colombia, geographical indications may be registered as trademarks, which is essentially consistent with US practice and less restrictive than the special forms of protection advocated by the European Union.

Provisions of the FTA essentially extend trademark protection to certification marks, recognize that geographical indications and indications of origin may be registered as certification or collective marks, and further strengthen the rights afforded without formalities to owners of well-known trademarks. These changes were relatively noncontroversial as regards the preferences of both Colombian and US negotiators. Beyond those elements, the agreement clarifies that the registration of geographical indications may be blocked if the logos or images chosen for them are confusingly similar to established trademarks.

As might be expected, the main US objective in this regard was a significant improvement in Colombia's enforcement of trademarks against counterfeiting and trade in counterfeit goods (USTR 2004a). In this regard, Decision 486 implemented expanded enforcement procedures, including preventive injunctions, suspension of infringing acts, removal of goods from circulation, temporary closure of infringing establishments, seizure of assets, fines tied to damages, the prospect of criminal prosecution, and the ability of judicial and administrative authorities to undertake enforcement actions on their own initiative. These procedures were further strengthened in the FTA, which, inter alia, will require changes in Colombian law to establish minimum fines for infringement that may be invoked at the discretion of rights holders. In general terms, the FTA enforcement provisions are more prescriptive than the broader language of TRIPS but are otherwise standard.

Copyrights and Related Rights

The current copyright laws of Colombia are based on Law 44 of 1993 and Andean Community Decision 351 of 1994. Colombia is also a member of the Berne Convention and several other copyright treaties relating to the rights of performers and broadcasters. These are modern copyright regimes, anticipating the standards of TRIPS, which largely incorporate the requirements of the Berne Convention. Thus, Colombia offers copyright protection for literary and artistic works lasting the life of the author plus 50 years. It also recognizes the rights of performers, broadcasting organizations, and producers of recorded media to exclusive distribution of their works. Given the civil law background of Andean nations, Colombia also recognizes moral rights for authors and creators, such as the right to benefit from a share of future sales of paintings after the first sale. This is an issue with respect to the United States, which does not provide such rights. Colombia also protects copyrights in computer programs, though its law does not classify software as a literary work.

In terms of these issues, Colombia has agreed in the FTA to offer copyright protection for the life of the author plus 70 years or, in the case of copyrights owned by corporations or other entities (as opposed to individuals), for 70 years. Both standards accord with US law, which recently extended these terms from 50 to 70 years essentially in order to prevent older Disney copyrights from lapsing into the public domain. The FTA also clarifies that there can be no legal hierarchy of copyrights between authors and performers (such as musicians, actors, and directors), providing all groups equal protection under the law. As noted earlier, Colombia did not agree to extend patents to computer programs. Finally, the agreement is silent on moral rights, permitting them to continue.

Most significantly, Colombia earlier had ratified both of the World Intellectual Property Organization's (WIPO) so-called Internet treaties. These include the WIPO Copyright Treaty (WCT) and the WIPO Performances and Phonograms Treaty (WPPT), both of which came into force in Colombia in 2000. These treaties are designed to provide a legal framework within which countries may permit copyright owners to control copies and gain compensation for their use in cyberspace. The main issue relates to the legality of actions that avoid or circumvent the technological protection mechanisms embodied in digital products. The Colombian Penal Code of 2001 establishes that such actions may carry both civil and criminal liability, as may also efforts to alter or eliminate essential copyright information on digital products. These provisions already go some way toward satisfying the US "digital agenda" in trade policy, discussed in the next section, though significant questions remain about the scope of what is permissible fair use of digital goods.

Three other structural copyright issues existed prior to the negotiations. First, Colombia was not a member of the Brussels Convention relating to the distribution of satellite transmissions, and the agreement calls for it to ratify or accede to the convention upon entry into force of the FTA. Second, according to USTR (2004b), the Colombian authorities had not taken effective actions to reduce the unauthorized use of television programs through a strong licensing program. The FTA has extensive language regarding new protection to be provided to satellite transmissions, wireless transmission, and television broadcasts. In particular, Colombia has committed not to issue compulsory licenses for permitting unauthorized reception of such transmissions, a provision that actually goes beyond American law and practice.

Finally, as with trademarks, the most pressing issue from the US standpoint was the high rate of copyright piracy in Colombia. This refers most readily to copying of printed media, digital entertainment products, and software, but applies equally to unauthorized downloading and distribution of digital goods on the Internet. Regarding the former, the enforcement provisions highlighted above regarding trademarks apply equally to copyrighted goods. In terms of the latter, protection of electronic materials on the Internet commanded extensive language in the FTA. In particular, US negotiators were successful in extending rights that closely mirror those in the United States. For example, the temporary downloading of virtual (electronic) copies of products without authorization is made illegal. Other rights, explained further in the following section, establish civil and criminal liability for willfully downloading electronic materials without authorization, distributing such materials in a commercial volume (even if no commercial advantages were gained), and developing or using technologies to circumvent legal or technical copyright protection mechanisms. Further, while libraries, archives, and other noncommercial public entities retain some rights to download such materials, the scope of fair use for such entities is significantly limited under the FTA. These provisions are a significant victory for copyright interests in the United States.[11]

The US TRIPS-Plus Agenda

In popular parlance, the expression "TRIPS-plus" refers to demands made by the United States and other developed economies that trading partners agree to IPR standards that exceed those required in the WTO rules. In the area of pharmaceuticals, the Doha Declaration built on and clarified TRIPS by permitting the least developed countries to delay implementation and enforcement of patent rules until 2016, stating that governments could accord priority to public health needs over intellectual property requirements and asserting that developing nations could take full advantage of

---

11. See *The U.S.-Peru Trade Promotion Agreement (TPA): The Intellectual Property Provisions*, Report of the Industry Trade Advisory Committee on Intellectual Property Rights (ITAC-15), February 1, 2006, www.ustr.gov (accessed June 29, 2006).

the flexibility in TRIPS. In its negotiations of bilateral FTAs, the United States has systematically ignored these provisions in favor of strong protection in pharmaceuticals, in particular, and in IPRs more generally.[12]

In operational terms, TRIPS-plus means the following. First, for items that are not negotiated within an FTA, the relevant TRIPS standards pertain, since virtually all countries are WTO members or preparing to become members. Second, the FTA might negotiate standards that exceed those of TRIPS. Third, newer areas of intellectual property rights that were not covered by TRIPS may be subject to negotiations in FTAs, a phenomenon especially prevalent in the digital age.

It should be noted that the United States has negotiated intellectual property rights in FTAs with a requirement of nondiscrimination, implying that most favored nation treatment applies. This is only practical because IPRs are competition rules rather than taxes, and it would be difficult and unwieldy to administer different sets of rules for applicants from different countries. Moreover, the TRIPS agreement itself does not have language permitting regionally differentiated standards. Accordingly, stronger IPRs that are reached in bilateral agreements must extend unconditionally to registrants of intellectual property from third countries. Thus, while particular standards vary across agreements, the trading partner involved must offer those terms to third parties. In terms of US strategy, this is an important means of ratcheting up global standards of protection.

Negotiating Objectives in Intellectual Property Rights

In granting trade promotion authority, the US Congress set out in the Trade Act of 2002 an extensive list of negotiating priorities, several of which pertain to intellectual property rights. One calls for the "accelerated and full implementation" of the TRIPS agreement, particularly with respect to its enforcement obligations. Another is to ensure that the intellectual property rights provisions of FTAs ". . . reflect a standard of protection similar to that found in U.S. law." A third is to provide strong protection for new and emerging technologies and products embodying intellectual property. A fourth is to ensure that standards keep pace with technological developments, especially in the area of digital copyrights, providing rights holders have the ". . . legal and technological means to

---

12. The United States is not alone in this regard. For example, the members of the European Free Trade Association have joined the United States in pressing the South African Customs Union to introduce five- to ten-year data exclusivity, even where a medicine is not patented or is subject to compulsory license ("Intellectual Property Protection Dogs Regional Trade Deals," *Bridges*, January 2005). See Fink and Reichenmiller (2005) for a full discussion of negotiated standards that go beyond TRIPS.

control the use of their works through the Internet . . . and to prevent the unauthorized use of their works."[13]

These four objectives encapsulate precisely the nature of recent and current US negotiations on IPRs on a bilateral and multilateral basis. The priorities are enforcement, exporting US laws, upgrading standards, and technological protection of digital content. These objectives have been central to the negotiations with Colombia and Peru, building on prior agreements with, especially, Jordan, Morocco, Singapore, and the members of CAFTA-DR. Effective intellectual property protection is also expected of developing countries hoping to benefit from trade preferences in the US market. For example, Colombia is a beneficiary country of the generalized system of preferences and the Andean Trade Preference Act (ATPA), which was recently replaced by the Andean Trade Promotion and Drug Eradication Act, all of which impose high standards for intellectual property rights (Ferrero 2004).

Main Elements of TRIPS-Plus

What might be called the "TRIPS-plus agenda" has evolved over time, reflecting both stronger US interests in expanding protection and the perceived need to upgrade and develop standards as technologies change. For example, the chapter on intellectual property rights in the North American Free Trade Agreement (NAFTA) anticipated TRIPS, the language of which in many cases came from the former agreement. Accordingly, NAFTA embodies similar standards and flexibility, leaving much to national discretion. The US-Chile FTA has stronger requirements, particularly in the areas of patents and trade secrets, but generally relies on TRIPS as its model. However, in succeeding FTAs with Morocco, Singapore, Australia, and Jordan, the United States has pushed for increasingly protective standards. Indeed, in the language of US trade diplomats, the US-Jordan FTA is the "gold standard" for introducing strong intellectual property protection. That agreement appeared to be the model under which US negotiators with Colombia operated.[14]

Therefore, it is important to understand the major elements of this approach. The primary items, none of them required by TRIPS, are described below.

---

13. See Trade Act of 2002, Section 2102 (b) (4), www.sice.oas.org (accessed June 30, 2006).

14. Author's conversation with officials at the US Department of Commerce, February 2005. Other observers noted that the initial US negotiating text was more similar to the agreement with Bahrain.

Patents

The United States prefers that countries provide extensions to the coverage and scope of patents in a number of ways. One way is to narrow the exclusions from patentability and, in particular, to make life forms, including genetic sequences, eligible. Other areas in which patents could be provided are plant varieties, software, and business methods (typically as embodied in computer programs). As noted earlier, patents in plant varieties would restrict research use and reduce the scope of the farmer's privilege.

A second issue is to provide patent-term extensions for drugs in cases where health authorities issued patents with undue delay. Another is to issue second-use patents, as defined above, which effectively extend patent protection for chemical entities beyond original terms. Yet another is to limit experimental use of patented materials and also to restrict their use by potential generic firms in preparation for entry as patents expire. Perhaps most significant is the demand that health authorities ban the registration of any generic drugs during the lifetime of a patent, effectively ending access to compulsory licensing except in rare circumstances. This last plank was successfully introduced into CAFTA-DR and the FTAs with Chile, Morocco, and Singapore.

Considering this agenda, US negotiators had mixed success in the FTA with Colombia. There is little expansion in patent eligibility, though the promised extension of patents to plant varieties and transgenic plants is significant. Patent-term extensions in response to delays in approvals are now required, a victory for pharmaceutical companies, but second-use patents do not appear. Perhaps most frustrating for US interests, there are no significant limitations in the FTA on compulsory licensing beyond the difficult formalities of TRIPS.

Test Data

As mentioned earlier, a central demand of the United States is that there be exclusive usage rights for test data on behalf of original applicants for a period of at least five years for pharmaceutical products and agricultural chemicals. Some FTAs go beyond this and effectively permit 10-year exclusivity (by giving firms up to five years to apply for marketing approval in the country and then adding data rights) before data may be used. This is a strong restriction on competition, even in medicines where no patent is issued.

In this area, the FTA fully reflects US preferences. There are lengthy periods of confidentiality, and generic companies cannot access international data for marketing approval. Expiration of patents cannot be used to accelerate the release of confidential data. In effect, these provisions provide strong exclusive rights for research-based pharmaceutical companies in Colombia.

Digital Copyright Protection

The demands put forward by the USTR in this area involve several items, as described in Wunsch-Vincent (2003). First is that countries ratify and implement the WIPO Internet treaties mentioned earlier. The significance is that both the WCT and WPPT enjoin countries to recognize copyrights in digital products, including those distributed electronically, while taking steps to penalize efforts to circumvent technical protection measures. However, those treaties are not very prescriptive when it comes to methods for accomplishing these goals, while they are largely silent on the issue of permissible fair use. Thus, for example, many countries do not consider temporary (virtual) copies to be copyrighted, while they provide leeway for making personal copies and copies for educational and scientific purposes. Countries also have latitude in defining areas within which compulsory licenses may be issued to ensure that access to digital content is available in remote areas, schools, and libraries.

In contrast, the United States has adopted extremely strong copyright protection for digital products under the Digital Millennium Copyright Act (DMCA), which is highly controversial among legal scholars. Under the DMCA, even inadvertent copying and circumvention can be subject to civil and criminal penalties, while the scope of fair use is heavily curtailed. The US negotiating strategy in recent FTAs, such as those with Morocco and Jordan, has been to export DMCA-like protection to trading partners. Interestingly, among all the TRIPS-plus agenda items, enhanced protection for digital copyrights has the full and unwavering support of the US Congress. Recorded music, software, video games, and movies form a potent lobby for international trade policy.

Here again, the United States achieved its objectives in the FTA. The rules to which Colombia agreed closely mirror those of the DMCA, including provisions for criminal penalties for circumvention and the limited liability of Internet service providers tied to their willingness to monitor the legality of content available on their systems. In brief, FTA provisions sharply restrict the scope of fair use in copyrights and could raise roadblocks to the access of scientists, educators, and students to technical information and data.

Exhaustion of Rights

The exhaustion doctrine governs the point of distribution at which an IPR holder loses the ability to control additional movement and sale of goods. Under international exhaustion, these rights disappear upon first sale by the rights holder anywhere in the world. In consequence, countries following this approach are open to parallel imports, though this may vary as regards patented, copyrighted, and trademarked goods. Under national exhaustion, the rights to exclude imports are not ended upon sale outside the country, meaning that parallel imports are not permitted.

The United States bars parallel imports in patented and copyrighted goods, though it is relatively open to products protected by trademarks (Maskus 2000b). In contrast, Colombia and the other Andean economies generally follow a doctrine of international exhaustion. The global research-based pharmaceutical companies and copyright industries would prefer that this doctrine be changed and that parallel imports be restricted. US negotiators have expanded the use of national exhaustion in a number of bilateral FTAs. For example, in both the Jordan and Morocco agreements, copyright holders are given the rights to block parallel imports. As discussed earlier, however, the US-Colombia FTA is silent on the issue of parallel trade, preserving autonomy in this regard on behalf of Colombian trade policy.

Trademarks and Geographical Indications

The United States protects geographical indications through collective and certification marks. During negotiations, US officials pushed for the Colombian system of geographical indications to protect American collective and certification marks. Further, the United States requested that preexisting trademarks block any registration of new marks for geographical indications that would be confusingly similar. Regarding trademarks, the major American interest, like that in copyrights, is an improved enforcement system and more resources devoted to punishing counterfeiting and piracy in the region. It is evident from the earlier discussion that the United States achieved the bulk of this negotiating agenda.

Enforcement Commitments

A final central plank of the TRIPS-plus agenda is to commit trading partners to considerably stronger efforts to establish effective enforcement mechanisms to deal with infringement. The TRIPS agreement has extensive language on the nature of enforcement expected of member countries, ranging from border measures to civil penalties. However, it does not require any allocation of resources to the task, nor does it require the establishment of specific means related to intellectual property rights, such as specialized courts.

Several of the US bilateral FTAs go beyond these general statements to specific obligations. For example, in the US agreements with Chile and Morocco, those countries are not permitted to invoke resource constraints (such as limits on administrative budgets) as justifications for failing to comply with enforcement obligations. In several FTAs there is now an obligation to apply criminal procedures in cases of willful infringements, with stronger commitments in the case of counterfeit labels attached to copyrighted works.

Similar to CAFTA-DR and agreements with Jordan and Morocco, the principles struck in the US-Colombia FTA offer extensive commitments on enforcement, though no formal pledge to minimum expenditures or special courts is made. In general, the rules for enforcement, penalties, administrative actions, and judicial oversight closely track those of US law and establish wide-ranging obligations for preliminary injunctions, alternative fines, criminal penalties, and border controls. Perhaps most significant is the injection of DMCA-like rules into copyright infringement on the Internet. Whether Colombia has the resources and the will to carry out these commitments remains to be seen, but on paper the enforcement rules are on a par with those in the most advanced industrial nations.

A Tentative Evaluation

The sections that follow evaluate the nature of US-Colombian technology trade and the existing situation regarding intellectual property rights in Colombia. As might be expected, Colombia has a significant comparative disadvantage relative to the United States in developing and trading new goods and advanced technologies, implying that its underlying interests are for rather weaker intellectual property rights. The terms of the FTA raise some problematic issues in this context.

Comparative Advantage in Technology Trade

The pursuit of stronger intellectual property protection through bilateral FTAs is understandable from the US perspective. The United States remains the largest developer of new technologies, medicines, and plant varieties, while its cultural industries generate the bulk of new content, especially in digital formats. Commercial interests in the United States would achieve considerable gains from stronger international copyright rules and patent protection. Moreover, the nondiscrimination aspects of IPR standards have the effect of ratcheting up global standards over time.

The more fundamental question is whether acceptance of TRIPS-plus requirements makes sense for developing countries such as Colombia that reach trading agreements with the United States. It is impossible to answer this question with certainty, because the nature of intellectual property rights, like other regulatory standards, is to deal with market failures in inherently second-best ways. The essential balance in IPRs is to absorb

Table 7.1   Utility patents granted, 2000–2003

Patents	2000	2001	2002	2003
Granted by United States to residents of:				
Argentina	54	54	51	63
Bolivia	2	0	0	0
Chile	15	12	11	11
Colombia	8	12	6	10
Ecuador	0	4	0	3
Peru	2	4	1	4
Venezuela	27	26	30	19
Granted by Colombia to residents of:				
Colombia	21	13	12	n.a.
United States	329	189	n.a.	n.a.
Other	245	161	360	n.a.

n.a. = not available

Sources: US Patent and Trademark Office; World Intellectual Property Organization.

short-run increases in market power on behalf of rights holders in return for the promise of long-run gains in greater innovation and technology transfer; that is, to sacrifice static competition in return for greater dynamic competition and growth.

A Question of Technology Balance

To gain some perspective, consider the relative positions of the two nations regarding the development and use of new technologies. It is no surprise to learn that, like other lower- to middle-income developing economies, Colombia lags far behind the United States in generating patentable new inventions. As shown in table 7.1, Colombian inventors in recent years have averaged around nine US-issued patents per year, ranking well behind Argentina and Venezuela (which are much larger economies) and approximately the same as Chile. In contrast, the Colombian authorities have granted 15 to 20 patents a year to domestic residents, but an average of 260 a year to US residents. US inventors accounted for more than 50 percent of Colombian patent grants in the early part of this decade.

As such figures might suggest, the United States has a strong bilateral comparative advantage in innovation, underscoring its interests in establishing strong IPRs in as many trading partners as possible. This situation is also evidenced by the fact that, in 2000, the US-sourced foreign direct investment stock in Colombia was around $5.3 billion, while the Colombiansourced foreign direct investment stock in the United States was approximately 10 percent of that total, at $585 million.[15] The United States also sustains a bilateral trade surplus with Colombia in medicines, machinery, equipment, and high-technology goods. All of these items are channels of net technology flows to Colombia.

Economic Development Potential

Multinational enterprises headquartered in the United States naturally wish to enjoy exclusive rights to exploit the technologies they transfer to Colombia. Exclusive rights can be established both through natural lead-time advantages and technological sophistication that makes imitation difficult and costly and through legal means involving intellectual property rights. Advocates of strong intellectual property protection claim that it encourages more inward technology transfer by raising certainty and reducing the costs of transferring information and know-how (Sherwood 1997). At the same time, even if technology flows were to increase, strong protection of intellectual property rights could permit patent holders to reduce access, raise licensing fees, segment markets, and limit competition (Correa 2005).

Empirical studies of this trade-off bear mixed messages. According to one extensive study, nations that have adopted stronger patent rights have not seen increases in domestic inventive activity for a lengthy period of time. Rather, the medium-term economic gains accrued to foreign inventors who registered more intellectual property in those countries (Lerner 2002). These results have been supplemented by recent microeconomic studies of changes in the Japanese patent system (Sakakibara and Branstetter 2001) that led to no detectable increase in innovation within Japan for at least five years. On this evidence, Colombia, a developing economy with relatively small science and technology sectors, is unlikely to see much gain in domestic innovation. At the same time, these same studies suggest that greater foreign patenting in countries that improve their IPRs reflects an intention to transfer more technology through protected channels, a finding that is consistent with the majority of macro-level investigations of foreign direct investment and licensing.[16]

None of these studies considered the question of innovation and technology flows in the context of a free trade agreement, which raises a number of complications. First, the TRIPS-plus agenda is focused on pharmaceuticals and digital products more than on general technological

---

15. Figures are from UNCTAD's *World Investment Directory*, www.unctad.org (accessed May 22, 2006).

16. Maskus (2000a) reviews such studies extensively, while they are updated in several papers in Fink and Maskus (2004).

development. As such, it seems unlikely that adoption of these higher standards can do much to expand innovation and technology flows beyond the incentives established in TRIPS. Second, an FTA itself, even in terms of standard trade liberalization, is discriminatory and not necessarily beneficial because of the possibility of trade diversion. When added to the second-best aspects of IPRs, the potential welfare implications become complex and economists cannot make general predictions.

Consider, for example, the fact that Colombia would be making permanent and highly protective changes in its IPR system, offered to inventors and creators from everywhere in the world, in return for preferential market access in the United States. This preferential access presumably would exist largely in agriculture and a few labor-intensive goods, given that US most favored nation barriers in other goods are low. These preferences are likely only to be temporary, given the US mandate to negotiate additional FTAs and the potential outcomes of the Doha Round of multilateral trade negotiations. Indeed, they would be effectively eliminated upon the successful conclusion of the FTAA.

There may be other reasons for Colombia to reach an agreement. As has often been claimed, FTAs have the potential to lock in trade reforms so credibly that they cannot later be rescinded due to changes in government. While locking in the TRIPS-plus reforms of IPRs may be of questionable value when considered in the context of larger domestic reforms in services, infrastructure, and trade barriers, the Colombian economy may see net efficiency gains. In that sense, stronger IPRs are a necessary cost of achieving the credibility that an FTA with the United States would provide and a useful signal to domestic and foreign investors.

Wider Concerns for Colombia

The broader concerns over intellectual property rights reflect more than their potential impact on innovation, technology transfer, and information diffusion. IPRs also affect fundamental social and development objectives in health, agriculture and nutrition, biodiversity, education, and science (Maskus and Reichman 2005). Thus, standards for protecting intellectual property, negotiated in the context of a trade policy initiative, have far-reaching implications for the preservation and provision of public goods in the Colombian and Andean economies. It is this feature that explains why IPRs are intensely controversial in the region.

Significantly more protective IPRs have effects on social objectives that, while perhaps difficult for economists to quantify, should be accounted for in any reckoning of the potential gains and losses from the FTA. Most prominently, the requirements for patent-term extensions and test data protection are designed explicitly to delay the onset of generic competition in medicines. An extensive body of statistical evidence documents that the presence, or threat, of generic competition places strong downward pressure on pharmaceutical prices and increases access to medicines. Colombian authorities need to think carefully about the potential implications of these restrictions.[17]

One can make similar claims about other aspects of the TRIPS-plus agenda that emerged in the US-Colombia FTA. Awarding patents to plant varieties may have some positive impact on the willingness of life science firms to locate innovative activities in Colombia. However, there would be costs for farmers and researchers in the medium run. Similarly, strong anticircumvention rules in digital copyrights can result in serious constraints for students, libraries, and researchers trying to gain access to scientific and literary information available on the Internet. In both of these areas, and others, Colombian policymakers should consider the scope of fair use that makes sense for their economy.

Taking a more balanced view, the potential for net gains depends on particular circumstances and may vary over the time horizon considered (Maskus 2004). What really matters is that intellectual property standards be selected in a way that increases certainty while encouraging effective dynamic competition (World Bank 2001). Such standards also need to be complemented by appropriate regulatory and development policies, as noted below.

A Broader Strategy

The discussion in this chapter has at times been critical of the wisdom of Colombia's decision to adopt considerably stronger intellectual property rights under its free trade agreement with the United States. This pessimism may be misplaced, for extended protection bears the prospect of longer-term advantages for innovative and creative industries in Colombia. In that context, it is useful to conclude by discussing briefly what Colombia might do in incorporate the new intellectual property obligations into a broader development strategy in order to maximize the potential for long-term gains.

Authorities should retain as much flexibility as possible in terms of policies to deal with access to public health. The FTA establishes strong protection of private rights to confidential data, marketing privileges, and patent terms, all of which will delay generic competition, with, it would seem, relatively little prospect for domestic innovation in medicines. Thus,

---

17. Again, in recent FTAs, including the US-Colombia pact, the United States has agreed to side letters that affirm the priority of public health over commercial rents from IPRs. These side letters satisfy the negotiating objective of the trade promotion authority to respect the spirit of the Doha declaration on public health. However, the legal obstacles countries must surmount to actually avail themselves of such flexibility as compulsory licensing, in the presence of TRIPS-plus standards, would be daunting.

ensuring access to medicines through purchasing programs, insurance systems, and price regulations will be important.

In a similar vein, it may be sensible for members of the Andean Community to establish a policy of regional exhaustion in patents and copyrights in order to benefit from access to the lowest-cost medicines, agricultural technologies, and other products in the area. Using that approach, member nations would be open to parallel trade among themselves. These countries might also consider means of supporting regional production capacity for generic producers of pharmaceuticals, agricultural chemicals, and seed varieties.

Colombian officials could look at copyright laws around the world for an understanding of the potential scope of fair use that remains consistent with the general provisions of the World Intellectual Property Organization's Copyright Treaty and Performances and Phonograms Treaty, while not violating the new FTA provisions. Colombia did retain some room for fair-use access by libraries, universities, and other public, noncommercial enterprises, and it will be important to retain such flexibility. However, the wholesale adoption within the FTA of many provisions of the US Digital Millennium Copyright Act is not likely to work in Colombia's favor.

It is important for Colombian authorities to coordinate views among the nation's ministries and interested citizens and businesses on how to move forward with the new system of IPRs as it is implemented. It makes little sense for a commercially driven trade ministry to undertake regulatory commitments that affect health, education, science, and technology without extensive consultation. But that effectively is what happened in this instance. The new rules, whenever implemented, will need to be complemented by broader support systems within the economy, and early consultation on these needs is essential. For example, an effective competition policy can help blunt the monopoly powers inherent in stronger IPRs. Also important are steps to encourage the development of human capital and innovation capacity within the domestic economy (Maskus and Reichman 2005).

8

Conclusions

JEFFREY J. SCHOTT

The launch of free trade negotiations between the United States and Colombia, Ecuador, and Peru in May 2004 created important opportunities and challenges for each of the participating countries. This chapter summarizes some of the most salient aspects of the initiative.

Considering the modest level of trade and investment between the partner countries and the generally open access to the US market afforded under the Andean Trade Preference Act (ATPA), it is not surprising that the welfare gains from a prospective free trade agreement—as detailed in the modeling results reported in chapter 4—are relatively small. The United States can expect significant increases in exports to the region from a small base and positive, albeit minimal, GDP gains in relation to the huge size of the US market. In contrast, aggregate welfare gains for Colombia should exceed 0.4 percent of GDP due to both large terms of trade effects and improved efficiency in its domestic production. Since the models deployed omit key sectors such as services and give short shrift to dynamic gains generated by enhanced competition and increased investment in the economy due to changes in the policy regime, these results undoubtedly underestimate the potential gains for both sides.

That said, the economic impact of an FTA will vary depending on the scope of reforms generated by other bilateral, regional, and multilateral trade initiatives in which the United States and Andean countries also participate. Indeed, the applied general equilibrium model results in chapter 4 indicate that Colombia's welfare gains are cut in half if one simulates the bilateral FTA with the United States together with the other FTAs that the

Jeffrey J. Schott is a senior fellow at the Institute for International Economics.

United States has signed or is currently negotiating. Completion of the Free Trade Area of the Americas (FTAA) would further dilute Colombia's advantage in the US market compared to its South American neighbors; so too would the results of the Doha Round of multilateral trade negotiations if those talks produce significant cuts in tariffs applied on a most favored nation basis that reduce the value of all FTA tariff preferences.

To achieve the gains promised by the economic models requires the foresight to offer "concessions" to the other trading partners. An open secret of trade policy is that the bulk of the welfare gains that can be garnered in a trade negotiation generally derive from reforms of one's own restrictions on trade and investment in goods and services. Getting your trading partner to "pay" for this self-promotion is often a prerequisite for domestic political support for the desired policy changes. That's why trade negotiators describe their final outputs as "win-win" propositions.

For the United States, with low most favored nation trade barriers and extensive tariff preferences accorded to Colombia and many other developing countries, the changes required by FTAs are limited. However, the ATPA expires at the end of 2006; an FTA would turn those unilateral and time-limited preferences into permanent and contractual obligations of the United States. In addition, the few remaining US barriers protect sectors (e.g., apparel, sugar) where trade liberalization could create substantial new export opportunities for developing countries. Selling such policy reforms to the US Congress has become increasingly difficult, as witnessed by the strident debate and razor-thin margin of passage of the Central American Free Trade Agreement–Dominican Republic (CAFTA-DR).

US officials have drawn two clear lessons from the CAFTA-DR experience for ongoing and prospective free trade agreements: first, future trade deals must be at least as comprehensive as CAFTA-DR in terms of coverage and perhaps go even farther with respect to labor and environmental provisions; and second, US negotiators need to be circumspect in putting forward proposals for textile, apparel, and sugar reforms. Of these products, the sugar industry has been the most resistant to trade liberalization, and it is thus notable that US negotiators agreed to increase the sugar quota for Colombia to 75,000 metric tons (plus a small annual growth factor). In the US FTA with Australia, sugar was fully exempted from the free trade regime, and CAFTA-DR called for only a very modest expansion of US sugar quotas, which the Congress approved only grudgingly. Additional liberalization—whether via an FTA with the Andean countries, a Doha Round accord, or implementation of existing North American Free Trade Agreement (NAFTA) commitments to Mexico—would likely render untenable the current US sugar programs and thus require extensive reform of US sugar policy. Such reform would make sense from an economic, environmental, and health policy perspective; to date, however, Congress has not regarded these advantages as compelling enough to override the demands of special interest politics.

For Colombia, an FTA will require more substantial changes in current policies that protect manufacturing, farming, and services. The pact should, however, afford reasonable transition periods before the free trade obligations are fully implemented to allow an orderly adjustment for workers and firms. The agricultural sector will undoubtedly pose the most vexing adjustment problems, particularly when the FTA provisions are coupled with ongoing efforts to promote alternative crops to the lucrative but illegal drug trade. Colombian farmers continue to oppose lowering trade barriers to temperate agricultural imports from the United States, and they charge such products benefit from extensive government subsidies. The availability of safeguard measures will be important; so, too, will adjustment programs to help restructure the rural economy and facilitate new investment, particularly in basic infrastructure (as has been offered to Central American countries through the Millennium Challenge Corporation and other bilateral assistance programs).

In addition, the CAFTA-DR ratification debate in the United States underscored the salience and sensitivity of labor rights and protections in partner countries. As noted in chapter 6, this issue could be even more contentious for the Andean countries. Developing a credible program of labor initiatives under the complementary labor cooperation agreement, including the provision of adequate financial resources for labor programs and their implementation and enforcement, should be a high priority. Indeed, it may be a prerequisite to closing the overall trade deal.

Colombia's special relationship with the United States, and in particular its alliance in the war against drug trafficking, provides some advantages vis-à-vis other US trading partners. As noted in chapter 1, that alliance was a crucial consideration in launching trade talks in 2004 and will be highly influential in congressional consideration of the final agreement. As such, if the terms of the prospective pact are comparable to other agreements ratified by the Congress, the special relationship should make the ratification debate less contentious than the strident and sharply divided vote on CAFTA-DR in the summer of 2005. But, again, such an outcome depends importantly on how labor problems in Colombia are addressed both in the FTA and in domestic regulation and enforcement.

The United States has a vested interest in Colombia's economic development and in its success in the war against drugs and in ending the prolonged armed insurrection in the country. These foreign policy objectives are integrally linked with progress on the economic front; indeed, they are what makes the US-Colombia relationship "special" and a key reason why Colombia rose to the top of the FTA queue with the United States. Nonetheless, Colombia's special relationship does not translate into exemptions from the comprehensive reforms required of other US trade agreement partners. Given the CAFTA-DR aftershocks, it is clear that Colombia should not expect a payoff in terms of extraordinary trade concessions on import-sensitive products.

At the same time, however, in light of US geopolitical objectives in an FTA with Colombia, US officials probably will continue and possibly expand current levels of financial, technical, and military assistance to reinforce Colombia's economic development and security needs. In other words, because of the special relationship, the United States may be more inclined to support more capacity-building initiatives than provided to other FTA partners (with the exception of Mexico). In particular, the United States should be willing to contribute to investment in economic infrastructure and channels for microfinance for small enterprises in both urban and rural areas in Colombia. Such programs could be integrated into the overall package of agreements associated with the trade pact, though on a more discrete scale than the North American Development Bank that was appended to the NAFTA primarily to provide financial assistance to border communities affected by the trade pact.

In short, an FTA will demand much more of Colombia than of the United States—just as it has of all the other FTA partners with which the United States has negotiated trade pacts. Most of the changes will involve domestic policies that Colombia would need to restructure in any event as it strives to keep pace with foreign competition at home and in its key export markets. An FTA provides additional impetus to do so by offering both economic and political benefits in the form of increased bilateral trade and investment, which in turn will create a stronger foundation for the overall bilateral relationship between Colombia and the United States.

Using the Free Trade Agreement to Promote Colombian Economic Development

Free trade agreements do not provide a ticket to prosperity. Trade reforms should be seen as an integral, albeit minor, part of a broader development strategy. If implemented in conjunction with domestic economic reforms, FTAs can give a powerful boost to economic growth. If Colombia is to use its FTA with the United States most effectively, it would do well to heed the lessons derived from past experience with such agreements.

First, FTAs create opportunities; they do not guarantee sales. Firms need to be able to take advantage of the market opening by producing goods or services of sufficient quality and price to garner sales. Tax and regulatory policies that blunt productivity and impose obstacles to investment will leave unfulfilled the economic potential of trade agreements.

Second, FTA preferences offer only temporary advantage. The value of the negotiated tariff preferences declines over time due to most favored nation trade liberalization negotiated in the World Trade Organization (WTO) and to the granting of similar preferences in other preferential trading arrangements. So it is critical to use the transition period during which trade liberalization is phased in to undertake structural adjustments that enable firms and workers to meet the challenges from foreign competitors in the home and third-country markets. This is an area where Mexico has fallen short, particularly in the agricultural sector. Although Mexico's agrarian reforms predated the signing of NAFTA and sensitive farm products were given lengthy periods to phase in NAFTA liberalization, the Mexican government did very little to revamp its farm programs while the protection remained intact.

Third, an FTA should be designed primarily to spur competition and investment in the economy. Its major benefit is not the extension of trade preferences but rather its role as an "insurance policy" against new protectionism at home and abroad, because the contractual obligations of the trade pact effectively raise the cost of policy reversals. This insurance applies both to domestic policies and to the foreign market access commitments secured in the trade pact. In essence, an FTA locks in policy reforms and in so doing contributes to a more stable and attractive environment for investment. If the overall policy mix is right, an FTA could help raise Colombia's profile among international investors.

Fourth, FTAs can help propel integration among the partner countries negotiating with the United States. One of the major achievements of CAFTA-DR was spurring regional integration among the Central American countries, in addition to deepening trade and investment ties with the United States. By unifying formerly fragmented markets, CAFTA-DR also is helping to spur the physical integration of the region by making more viable investment in transport, energy, and telecommunications infrastructure that facilitates trade in goods and services within Central America. While the Andean countries already have worked out an incomplete customs union, the development of common obligations with the United States in an FTA could help harmonize areas of policy friction within the Andean Community (at least among those members who partner with the United States) and spur investment in a similar fashion.

Unfortunately, political differences among the Andean countries seem to be working in the opposite direction. Venezuela's notification in April 2006 that it intends to withdraw from the Andean Community demonstrated starkly how difficult it has been, and will be, for the Andean neighbors to work together for their mutual benefit. The main exceptions to this dire forecast may be Colombia and Peru, which have both instituted market-oriented policies to address the challenges of global competition in general and free trade with the United States in particular.

Finally, an FTA does not ensure that the gains from trade will spread evenly throughout the country. Trade liberalization generates winners and losers, and often there is a wide gap between those that benefit from new trade and investment opportunities and those that are unable to compete in a more competitive environment. In Mexico, the income gap between northern and southern states has widened substantially since NAFTA entered into force, and some components of the agricultural economy have suffered. Several factors contributed to such skewed growth, but inadequate investment—particularly in economic infrastructure—has been the main culprit (Hufbauer and Schott 2005). Due to tight fiscal and monetary policies required by the initial response to the peso crisis in 1995 and political gridlock that has prevented the passage of needed tax and energy reforms, Mexico has not invested enough in physical and human capital to take full advantage of the new opportunities created by NAFTA.

In sum, an FTA can succeed in promoting economic growth if the trade bargain catalyzes economic reforms in each partner country. The challenge for policymakers is to create a policy environment conducive to trade and investment that will open new opportunities for firms and workers, while providing a more reliable social safety net to facilitate the adjustment of those workers and their communities that fall behind in the new competitive environment. For Colombia, this challenge is complicated by the production and trafficking of illicit drugs that have such a distorting impact on its rural economy. Helping its partner overcome this problem is, in essence, the main challenge and the ultimate prize that can be achieved for the United States as well.

Implications of Andean Free Trade Agreements for Broader Hemispheric Integration

The US-Colombia FTA and the US-Peru Trade Promotion Agreement are highly similar but separate pacts. They were designed to be implemented as stand-alone initiatives but also to be agglomerated into a broader free trade regime linking countries in North and South America.

The original vision of hemispheric trade integration, set forth at the Miami Summit of the Americas in December 1994, was to negotiate the FTAA. As mandated by the summit leaders, the FTAA was to be a self-contained negotiation among the 34 democratic countries in the hemisphere. FTAA negotiations formally began after the Santiago Summit of the Americas in April 1998. However, the negotiations soon bogged down and have been moribund since the November 2003 meeting of Western Hemisphere trade ministers in Miami. The deadline for concluding the talks passed virtually unnoticed in January 2005. The cochairs of the negotiations, the United States and Brazil, have focused efforts instead on the Doha Round in the WTO and on other bilateral FTAs.

Can the US-Colombia and US-Peru pacts restore momentum toward the creation of a broader free trade regime in the Americas? At present, the signs are not positive. First, the pacts have provoked the fragmentation rather than deeper integration of the Andean Community. Venezuela announced its intention in April 2006 to withdraw from the Andean Community in protest over the deepening ties with the United States. Trade talks with Ecuador lagged those with Colombia and Peru and were at least temporarily suspended in May 2006 due to energy sector investment problems. Bolivia has been a casual observer of the FTA process, but as a result of policy changes undertaken by the new administration of President Evo Morales, the country has dimmed prospects for a future trade deal with the United States. The Andean Community never had a fully integrated market, and intraregional trade is now under increasing stress.

Second, both the Colombian and Peruvian pacts face domestic opposition. In Colombia, the FTA has generated sharp criticism, particularly from agricultural interests, but is likely to be ratified. In Peru, the administration of President Alejandro Toledo ratified the pact before it left office in late July, with muted support from incoming president, Alan Garcia, who had been critical of the agreement during the election campaign. Ensuring that the new Peruvian government fully implements the pact will be a central focus of US legislators when they address implementing legislation in the second half of 2006, in addition to concerns about abusive labor practices raised by Democrats in the House of Representatives.[1] Since congressional notification of the US-Colombia FTA was delayed throughout the spring of 2006, it is unlikely that the US Congress will pursue the ratification process until 2007. In the interim, Congress should extend the ATPA preferences to avoid disruptions in Andean exports to the United States that could occur if ATPA benefits expire.

Third, many Latin American countries seem distracted by pressing economic and political problems at home; all face the challenge of adjusting to rapidly changing conditions in the global economy generated by technological innovation and by the emergence of the Chinese trading juggernaut. Some have denounced the FTAA process; others have openly questioned its continued viability or desirability.

However, like Mark Twain reading his obituary, news of the death of the FTAA may be premature. Although the talks have drifted, concrete trade negotiations have advanced among subsets of FTAA participants. There already are numerous FTAs linking countries in North and South America, FTAs or customs unions among Latin American neighbors, and a variety of "partial scope" trade accords that grant sector-specific benefits to bilateral trading partners. To be sure, except for NAFTA, most of these accords involve small volumes of trade, but this is not necessarily bad for prospects for an FTAA.

US officials have deliberately moved forward with bilateral FTAs with a number of Latin American and Caribbean countries, challenging Brazil and its Southern Cone Common Market (Mercosur) partners to catch up when they are ready to negotiate actively in the FTAA. CAFTA-DR and pacts with Chile, Colombia, Peru, and possibly Panama—along with deepening integration in the NAFTA region—are designed to maintain momentum and establish negotiating precedents for the broader FTAA ex-

---

1. See *Inside US Trade*, March 31, 2006.

ercise. In addition, US unilateral tariff preferences have been extended through September 2008 under the Caribbean Basin Trade Partnership Act of 2000 (CBTPA) for most Caribbean exports not covered by the original Caribbean Basin Initiative (CBI).[2] What remains that is not subject to free trade commitments is mainly US trade with Mercosur and with Venezuela and Bolivia.

If the bilateral and subregional accords accelerate the pace of economic reform, they will contribute importantly over time to the ability and willingness of Latin American and Caribbean countries to undertake the reciprocal obligations of the broader hemispheric pact. Indeed, that is one of the advantages that the Colombia and Peru pacts bring to the broader hemispheric trade initiative.

Even if not all of the original 34 countries participate, revival of the FTAA process is possible if driven by two separate events: the Doha Round of multilateral trade negotiations and the evolution of new Asia-Pacific trade linkages. First, if the Doha Round succeeds, commitments to reduce agricultural subsidies will remove a major substantive barrier to trade talks between the United States and Mercosur. Uruguay is already pressing its Mercosur partners to move in this direction, and the others could follow suit if the impasse over agricultural reforms is broken. On the other hand, if the Doha Round fails, or concludes with a minimalist package of trade reforms, then the Mercosur countries may turn back to the hemispheric talks with even greater ardor—since they will be at a distinct disadvantage vis-à-vis most of the countries on the west coast of South America, plus Central America and the Caribbean, that already have preferential access to the US market.

Second, several Latin American countries are forging new trade pacts with East Asian countries. Chile has concluded deals with China and Korea; Mexico has an FTA with Japan and is talking about closer trade ties with Korea; and Peru is negotiating with Thailand. To take advantage of these new opportunities and to encourage the inflow of new foreign direct investment in their economies, these countries will need to pursue the types of trade and regulatory reforms required by US-style free trade agreements. This should build support for cumulating the gains from individual FTAs into an integrated regional free trade regime.

Such considerations could well drive the revival of FTAA talks, led by Colombia, Peru, Chile, and other US trading partners that already have concluded bilateral deals with their principal trading partners in the hemisphere. The allure of such an alliance may prove attractive for Brazil and Argentina as well.

---

2. The CBTPA provides "NAFTA parity" for products (mostly textiles and apparel) excluded from the Caribbean Basin Economic Recovery Expansion Act of 1990, known as CBI II. Unlike the CBI preferences that have no termination date, the supplementary benefits under CBTPA must comply with NAFTA rules of origin and expire on September 30, 2008.

Technical Appendix
Applied General Equilibrium Simulation of the Proposed US-Colombia FTA

JOHN P. GILBERT

This technical appendix presents a series of applied general equilibrium (AGE) simulations to assess the likely implications of a proposed FTA between the United States and Colombia. Extending the simulation presented in chapter 4, this appendix presents the full model results for the revised simulations of the US-Colombia FTA, incorporating existing FTAs into the database and the results of a multilateral benchmark exercise. The simulations have been undertaken using a common framework and database, the standard Global Trade Analysis Project (GTAP) model (Hertel 1997) and the GTAP5.4 database (Dimaranan and McDougall 2002).

AGE Simulation and the GTAP Model

AGE models are numerical models based on general equilibrium theory and constructed with the objective of turning the abstract models of theory into a practical tool for policy analysis. A number of features distinguish AGE models from other widely used tools of trade policy analysis (partial equilibrium and gravity models). They are multisectoral and in many cases multiregional, and the behavior of economic agents is modeled

John P. Gilbert is associate professor of economics in the Department of Economics, Utah State University, Logan, Utah.

explicitly through utility and profit maximizing assumptions. In addition, economywide resource and expenditure constraints are rigorously enforced. Distortions in an economic system will often have repercussions beyond the sector in which they occur. By linking markets into a single system, AGE techniques are effective in capturing relevant feedback and flow-through effects associated with changes in trade policy. AGE simulation has become a widely accepted tool of trade policy analysis and is particularly well-suited to the examination of proposed FTAs, where multisectoral reform is to be undertaken in at least two economies simultaneously, and where the potential second-best consequences of the discriminatory aspect of the trade reform are well known (Panagariya 2000).

Against these significant advantages, AGE models are also highly data intensive and subject to uncertainties of specification, experimental design, and parameterization. Hence, it is important to evaluate AGE simulation results carefully.[1]

The simulations presented here were undertaken using the GTAP model. This is a publicly available model that is in widespread use and has a structure typical of many AGE models. The model is fully documented in Hertel (1997), while the database on which the initial point is calibrated is documented in Dimaranan and McDougall (2002). The GTAP is a multiregional and multisectoral AGE model with perfect competition and constant returns to scale. Bilateral trade is handled via the Armington assumption, which treats goods from alternative sources as imperfect substitutes. Import demand functions are separated by agent (sometimes called the Salter specification). Production is modeled using nested constant elasticity of substitution (CES) functions, with intermediate goods used in fixed proportions. Representative household demand uses a nonhomothetic function that takes into account changes in demand structures as incomes rise.[2]

Experimental Design

The experimental design used was discussed extensively in chapter 4. The simulations in this appendix use an aggregation of 30 regions and 23 sectors, as presented in table 4.2 in chapter 4. Regional aggregation reflects the proposed US FTA partners that can be identified in the GTAP5.4 data-

---

1. For recent surveys of the application of AGE models to regional trade negotiations, see Scollay and Gilbert (2000, 2001), Gilbert and Wahl (2002), and Robinson and Thierfelder (2002). See Gilbert (2003) for an examination of unilateral reform in Colombia and other economies of the Americas.

2. For further details, see Hertel (1997) and the GTAP Web site, www.gtap.org. For a recent application of the GTAP model to the issue of US bilateral FTAs, see DeRosa and Gilbert (2004).

base and the extent of trading relations with Colombia and the United States. Sectoral aggregation highlights important commodities in the total trade (exports plus imports) of Colombia and the United States and in the bilateral trade of these two economies.

As noted in chapter 4, the basic simulation design mirrors that used in DeRosa and Gilbert (2004), with some extensions to account for overlapping FTAs in the Americas. The proposed FTA between the United States and Colombia is first simulated independently of the existence of other potential agreements, and the results thus reflect the estimated effect of the proposal in isolation. An "all partners" experiment is then considered in which the proposed US-Colombia FTA is implemented simultaneously with other current and prospective US FTAs, with the United States as the FTA hub. In all cases, the arrangements are assumed to be implemented "clean," meaning that all import tariffs are reduced to zero in the participating economies, on a preferential basis. All other tariffs (i.e., those applied to nonparticipating economies) are left in place. In the experiment with all FTAs, it is assumed that the agreements are implemented simultaneously with the United States only. That is, preferential liberalization among the proposed partner regions is not considered. These results were presented in chapter 4.

We then ran a benchmarking exercise, where simulated multilateral reform is considered. Under this scenario, all economies in the model are assumed to eliminate all tariffs on a most favored nation basis. The results of this exercise are presented in this appendix.

Finally, because of the limited number of existing preferential agreements accounted for in the GTAP5.4 protection data, as noted in chapter 4, we estimated the impact of the implementation of existing agreements by simulation, producing a new equilibrium dataset in which those agreements are present.[3] The set of experiments described above was then repeated, using this new equilibrium as the baseline. The interpretation is as follows: We first estimate how the economies of the model would have looked had relevant FTAs been completed in the base year, and from that point we simulate the proposed new agreements. This avoids a potential confounding of the results (i.e., attributing effects to the US-Colombia FTA that might not occur given, for example, the completion of trade reform within the Andean Community). These results are presented in full in this appendix.

All of the simulations are run as comparative statics. The factor market closure allows full mobility of capital and labor (skilled and unskilled) across domestic activities, hence the implicit time period is the long run. Land is treated as imperfectly mobile across agricultural activities, while

---

3. This method has been used to estimate the effect of the following FTAs: EU-Chile, EU-Mexico, EU-Mercosur, CAFTA-DR, Southern Cone Common Market (Mercosur), Andean Community, and Chile-Andean.

natural resources are assumed to be specific factors. The parameters used in the model that govern the degree of substitutability between imports and domestic goods and imports from various sources are the default values in the GTAP5.4 database, and they range from 2 to 5 and 4 to 10, respectively. Table A.1 presents more details on the Armington elasticities.

The Multilateral Reform Scenario

The multilateral benchmark scenario assumes complete tariff reform in all world economies on a most favored nation basis. This scenario, while not a particularly likely outcome at present, provides a useful benchmark for evaluating the significance of preferential agreements in terms of direction and magnitude of expected effects. In particular, note that the total world benefits from multilateral reform are positive and significant, while the total world welfare impact of most preferential trading agreement scenarios is generally negative, reflecting the consequences of trade diversion (table A.2).

Effects Assuming Existing Preferential Trading Agreements

The simulations are repeated starting from a baseline that incorporates the presence of important existing FTAs on which the GTAP5.4 database does not include information, as described above. The full results of this exercise are contained in tables A.3 to A.14.

The "refined" results indicate slightly larger welfare gains to Colombia and slightly smaller welfare gains to the United States under the proposed FTA (chapter 4 tables 4.4 and 4.11). Under the simulation with other proposed US FTAs implemented simultaneously, the estimated net welfare effect is slightly smaller for Colombia (comparing table A.8 with table 4.10 in chapter 4). The negative effect of the agreement on the other economies of the Andean Community is somewhat exacerbated relative to the simulation set described in chapter 4. This result reflects the fact that the starting point takes into account preferential access to the Colombian market under the Andean Community. The degree of preferential access is diminished when Colombia extends preferential tariffs to the United States under the proposed agreement. This is the preference dilution effect noted in chapter 4. However, the net welfare effect on the Andean partners remains small (comparing appendix table A.6 with table 4.8 in chapter 4), and as before, it is reversed for countries except Venezuela under the assumption that the other economies simultaneously implement an FTA with the United States (table A.12).

The broad pattern of anticipated sectoral changes is unchanged, but the estimated magnitude of changes is subdued (comparing tables A.3 and A.4 with tables 4.5 and 4.6 in chapter 4 and tables A.9 and A.10 with tables 4A.1 and 4A.2 in the appendix to chapter 4).

Concluding Comments

This technical appendix has presented further results of a series of simulations designed to explore the potential economic implications of a proposed US-Colombia FTA using an applied general equilibrium model of the world economy. This type of modeling provides indications of the magnitude of certain types of expected benefits of such an agreement, in particular the efficiency effects of reallocation of resources and the potential costs of reallocating import sources. It should be recognized that this is only one type of cost/benefit analysis and that other costs and benefits that are not easily captured by this type of modeling approach may also be significant (in general, the net benefits indicated by this type of model are regarded as very much lower bounds). Nonetheless, the simulations indicate significant welfare gains for Colombia and smaller welfare gains for the United States from a FTA. Sectoral adjustments are likely to be insignificant for the United States and more significant for the Colombian economy.

Table A.1   Armington import elasticities

Sector	Lower-level	Upper-level
Grains	2.20	4.40
Vegetables and fruits	2.20	4.40
Other crops	2.20	4.40
Other agriculture	2.61	5.47
Forestry and fisheries	2.80	5.60
Coal	2.80	5.60
Oil and gas	2.80	5.60
Food products	2.39	4.71
Textiles	2.20	4.40
Wearing apparel	4.40	8.80
Lumber	2.80	5.60
Pulp and paper	1.80	3.60
Petroleum and coal products	1.90	3.80
Chemical	1.90	3.80
Nonmetallic minerals	2.80	5.60
Metals	2.80	5.60
Fabricated metal products	2.80	5.60
Motor vehicles	5.20	10.40
Other transportation equipment	5.20	10.40
Electronic equipment	2.80	5.60
Machinery	2.80	5.60
Other manufactures	2.80	5.60
Services	1.94	3.84

Source: GTAP5.4 database (Dimaranan and McDougall 2002).

Table A.2   Estimated changes in net welfare by region: Multilateral benchmark results (millions of 1997 dollars)

Country/region	Initial GDP	Total benefits	Allocative efficiency	Terms of trade
Australia	392,832.2	2,825.1	321.0	2,504.0
Botswana	4,774.8	130.3	78.5	51.8
China	994,719.3	6,278.2	7,357.8	−1,079.6
European Union	7,957,874.0	−4,693.8	7,442.4	−12,136.2
Japan	4,255,576.5	14,072.8	10,973.6	3,099.3
Korea	445,523.8	9,985.7	6,887.5	3,098.2
Morocco	34,946.6	985.7	753.6	232.1
New Zealand	65,078.6	3,413.5	388.5	3,025.0
Rest of Southern African Customs Union	139,040.8	1,589.6	1302.1	287.5
Sri Lanka	15,592.4	4,48.2	304.0	144.2
Taiwan	299,662.4	3,541.8	905.3	2,636.5
Rest of world	3,195,647.3	21,801.6	27,842.0	−6,040.4
Argentina	325,978.2	3,037.5	1,168.8	1,868.7
Brazil	789,792.2	4,534.0	4,920.4	−386.4
Central America and Caribbean	94,073.2	1,660.3	741.9	918.4
Chile	76,151.1	490.1	154.9	335.2
Colombia	94,561.2	303.4	234.9	68.5
Peru	64,919.8	760.8	509.4	251.5
Uruguay	19,060.2	717.3	244.3	473.0
Venezuela	83,736.4	674.8	335.6	339.2
Rest of Andean Community	27,248.1	436.6	181.9	254.7
Rest of South America	10,605.8	445.3	117.0	328.3
Indonesia	208,823.4	3,017.9	2,673.4	344.5
Malaysia	106,086.1	1,447.8	898.5	549.3
Philippines	78,356.6	612.8	822.0	−209.2
Singapore	79,791.7	1,990.5	128.3	1,862.2
Thailand	157,789.5	2,891.0	2,165.2	725.8
Total Association of Southeast Asian Nations	630,847.1	9,960.0	6,687.4	3,272.6
Canada	631,155.3	1,509.6	1,200.8	308.8
United States	7,945,411.0	−718.1	1,717.2	−2,435.3
Mexico	388,840.3	−509.9	1,501.6	−2,011.4
Total NAFTA	8,965,406.7	281.6	4,419.6	−4,138.0
Total world	28,983,648.3	83,680.4		

Source: Initial data from the GTAP5.4 database (Dimaranan and McDougall 2002). Estimates from simulation results.

Table A.3 **Estimated changes in the sectoral pattern of production (refined): US-Colombia FTA**

	United States		Colombia	
Sector	Initial value (millions of 1997 dollars)	US-Colombia FTA (percent change in volume)	Initial value (millions of 1997 dollars)	US-Colombia FTA (percent change in volume)
Grains	53,900.0	.15	960.3	−6.92
Vegetables and fruits	34,953.2	.01	4,132.0	−1.26
Other crops	50,922.8	−.55	4,163.1	9.36
Other agriculture	109,960.0	.01	5,811.0	.17
Forestry and fisheries	15,370.8	−.01	995.9	−.22
Coal	32,701.1	0	962.6	−.65
Oil and gas	83,149.9	−.02	5,252.1	−.73
Food Products	556,329.6	.01	20,954.9	.42
Textiles	111,569.7	.06	2,160.1	1.27
Wearing apparel	102,131.5	−.01	3,710.4	10.01
Lumber	176,993.5	0	1,047.6	−1.73
Pulp and paper	310,167.5	.02	3,300.7	−1.68
Petroleum and coal products	165,142.6	.01	2,343.4	−.20
Chemical	573,930.6	.04	8,244.8	−2.46
Nonmetallic minerals	94,685.0	.04	2,035.0	−2.98
Metals	201,119.0	.01	1,425.7	−4.71
Fabricated metal products	224,697.7	.02	1,248.0	−5.34
Motor vehicles	366,300.8	.01	1,580.0	−3.16
Other transportation equipment	158,054.6	−.05	293.9	−3.84
Electronic equipment	290,664.6	−.02	429.1	−8.49
Machinery	633,468.4	.04	2,462.1	−7.78
Other manufactures	46,886.9	.08	1,113.6	−3.85
Services	9,958,251.0	0	94,734.9	−.19

Source: Initial data from the GTAP5.4 database (Dimaranan and McDougall 2002). Estimates from simulation results.

Table A.4   Estimated changes in the sectoral pattern of exports (refined): US-Colombia FTA

| | United States | | | | | | Colombia | | | | | |
| | Initial value (millions of 1997 dollars) | | US-Colombia FTA (percent change in value) | | | | Initial value (millions of 1997 dollars) | | US-Colombia FTA (percent change in value) | | | |
Sector	Total	To Colombia	Total	To Colombia			Total	To United States	Total	To United States		
Grains	10,924.9	234.6	.68	37.49			1.3	0.2	-7.53	0		
Vegetables and fruits	5,053.1	15.9	.19	84.79			522.5	169.0	-2.00	11.39		
Other crops	13,610.7	92.9	.68	48.43			2,739.7	1,020.9	22.24	85.00		
Other agriculture	2,939.6	9.3	.04	54.02			40.5	11.2	-11.72	-11.64		
Forestry and fisheries	2,648.2	1.1	-.05	55.06			10.5	3.9	-5.17	-3.77		
Coal	3,388.4	0	0	0			838.5	80.4	-.42	0		
Oil and gas	3,032.3	6.7	-.03	28.53			2,644.7	2,125.6	-.23	.19		
Food products	30,674.1	188.9	.51	107.48			925.2	255.5	21.52	118.76		
Textiles	11,484.6	118.6	.69	79.25			299.2	46.3	4.88	62.32		
Wearing apparel	9,126.5	96.9	2.19	205.31			585.5	329.7	71.75	187.51		
Lumber	9,473.4	24.4	.14	108.80			30.5	7.4	-3.83	5.70		
Pulp and paper	19,912.9	142.4	.24	43.28			230.7	26.6	-2.23	.91		
Petroleum and coal products	6,383.0	23.4	.07	42.57			215.2	122.7	3.64	7.735		
Chemical	84,186.3	1,015.3	.25	26.23			1,143.6	125.3	-.91	15.97		
Nonmetallic minerals	11,920.5	76.8	.42	87.27			183.5	52.8	-1.78	9.25		
Metals	20,523.8	90.1	.18	73.88			294.5	90.4	-1.19	7.16		
Fabricated metal products	13,714.1	103.2	.44	77.41			109.7	13.5	-2.92	12.62		
Motor vehicles	56,832.5	200.2	.21	279.47			96.1	2.9	-1.66	13.33		
Other transportation equipment	45,807.6	240.7	-.09	22.73			14.6	0.8	-1.00	20.00		
Electronic equipment	109,331.5	756.6	.02	17.57			13.6	2.3	-3.36	5.83		
Machinery	160,560.8	1,382.6	.22	37.90			340.0	12.4	-4.09	10.93		
Other manufactures	11,322.0	69.3	.45	96.26			186.7	86.3	-3.06	-.01		
Services	210,090.1	696.4	-.09	3.17			3,794.9	698.0	-4.54	-4.49		

Source: Initial data from the GTAP5.4 database (Dimaranan and McDougall 2002). Estimates from simulation results.

Table A.5 Estimated changes in the regional pattern of exports (refined): US-Colombia FTA

Country/region	Initial value (millions of 1997 dollars)			US-Colombia FTA (percent change in value)		
	Total	To United States	To Colombia	Total	To United States	To Colombia
Australia	70,568.6	7,770.0	84.4	−.01	−.04	−3.72
Botswana	2,912.2	86.1	0.7	−.02	−.05	2.90
China	292,747.5	75,785.2	215.7	−.03	−.14	−6.59
European Union	2,360,091.5	221,163.9	4,030.1	−.02	0	−6.32
Japan	490,466.4	127,323.8	1,200.1	−.01	.05	−9.00
Korea	149,305.6	25,365.0	383.5	−.02	−.01	−8.31
Morocco	8,789.0	763.8	5.7	−.02	−.09	1.03
New Zealand	17,027.0	2,066.9	27.8	−.02	−.23	−2.16
Rest of Southern African Customs Union	34,388.6	3,567.7	45.7	−.01	−.04	−3.45
Sri Lanka	4,781.2	1,779.3	7.4	−.05	−.37	−1.06
Taiwan	136,412.9	35,280.6	178.6	−.02	−.01	−10.30
Rest of world	835,098.5	100,689.7	1,013.1	−.02	−.14	−4.65
Argentina	28,565.5	2,504.1	186.9	−.03	−.47	−8.43
Brazil	57,882.7	10,302.5	527.0	−.03	−.47	−9.77
Central America and Caribbean	39,264.9	16,076.4	148.3	−.04	−.49	−6.10
Chile	18,801.1	2,627.0	231.9	−.09	−.15	−7.33
Colombia	15,306.9	5,159.8	0	7.08	36.93	0
Peru	7,829.8	1,925.9	159.2	−.17	−.46	−7.65
Uruguay	3,989.8	423.3	20.5	−.03	−.12	−4.05
Venezuela	235,15.0	12,644.9	1,377.9	−.37	.33	−6.92
Rest of Andean Community	6,946.2	2,492.8	429.6	−.45	.02	−6.40
Rest of South America	4,436.6	465.1	7.9	−.02	−.11	−4.39
Indonesia	56,891.9	10,537.8	40.6	−.05	−.46	−6.24
Malaysia	95,089.8	18,817.8	64.6	−.01	−.01	−1.42
Philippines	40,995.1	11,849.6	51.0	−.02	−.11	1.28
Singapore	125,733.8	22,395.5	117.7	−.01	0	1.38
Thailand	70,705.3	14,566.9	59.8	−.02	−.16	−1.32
Total Association of Southeast Asian Nations	389,415.9	78,167.6	333.7	−.02	−.11	−.57
Canada	230,960.7	168,165.2	339.8	−.01	−.01	−6.14
United States	852,807.6	0	5,584.1	.16	0	39.74
Mexico	115,222.0	864,09.2	575.1	−.03	0	−9.69
Total NAFTA	1,198,990.2	254,574.4	6,499.0	.11	−.01	33.20
Total world	6,197,533.7	989,005.8	17,114.4	.12	.42	14.49

Source: Initial data from the GTAP5.4 database (Dimaranan and McDougall 2002). Estimates from simulation results.

Table A.6   Estimated changes in net welfare by region (refined): US-Colombia FTA (millions of 1997 dollars)

Country/region	Initial GDP	Total benefits	Allocative efficiency	Terms of trade
Australia	392,832.2	−6.9	−0.8	−6.1
Botswana	4,774.8	−0.1	0	−0.2
China	994,719.3	−46.2	−20.0	−26.2
European Union	7,957,874.0	−144.2	−22.0	−122.2
Japan	4,255,576.5	−17.9	2.0	−19.9
Korea	445,523.8	−10.8	−3.5	−7.3
Morocco	34,946.6	−0.5	−0.2	−0.3
New Zealand	65,078.6	−2.8	−0.3	−2.5
Rest of Southern African Customs Union	139,040.8	−1.7	−0.4	−1.3
Sri Lanka	15,592.4	−3.4	−1.4	−2.0
Taiwan	299,662.4	−8.6	−1.1	−7.5
Rest of world	3,195,647.3	−80.9	−25.4	−55.5
Argentina	325,978.2	−10.8	−4.1	−6.8
Brazil	789,792.2	−38.7	−20.0	−18.7
Central America and Caribbean	94,073.2	−51.0	−19.2	−31.9
Chile	76,151.1	−11.1	−1.8	−9.4
Colombia	94,561.2	480.3	132.5	347.8
Peru	64,919.8	−14.2	−3.9	−10.4
Uruguay	19,060.2	−0.2	−0.1	−0.1
Venezuela	83,736.4	−49.9	10.6	−60.5
Rest of Andean Community	27,248.1	−37.6	−8.1	−29.5
Rest of South America	10,605.8	−0.1	−0.1	0
Indonesia	208,823.4	−13.5	−1.9	−11.7
Malaysia	106,086.1	−2.1	−0.8	−1.3
Philippines	78,356.6	−6.4	−3.3	−3.1
Singapore	79,791.7	1.3	−0.7	2.0
Thailand	157,789.5	−9.8	−1.8	−7.9
Total Association of Southeast Asian Nations	630,847.1	−30.5	−8.4	−22.1
Canada	631,155.3	−50.7	−2.4	−48.3
United States	7,945,411.0	186.6	10.3	176.3
Mexico	388,840.3	−36.8	1.2	−37.9
Total NAFTA	8,965,406.7	99.2	9.1	90.1
Total world	28,983,648.3	11.4		

Source: Initial data from the GTAP5.4 database (Dimaranan and McDougall 2002). Estimates from simulation results.

Table A.7   Estimated changes in real returns to factors of production (refined): US-Colombia FTA

Factor	United States	Colombia
Land	–.22	13.36
Unskilled labor	.01	.86
Skilled labor	.01	.52
Capital	.01	.63
Natural resources	–.07	–4.26

Table A.8   Estimated changes in key economywide variables (refined): US–all partners FTA

Variable	United States	Australia	Botswana	Chile	Colombia	Morocco	Peru	Venezuela	Rest of Andean Community	CAFTA-DR	Singapore	Thailand	Rest of SACU
Import value (percent change)	1.95	1.21	-.96	1.49	4.26	3.82	6.06	4.19	3.24	15.23	.18	4.47	2.45
From partner(s)	24.14	15.73	33.42	44.89	35.04	92.94	55.18	50.21	43.71	64.80	-.76	60.36	43.52
From rest of world	-.27	-2.62	-2.40	-8.75	-8.59	-5.23	-8.71	-19.78	-8.05	-6.56	.35	-4.46	-3.65
Export value (percent change)	2.16	.89	-.94	1.11	4.36	4.35	5.79	1.08	2.84	11.94	.14	2.91	1.68
To partner(s)	34.94	12.36	.54	16.56	35.06	19.26	38.83	4.87	24.66	60.51	6.11	32.33	17.81
To rest of world	-1.60	-.52	-.99	-1.11	-8.70	2.93	-4.39	-2.67	-6.75	-18.67	-1.14	-4.72	-.19
Tariff revenue (dollar change)	-2,769.5	-558.2	-7.1	-470.9	-571.4	-294.6	-336.6	-1,052.2	-213.0	-2,480.5	-30.5	-1,500.5	-462.9
From partner(s)	-2,190.6	-437.4	-2.1	-389.7	-483.9	-118.3	-274.9	-693.2	-176.4	-2,271.4	-25.5	-829.3	-237.9
From rest of world	-578.9	-120.9	-5.0	-81.2	-87.6	-176.3	-61.7	-359.0	-36.6	209.1	-5.0	-671.1	-225.0
Welfare as a percent of GDP	.05	-.01	-.07	-.02	.18	-.27	.23	-.10	.34	3.34	.29	.56	-.06
Total equivalent variation (millions of dollars)	4,050.2	-51.5	-3.2	-15.4	166.7	-93.6	6.43	1.58	91.4	3,138.1	223.5	878.4	-89.1
Allocative efficiency	574.6	-40.8	.1	-1.1	8.8	-20.8	38.96	4.99	25.5	1,456.2	9.7	4.4	-54.7
Terms of trade	3,475.6	-10.7	-3.3	-14.2	157.9	-72.7	-11.29	-6.87	65.9	1,682.0	223.8	874.0	-34.4

CAFTA-DR = Central American Free Trade Agreement–Dominican Republic
SACU = Southern African Customs Union

Table A.9 Estimated changes in the sectoral pattern of production (refined): US–all partners FTA (percent change in volume)

Variable	United States	Australia	Botswana	Chile	Colombia	Morocco	Peru	Venezuela	Rest of Andean Community	CAFTA-DR	Singapore	Thailand	Rest of SACU
Grains	.72	–.14	–1.33	–.44	–5.80	–2.93	–2.99	–1.29	–2.92	–6.19	–1.09	.52	–4.78
Vegetables and fruits	.06	.01	.25	.72	–.79	.06	–.36	.02	–1.36	–3.99	–1.85	–2.05	.47
Other crops	–1.13	–.12	.28	6.31	9.34	–1.01	3.32	.46	5.92	–.25	1.09	.33	.69
Other agriculture	.12	.43	–.28	.23	.20	–.35	.13	.18	1.68	.71	–1.14	.20	.09
Forestry and fisheries	–.02	.04	.15	.19	–.18	.20	0	–.05	.30	–2.14	–.21	–.76	–.01
Coal	–.09	–.03	.07	–.20	–.02	.17	–1.13	–.07	–1.44	–3.64	–.08	–.66	.06
Oil and gas	–.18	–.10	.40	.13	–.03	.75	–.41	.33	–.30	–5.33	–.65	–1.84	0
Food products	.16	1.18	–.57	.49	.42	–4.77	.30	.43	3.18	–.32	.78	.78	.05
Textiles	1.29	.57	.01	–.44	.91	3.19	2.19	–.82	–.98	17.95	9.08	8.84	1.69
Wearing apparel	.27	–.24	–5.45	.17	8.37	3.72	6.67	–.24	–1.14	47.66	36.17	18.35	12.15
Lumber	.02	–.09	.48	.24	–1.94	.32	–.26	–1.51	–.87	–12.57	–.04	–4.16	.07
Pulp and paper	.04	–.08	–.16	–.92	–1.67	–.35	–.70	–.07	–1.29	–5.39	–.41	–.94	–.24
Petroleum and coal products	.17	0	.55	–.77	–.34	–.25	.16	1.61	.06	–3.27	–.08	–.22	–.08
Chemical	.24	–.22	–.30	–.51	–2.34	.24	–1.05	–.32	–.92	–5.18	.31	–2.58	.15
Nonmetallic minerals	.24	–.51	.38	–.63	–2.88	–.65	–1.04	–.51	–1.65	–12.97	–.97	–2.26	–.05
Metals	–.01	–.35	1.89	.31	–2.71	1.03	–2.05	–.36	–1.68	–19.36	–1.17	–4.12	.37
Fabricated metal products	.35	–.20	–3.81	–1.17	–5.50	–.19	–.75	–2.24	–.36	–11.23	–.79	–5.67	–.13
Motor vehicles	1.05	–1.48	–9.73	–4.07	–22.49	.04	–3.50	–7.21	–13.77	–13.05	–1.64	–2.83	–2.70
Other transportation equipment	–.78	.86	2.38	–10.62	–1.88	–4.33	–2.41	1.41	–6.33	–12.80	–.59	–3.89	1.04
Electronic equipment	–.59	.52	1.64	–6.03	–7.17	1.93	–4.29	–.70	–2.26	–6.94	–.15	–2.38	–.13
Machinery	.12	–.66	–.73	–6.11	–9.37	.37	–4.39	–3.41	–3.48	–16.41	–.01	–1.58	–.71
Other manufactures	.21	–.10	–1.27	–1.55	–2.95	.05	1.83	–4.74	3.00	–14.09	–.69	–.47	.07
Services	–.03	.01	–.17	.04	–.19	–.11	.04	.16	.18	–.74	–.12	–.46	–.01

CAFTA-DR = Central American Free Trade Agreement–Dominican Republic
SACU = Southern African Customs Union

Table A.10 Estimated changes in the sectoral pattern of exports (refined): US–all partners FTA

Sector	United States Initial value (millions of 1997 dollars) Total	To Colombia	United States US–all partners FTA (percent change in value) Total	To Colombia	Colombia Initial value (millions of 1997 dollars) Total	To United States	Colombia US–all partners FTA (percent change in value) Total	To United States
Grains	10,924.9	234.6	3.67	35.20	1.3	0.2	-11.54	-30.00
Vegetables and fruits	5,053.1	15.9	3.78	79.25	522.5	169.0	-2.88	9.68
Other crops	13,610.7	92.9	3.23	44.75	2,739.7	1,020.9	19.25	72.69
Other agriculture	2,939.6	9.3	1.41	49.78	40.5	11.2	-10.32	-7.95
Forestry and fisheries	2,648.2	1.1	.14	45.45	10.5	3.9	-1.14	1.03
Coal	3,388.4	0	-.35	0	838.5	80.4	1.74	2.54
Oil and gas	3,032.3	6.7	.30	27.46	2,644.7	2,125.6	-11.24	-10.70
Food products	30,674.1	188.9	9.46	95.11	925.2	255.5	24.72	110.28
Textiles	11,484.6	118.6	16.08	73.80	299.2	46.3	8.20	77.21
Wearing apparel	9,126.5	96.9	40.68	183.88	585.5	329.7	102.46	195.41
Lumber	9,473.4	24.4	3.20	98.40	30.5	7.4	-4.75	18.24
Pulp and paper	19,912.9	142.4	1.39	39.52	230.7	26.6	-1.32	7.44
Petroleum and coal products	6,383.0	23.4	3.53	41.03	215.2	122.7	45.69	51.72
Chemical	84,186.3	1,015.3	1.75	23.54	1,143.6	125.3	-1.65	21.26
Nonmetallic minerals	1,1920.5	76.8	3.83	80.38	183.5	52.8	-1.89	15.78
Metals	20,523.8	90.1	1.20	70.29	294.5	90.4	3.34	13.43
Fabricated metal products	13,714.1	103.2	5.52	69.44	109.7	13.5	-3.36	22.74
Motor vehicles	56,832.5	200.2	9.06	198.89	96.1	2.9	-43.61	40.34
Other transportation equipment	45,807.6	240.7	-1.28	17.54	14.6	0.8	6.23	45.00
Electronic equipment	109,331.5	756.6	-.18	15.48	13.6	2.3	2.79	15.22
Machinery	160,560.8	1,382.6	1.68	34.31	340.0	12.4	-9.75	23.95
Other manufactures	11,322.0	69.3	3.46	88.50	186.7	86.3	7.93	12.90
Services	210,090.1	696.4	-1.07	0.21	3,794.9	698.0	0.17	0.59

Source: Initial data from the GTAP5.4 database (Dimaranan and McDougall 2002). Estimates from simulation results.

Table A.11 Estimated changes in the regional pattern of exports (refined): US–all partners FTA

Country/region	Initial value (millions of 1997 dollars)			US–all partners FTA (percent change in value)		
	Total	To United States	To Colombia	Total	To United States	To Colombia
Australia	70,568.6	7,770.0	84.4	.89	12.35	–5.37
Botswana	2,912.2	86.1	0.7	–.96	.52	–2.86
China	292,747.5	75,785.2	215.7	–.52	–2.47	–7.58
European Union	2,360,091.5	221,163.9	4,030.1	–.17	.21	–8.08
Japan	490,466.4	127,323.8	1,200.1	–.01	1.10	–14.12
Korea	149,305.6	25,365.0	383.5	–.31	–.33	–17.05
Morocco	8789.0	763.8	5.7	4.26	19.10	.70
New Zealand	17,027.0	2,066.9	27.8	–.38	–1.74	–4.32
Rest of Southern African Customs Union	34,388.6	3,567.7	45.7	1.65	17.75	–6.43
Sri Lanka	4,781.2	1,779.3	7.4	–.68	–6.43	–.81
Taiwan	136,412.9	35,280.6	178.6	–.26	–.33	–11.91
Rest of world	835,098.5	100,689.7	1013.1	–.19	–.87	–6.27
Argentina	28,565.5	2,504.1	186.9	–.41	–2.02	–9.07
Brazil	57,882.7	10,302.5	527.0	–.34	–.91	–11.70
Central America and Caribbean	39,264.9	16,076.4	148.3	13.07	58.38	–22.60

Chile	18,801.1	2,627.0	231.9	1.71	16.67	-8.52
Colombia	15,306.9	5,159.8	0	6.91	34.02	0
Peru	7,829.8	1,925.9	159.2	6.43	38.96	-11.29
Uruguay	3,989.8	423.3	20.5	-.37	-2.03	-4.93
Venezuela	23,515.0	12,644.9	1,377.9	1.58	4.99	-6.87
Rest of Andean Community	6,946.2	2,492.8	429.6	4.25	22.88	-15.71
Rest of South America	4,436.6	465.1	7.9	-.14	-.42	-5.06
Indonesia	56,891.9	10,537.8	40.6	-.46	-3.83	-7.22
Malaysia	95,089.8	18,817.8	64.6	-.21	-.33	-2.83
Philippines	40,995.1	11,849.6	51.0	-.44	-2.00	.12
Singapore	125,733.8	22,395.5	117.7	.13	6.07	-1.19
Thailand	70,705.3	14,566.9	59.8	2.89	32.14	-8.51
Total Association of Southeast Asian Nations	389,415.9	78,167.6	333.7	.40	6.83	-3.35
Canada	230,960.7	168,165.2	339.8	-.20	-.03	-8.56
United States	852,807.6	0	5,584.1	2.18	0	39.61
Mexico	115,222.0	86,409.2	575.1	-.20	.21	-11.26
Total NAFTA	1,198,990.2	254,574.4	6,499.0	1.50	.08	32.59
Total world	6,197,533.7	989,005.8	17,114.4	.33	1.96	6.56

Source: Initial data from the GTAP5.4 database (Dimaranan and McDougall 2002). Estimates from simulation results.

TRADE RELATIONS BETWEEN THE UNITED STATES AND COLOMBIA

**Table A.12   Estimated changes in net welfare by region (refined):
US–all partners FTA** (millions of 1997 dollars)

Country/region	Initial GDP	Total benefits	Allocative efficiency	Terms of trade
Australia	392,832.2	−51.5	−40.8	−10.7
Botswana	4,774.8	−3.2	0.1	−3.3
China	994,719.3	−1,230.2	−502.7	−727.5
European Union	7,957,874.0	−2,408.7	−612.0	−1,796.8
Japan	4,255,576.5	−1,167.6	−280.4	−887.2
Korea	445,523.8	−359.7	−108.2	−251.5
Morocco	34,946.6	−93.6	−20.8	−72.7
New Zealand	65,078.6	−56.5	−7.4	−49.0
Rest of Southern African Customs Union	139,040.8	−89.1	−54.7	−34.4
Sri Lanka	15,592.4	−63.5	−27.0	−36.5
Taiwan	299,662.4	−209.5	−17.9	−191.5
Rest of world	3,195,647.3	−11,77.0	−464.3	−712.7
Argentina	325,978.2	−166.4	−66.2	−100.2
Brazil	789,792.2	−491.5	−270.0	−221.4
Central America and Caribbean	94,073.2	3,138.1	1456.2	1,682.0
Chile	76,151.1	−15.4	−1.1	−14.2
Colombia	94,561.2	166.7	8.8	157.9
Peru	64,919.8	146.5	91.8	54.7
Uruguay	19,060.2	−7.7	−4.0	−3.8
Venezuela	83,736.4	−82.8	−26.0	−56.7
Rest of Andean Community	27,248.1	91.4	25.5	65.9
Rest of South America	10,605.8	−14.6	−5.7	−9.0
Indonesia	208,823.4	−195.4	−47.2	−148.2
Malaysia	106,086.1	−118.8	−26.9	−91.9
Philippines	78,356.6	−148.0	−76.4	−71.6
Singapore	79,791.7	233.5	9.7	223.8
Thailand	157,789.5	878.4	4.4	874.0
Total Association of Southeast Asian Nations	630,847.1	649.8	−136.3	786.1
Canada	631,155.3	−656.5	−52.3	−604.2
United States	7,945,411.0	4,050.2	574.6	3,475.6
Mexico	388,840.3	−514.3	−22.3	−492.0
Total NAFTA	8,965,406.7	2,879.4	500.0	2,379.4
Total world	2,8983,648.3	−616.6		

Source: Initial data from the GTAP5.4 database (Dimaranan and McDougall 2002). Estimates from simulation results.

Table A.13 Estimated changes in real returns to factors of production (refined): US–all partners FTA

Factor	United States	Australia	Botswana	Chile	Colombia	Morocco	Peru	Venezuela	Rest of Andean Community	CAFTA-DR	Singapore	Thailand	Rest of SACU
Land	1.12	.89	-1.89	4.61	14.23	-4.16	6.18	.53	10.62	-3.79	1.35	-2.98	-2.06
Unskilled labor	.13	.13	-.26	.39	.43	.87	.70	.73	1.34	7.31	.46	1.98	.39
Skilled labor	.12	.12	-.19	.32	.10	.91	.53	.88	.96	7.37	.36	1.65	.38
Capital	.13	.12	.19	.35	.25	.86	.47	.97	.58	8.50	.34	1.82	.35
Natural resources	-.95	-.26	2.33	1.47	0	3.91	-0.84	3.28	-.72	-17.56	-1.44	-5.27	.75

CAFTA-DR = Central American Free Trade Agreement–Dominican Republic
SACU = Southern African Customs Union

Table A.14   Estimated changes in net welfare by region (refined): Multilateral benchmark results (millions of 1997 dollars)

Country/region	Initial GDP	Total benefits	Allocative efficiency	Terms of trade
Australia	392,832.2	2,824.1	342.3	2,481.7
Botswana	4,774.8	126.5	78.4	48.0
China	994,719.3	6,576.8	7,431.9	−855.1
European Union	7,957,874.0	−5,837.7	6,886.3	−12,724.0
Japan	4,255,576.5	15,509.5	10,967.9	4,541.6
Korea	445,523.8	10,366.1	6,983.9	3,382.3
Morocco	34,946.6	1,020.1	759.9	260.2
New Zealand	65,078.6	3,420.1	389.5	3,030.6
Rest of Southern African Customs Union	139,040.8	1,656.3	1,321.0	335.3
Sri Lanka	15,592.4	451.1	304.7	146.5
Taiwan	299,662.4	3,637.7	870.7	2,767.0
Rest of world	3,195,647.3	22,353.5	28,103.8	−5,750.3
Argentina	325,978.2	−812.7	84.3	−897.0
Brazil	789,792.2	1,211.3	1,535.3	−324.0
Central America and Caribbean	94,073.2	1,207.6	615.9	591.8
Chile	76,151.1	387.8	220.3	167.5
Colombia	94,561.2	−15.7	56.8	−72.5
Peru	64,919.8	771.4	455.7	315.7
Uruguay	19,060.2	−54.7	9.1	−63.8
Venezuela	83,736.4	436.6	468.2	−31.6
Rest of Andean Community	27,248.1	229.7	105.0	124.8
Rest of South America	1,0605.8	498.5	121.8	376.7
Indonesia	208,823.4	3,031.0	2,679.2	351.8
Malaysia	106,086.1	1,471.8	888.2	583.6
Philippines	78,356.6	614.2	844.3	−230.1
Singapore	79,791.7	1,976.4	145.3	1,831.1
Thailand	157,789.5	2,919.7	2,170.5	749.2
Total Association of Southeast Asian Nations	630,847.1	10,013.0	6,727.6	3,285.5
Canada	631,155.3	1,441.4	1,193.8	247.6
United States	7,945,411.0	2,422.5	2,386.3	36.3
Mexico	388,840.3	−701.5	1,264.2	−1,965.7
Total NAFTA	8,965,406.7	3,162.4	4,844.3	−1,681.9
Total world	289,83,648.3	79,139.2		

Source: Initial data from the GTAP5.4 database (Dimaranan and McDougall 2002). Estimates from simulation results.

References

Andrianmananjara, Soamiely. 2000. Regionalism and Incentives for Multilateralism. *Journal of Economic Integration* 15, no. 1: 1–18.

Angel-Urdinola, Diego F., and Quentin Wodon. 2003. The Gender Wage Gap and Poverty in Colombia. *Archivos de Economia*, no. 239. Bogota: Colombia Department of National Planning, Office of Economic Studies (in English).

Armington, P. A. 1969. A Theory of Demand for Products Distinguished by Place of Production. *IMF Staff Papers* 16, no. 1: 159–78. Washington: International Monetary Fund.

Arndt, C. 1996. *An Introduction to Systematic Sensitivity Analysis via Gaussian Quadrature.* GTAP Technical Paper, no. 2. Center for Global Trade Analysis, Purdue University.

Balassa, Bela. 1965. Trade Liberalization and Revealed Comparative Advantage. *Manchester School of Economic and Social Studies* 33, no. 2: 99–123.

Baldwin, Richard. 1996. A Domino Theory of Regionalism. In *Expanding Membership of the European Union*, eds. Richard Baldwin, Pentti Haaparanta, and Jaakko Kiander. New York: Cambridge University Press.

Bergsten, C. Fred. 1996. *Competitive Liberalization and Global Free Trade: A Vision for the 21st Century.* Working Paper 96-15. Washington: Institute for International Economics.

Bora, B., A. Kuwahara, and S. Laird. 2002. *Quantification of Non-Tariff Measures.* Policy Issues in International Trade and Commodities Study Series, no. 18. Geneva: United Nations Conference on Trade and Development.

Bradford, Scott C., and Robert Z. Lawrence. 2004. *Has Globalization Gone Far Enough? The Costs of Fragmented Markets.* Washington: Institute for International Economics.

Bradford, Scott C., Paul L. E. Grieco, and Gary C. Hufbauer. 2005. The Payoff to America from Global Integration. In *The United States and the World Economy: Foreign Economic Policy for the Next Administration*, by C. Fred Bergsten and the Institute for International Economics. Washington: Institute for International Economics.

Charnovitz, Steve. 2004. *The Labor Dimension of the Emerging Free Trade Area of the Americas.* Working Paper 2004/02. New York: New York University Law School Center for Human Rights and Global Justice.

Choi, Inbom, and Jeffrey J. Schott. 2001. *Free Trade between Korea and the United States?* Washington: Institute for International Economics.

Coalition of Services Industries. 2004. Written Testimony on the Free Trade Agreement between the United States and the Andean Countries for the Trade Policy Staff, Committee of the Office of the United States Trade Representative, March 17. Available at www.uscsi.org/pdf/TPSC_testimony.pdf (accessed March 9, 2005).

Coinvertir (Colombia's National Investment Promotion Agency). 2004. Legal Framework for Foreign Investment. www.coinvertir.org (accessed March 9, 2005).

Correa, Carlos M. 2005. Can the TRIPS Agreement Foster Technology Transfer to Developing Countries? In *International Public Goods and Transfer of Technology under a Globalized Intellectual Property Regime*, eds. Keith E. Maskus and Jerome H. Reichman. Cambridge, UK: Cambridge University Press.

Dangond, M. E. 2000. Andean Community Decision 439 on Services Trade. In *Services Trade in the Western Hemisphere: Liberalization, Integration, and Reform*, ed. S. M. Stephenson. Washington: Organization of American States and Brookings Institution.

DeRosa, Dean, and John Gilbert. 2004. Quantitative Estimates of the Economic Impacts of US Bilateral Free Trade Agreements. In *Free Trade Agreements: US Strategies and Priorities*, ed. Jeffrey J. Schott. Washington: Institute for International Economics.

Dimaranan, B., and R. A. McDougall. 2002. Global Trade, Assistance, and Protection: The GTAP5 Database. Center for Global Trade Analysis, Department of Agricultural Economics, Purdue University. Available at www.gtap.agecon.purdue.edu.

ECLAC (Economic Commission for Latin America and the Caribbean). 2005. *Preliminary Overview of the Economies of Latin America and the Caribbean*. Santiago, Chile: United Nations.

Egger, P. 2002. An Econometric View on the Estimation of Gravity Models and the Calculation of Trade Potentials. *World Economy* 25 (February): 297–312.

Elliott, Kimberly Ann, and Richard B. Freeman. 2003. *Can Labor Standards Improve Under Globalization?* Washington: Institute for International Economics.

EIA (Energy Information Administration). 2005. Country Analysis Briefs: Colombia. Washington. Available at www.eia.doe.gov (accessed February 22, 2005).

Ferrero, Emilio. 2004. Colombia: A Country where Formalities Matter. *Managing Intellectual Property* (October). Euromoney Institutional Investor PLC.

Fink, Carsten, and Keith E. Maskus, eds. 2004. *Intellectual Property Rights and Development: Lessons from Economic Research*. Washington: World Bank and Oxford University Press.

Fink, Carsten, and Patrick Reichenmiller. 2005. Tightening TRIPS: The Intellectual Property Provisions of Recent U.S. Free Trade Agreements. World Bank Trade Note 20. Washington: World Bank. Available at http://siteresources.worldbank.org (accessed May 22, 2006).

Frankel, J. A. 1997. *Regional Trading Blocs in the World Economic System*. Washington: Institute for International Economics.

Freedom House. 2005. *Freedom in the World 2005*. Washington.

Fukase, E., and W. Martin. 2001. A Quantitative Evaluation of Vietnam's Accession to the ASEAN Free Trade Area. *Journal of Economic Integration* 16, no. 4: 545–67.

Gilbert, John. 2003. Trade Liberalization and Employment in Developing Economies of the Americas. *Économie Internationale* 95, no. 3: 155–74.

Gilbert, John, and Thomas Wahl. 2002. Applied General Equilibrium Assessments of Trade Liberalisation in China. *World Economy* 25, no. 5: 697–731.

Glick, R., and A. K. Rose. 2002. Does a Currency Union affect Trade? The Time-Series Evidence. *The European Economic Review* 46, no. 6: 1125–51.

Greenaway, D., and C. Milner. 2002. Regionalism and Gravity. *Scottish Journal of Political Economy* 49, no. 5: 574–85.

Harberger, A. C. 1971. Three Basic Postulates for Applied Welfare Economics: An Interpretive Essay. *Journal of Economic Literature* 9, no. 3: 785–97.

Hausman, J. A. 1978. Specification Tests in Econometrics. *Econometrica* 46, no. 6: 1251–71.

Hausman, J. A., and W. E. Taylor. 1981. Panel Data and Unobservable Individual Effects. *Econometrica* 49, no. 6: 1377–98.

Hertel, T., ed. 1997. *Global Trade Analysis: Modeling and Applications*. New York: Cambridge University Press.

Heston, Alan, Robert Summers, and Bettina Aten. 2002. Penn World Table Version 6.1. Center for International Comparisons, University of Pennsylvania (CICUP).

Hsiao, C. 2003. *Analysis of Panel Data*. Second Edition. Cambridge, UK: Cambridge University Press.

Hufbauer, Gary Clyde, and Jeffrey J. Schott. 1994. *Western Hemisphere Economic Integration*. Washington: Institute for International Economics.

Hufbauer, Gary Clyde, and Jeffrey J. Schott. 2005. *NAFTA Revisited: Achievements and Challenges*. Washington: Institute for International Economics.

Huff, Karen, and Thomas W. Hertel. 1996. Decomposing Welfare Changes in GTAP. GTAP Technical Paper 5. Center for Global Trade Analysis, Department of Agricultural Economics, Purdue University. Available at www.gtap.agecon.purdue.edu.

ICFTU (International Confederation of Free Trade Unions). 2004. *Annual Survey of Violations of Trade Union Rights 2004*. Brussels.

IIPA (International Intellectual Property Alliance). 2003. *Special 301 Report: Colombia*. www.iipa.com (accessed March 9, 2005).

ILO (International Labor Organization). 1997. *World Labour Report: Industrial Relations, Democracy, and Social Stability, 1997–98*. Geneva.

ILO (International Labor Organization). 2004. *General Report of the Committee of Experts on the Application of Conventions and Recommendations 2004*. Geneva.

IMF (International Monetary Fund). 2004. *Colombia: Third Review Under the Stand-by Arrangement*. Document 04/199 (July). Washington.

IMF (International Monetary Fund). 2005. Colombia: Fourth Review under the Stand-by Arrangement. Document 05/154 (April/May). Washington.

IMF (International Monetary Fund). 2006. *World Economic Outlook 2006*. Washington.

Josling, Tim. 1997. *Agricultural Trade Policies in the Andean Group: Issues and Options*. World Bank Technical Paper 364. Washington: World Bank.

Josling, Tim, and Dale Hathaway. 2004. *This Far and No Farther? Nudging Agricultural Reform Forward*. International Economics Policy Brief Number 04-1 (March). Washington: Institute for International Economics.

Josling, Tim, Donna Roberts, and David Orden. 2004. *Food Regulation and Trade: Toward a Safe and Global System*. Washington: Institute for International Economics.

Kenworthy, James. 2003. Analysis of Colombia's Trade and Investment Issues for Regional and Bilateral Negotiations. Report submitted to USAID/Colombia by Nathan Associates, CRECER Project. Lima, Peru (December).

Lerner, Josh. 2002. *Patent Protection and Innovation over 150 Years*. NBER Working Paper 8977. Cambridge, MA: National Bureau for Economic Research.

Lopez, Alejandro. 1997. *Why Did Colombian Private Savings Decline in the Early 1990s?* World Bank Policy Research Working Paper 1713. Washington: World Bank.

Maskus, Keith E. 2000a. *Intellectual Property Rights in the Global Economy*. Washington: Institute for International Economics.

Maskus, Keith E. 2000b. Parallel Imports. *World Economy: Global Trade Policy 2000*, no. 23: 1269–84.

Maskus, Keith E. 2004. *Encouraging International Technology Transfer*. ICTSD/UNCTAD Project on Intellectual Property Rights, Issue Paper 7. Geneva: International Centre for Trade and Sustainable Development the UN Conference on Trade and Development.

Maskus Keith E., and Jerome H. Reichman, eds. 2005. *International Public Goods and Transfer of Technology under a Globalized Intellectual Property Regime*. Cambridge, UK: Cambridge University Press.

Panagariya, A. 2000. Preferential Trade Liberalization: The Traditional Theory and New Developments, *Journal of Economic Literature* 38, no. 2: 287–331.

Robinson, S., and K. Thierfelder. 2002. Trade Liberalization and Regional Integration: The Search for Large Numbers. *Australian Journal of Agricultural and Resource Economics* 46, no. 4: 585–604.

Rose, A. K. 2002. *Do We Really Know That the WTO Increases Trade?* NBER Working Paper 9273. Cambridge, MA: National Bureau for Economic Research.

Rose, A. K. 2003. Which International Institutions Promote International Trade? Institute for International Economics, Washington. Photocopy (October 2).

Sakakibara, Mariko, and Lee Branstetter. 2001. Do Stronger Patents Induce More Innovation? Evidence from the 1988 Japanese Patent Law Reforms. *RAND Journal of Economics* 32, no. 1: 77–100.

Schott, Jeffrey J. 2001. *Prospects for Free Trade in the Americas.* Washington: Institute for International Economics.

Schott, Jeffrey J. 2004. Assessing US FTA Policy. In *Free Trade Agreements: US Strategies and Priorities*, ed. Jeffrey J. Schott. Washington: Institute for International Economics.

Scollay, Robert, and John Gilbert. 2000. Measuring the Gains from APEC Trade Liberalization: An Overview of CGE Assessments. *World Economy* 23, no. 2: 175–93.

Scollay, Robert, and John Gilbert. 2001. *New Regional Trading Arrangements in the Asia Pacific.* Washington: Institute for International Economics.

Sherwood, Robert M. 1997. The TRIPS Agreement: Implications for Developing Countries. *Idea: The Journal of Law and Technology* 37: 491–544.

Skully, D. W. 1998. *Auctioning Tariff Quotas for US Sugar Imports.* Sugar and Sweetener Document SSS-223 (May). Washington: Economic Research Service, US Department of Agriculture.

Tanner, Evan. 1994. The Impact of a US-Colombia Free Trade Area: The Case of Sugar. *North American Journal of Economics and Finance* 5, no. 1: 5–21.

UNCTAD (United Nations Conference on Trade and Development). 2004. *World Investment Report 2004.* New York and Geneva: United Nations.

UNDP (United Nations Development Program). 2003. *El Conflicto, Callejón con Salido: Informe Nacional de Desarrollo Humano por Colombia 2003.* Bogota: United Nations.

UNDP (United Nations Development Program). 2004. *Human Development Report 2004.* New York: United Nations.

US Department of State. 2004. *Country Reports on Human Rights Practices.* Washington.

USTR (United States Trade Representative). 2003a. First Report to the Congress on the Operation of the Andean Trade Preference Act as Amended. Washington. Available at www.ustr.gov (accessed March 9, 2005).

USTR (United States Trade Representative). 2003b. *2003 National Trade Estimate Report on Foreign Trade Barriers.* Washington. Available at www.ustr.gov (accessed March 9, 2005).

USTR (United States Trade Representative). 2004a. *2004 National Trade Estimate Report on Foreign Trade Barriers.* Washington. Available at www.ustr.gov (accessed May 22, 2006).

USTR (United States Trade Representative). 2004b. *Special 301 Report.* Washington.

USTR (United States Trade Representative). 2005. *2005 National Trade Estimate Report on Foreign Trade Barriers.* Washington. Available at www.ustr.gov (accessed May 22, 2006).

World Bank. 2001. *Global Economic Prospects and the Developing Countries 2002: Making Trade Work for the World's Poor.* Washington.

World Bank. 2003. *Doing Business in 2004.* Washington.

World Bank. 2006. *World Development Report 2006.* Washington.

WTO (World Trade Organization). 2004. General Council Report. WT/L/579 (August 1). Geneva.

Wunsch-Vincent, Sacha. 2003. The Digital Trade Agenda of the U.S.: Parallel Tracks of Bilateral, Regional, and Multilateral Liberalization. *Aussenwirtschaft* 58: 7–46.

Zoellick, Robert Z. 2003. Letter to The Honorable J. Dennis Hastert, Speaker of the US House of Representatives, notifying the Congress of the intent to initiate FTA negotiations with Colombia, Peru, Ecuador, and Bolivia, November 18, 2003. Washington: Office of the US Trade Representative.

Index

Argentina, US FDI in, 24
Armington assumption, 83, 176
    import elasticities, 180*t*
    price elasticities, 96*n*
ATPA. *See* Andean Trade Preference Act
ATPDEA. *See* US trade legislation,
    Andean Trade Promotion and Drug
    Enforcement Act
AUC. *See* United Self-Defense Forces of
    Colombia

bananas, 19*t*, 20
Bangkok Agreement, 79
Berne Convention, 153
bilateral merchandise trade, 16–17, 16*t*,
    17*t*, 20
Bingaman, Jeff, 142, 144, 144*n*
Bolivia, 10, 173
    drug eradication program, 5
    labor standards in, 135*t*
    participation in US FTA talks, 1*n*
    readiness indicators for, 65, 65*f*, 70*t*–71*t*
BP Amoco, 61
Brazil
    FDI in, 22, 24
    trade with Andean-3, 16*t*, 17*t*
broadcasting, satellite transmissions, 24
    protection of, 153–54
Brussels Convention, 153
Bush, George W., 4

CAFTA-DR. *See* Central American Free
    Trade Agreement–Dominican
    Republic
Caribbean, trade with US, 3*t*
Caribbean Basin Economic Recovery
    Expansion Act, 174*n*
Caribbean Basin Initiative (CBI), 174
Caribbean Basin Trade Partnership Act
    (CBTPA), 174, 174*n*
Cartagena Agreement, 33, 33*n*
Castro, Fidel, 72
Central America, US FDI in, 4*t*
Central American Free Trade
    Agreement–Dominican Republic
    (CAFTA-DR), 119
    achievements of, 171
    agricultural components of, 121*t*–22*t*
    congressional vote tallies, 141, 141*t*
    sensitive exports to US, 142, 143*t*
    similarities and differences with
        US-Colombia FTA, 140–43
    trade with US, 3*t*
    US lessons learned, 168, 169

CET. *See* common external tariff
Chàvez, Hugo, 72
chemicals
    antidumping investigations, 39*t*, 41
    US-Colombia trade, 18*t*, 19*t*
Chile
    FDI in, 4*t*, 22, 24
    price band system, 124, 124*n*
    trade agreements with Asian countries,
        174
    trade with US, 3*t*
China, 8, 174
    trade with Peru, Andean-3, 16–17, 16*t*,
        17*t*
coffee, 19*t*, 20, 30*n*, 48
Colombia. *See also* Andean Community
    agricultural sector in, 46, 47*t*, 48*t*, 117–19
        coffee, 48
        sugar, 36*n*
    Banco de República, 55, 58
    bank restructuring, 60–62
    budget discipline, 58
    child labor in, 135*t*, 136
    copyright laws, 152–53
    currency stability, 59
    current account, 48, 49*t*–50*t*
    drugs, trafficking of, 4–5, 7, 10, 62, 169,
        172
    external debt of, 59
    foreign direct investment (FDI) in,
        22–24, 22*t*, 23*t*
    financial sector of, 46, 47*t*, 48*t*
    GDP of, 45*t*, 46, 47*t*
    human development index (HDI) for,
        62
    inflation, price stability in, 55, 58
    intellectual property rights (IPR)
        protection efforts, 33, 36, 146
    Justice and Peace Law, 63
    labor standards, compared with other
        regions, 135*t*
    market openness of, 60–62
    mining and petroleum sector in, 46, 47*t*,
        48
    national savings in, 58
    patents issued to and by, 161, 161*t*
    Plan Colombia, 5, 10
    poverty rate in, 46, 46*n*
    purchasing power in, 44, 44*n*
    readiness indicators for, 56*t*–57*t*, 59,
        64–65, 65*f*, 72
    reform of criminal justice system,
        139–40
    reliance on trade taxes of, 60

rice, 123
RTA. *See* regional trade agreements (RTAs)

Sánchez de Lozada, Gonzalo, 72
sanitary and phytosanitary (SPS) measures
   of selected FTAs, 122*t*
   as trade barriers, 126
SAPTA. *See* South Asian Preferential Trading Arrangement
Schwab, Susan, 144
services trade, 20–22, 21*t*, 84*n*
Solidarity trade union, 131
South Africa, 131
South Asian Preferential Trading Arrangement (SAPTA), 79
SPS measures. *See* sanitary and phytosanitary (SPS) measures
Stiglitz, Joseph, 118*n*
sugar trade
   Colombia, Peru, 36*n*
   Colombian exports, 142
   quotas, 123
   US, 36, 36*n*, 168
   US-Colombia balance, 19*t*, 20
   US-Colombia negotiations, 7, 37
Summit of the Americas
   Mar del Plata, 11
   Miami, 4, 172
   Santiago, 172

tariff elimination schedules
   in FTAs, 120–21, 121*t*, 123
tariff-rate quotas (TRQs)
   products at issue in US FTAs, 123
   in selected FTAs, 121*t*
tariff protection, US and Colombian, 32–33, 36–37
technology trade
   broadcasting, 24
   digital, electronic media protection, 153–54, 158
   potential economic gain, innovation, 162–63
   telecommunications, 22, 61
   US-Colombia balance, 160–62
terms-of-trade effects, 95, 96*n*
textiles, clothing, and footwear
   Colombian exports of, 8
   RCA indices for US, Colombia, 27*t*
   US, Colombian protection of, 34*t*, 35*t*
   US-Colombia trade, 18*t*, 19*t*, 20
Thailand, 174

Toledo, Alejandro, 173
trademarks and geographical indications, protection of, 159
transport, travel services, 21, 21*t*
tuna, 116*n*

Union for the Protection of New Plant Varieties (UPOV), 151, 151*n*
United Self-Defense Forces of Colombia (AUC), drug trafficking and, 62, 62*n*
United States
   advantages, disadvantages in trade, 30–31
   exports to Colombia, 17, 18*t*, 20
   foreign direct investment (FDI)
      in Andean-3, 23–24, 23*t*
      in Latin America, Caribbean, 2, 4*t*
   generalized system of preferences, 36
   imports from Colombia, 19*t*
   merchandise trade with Colombia, 16, 17, 18*t*, 19*t*–20*t*, 20
   RCA indices for, 26*t*–29*t*
   relations with Andean Community, 2
   sugar trade, reform, 36, 36*n*, 168
   trade with Colombia, Andean-3, 6*t*, 16*t*, 17*t*
      services, 20–22, 21*t*
US Congress
   concerns over labor standards in Colombia, 144
   trade legislation voting preferences, 140–41, 141*t*, 142
US free trade agreements (FTAs), 11
   agricultural components of, 121*t*–22*t*
   agricultural issues, 12–13
      safeguards, subsidies, 124–25, 125–26
   criteria for partners, 44
   "fast track" implementation procedures, 8, 9*b*
   intellectual property rights provisions, 155, 156–60
   labor, environmental issues, 12
   labor standards in, 132–34
   with Latin America, Caribbean, 173–74
   ratification of, 2
   US objectives of, 11–12
US trade legislation
   Andean Trade Promotion and Drug Enforcement Act, 36, 119, 130, 156
      congressional vote tallies, 141, 141*t*
      and ratification of US FTAs, 2
   Digital Millennium Copyright Act, 158, 165

Other Publications from the Institute for International Economics

46 The National Economic Council: A Work in Progress* I. M. Destler
November 1996 ISBN 0-88132-239-3

47 The Case for an International Banking Standard Morris Goldstein
April 1997 ISBN 0-88132-244-X

48 Transatlantic Trade: A Strategic Agenda* Ellen L. Frost
May 1997 ISBN 0-88132-228-8

49 Cooperating with Europe's Monetary Union C. Randall Henning
May 1997 ISBN 0-88132-245-8

50 Renewing Fast Track Legislation* I. M. Destler
September 1997 ISBN 0-88132-252-0

51 Competition Policies for the Global Economy Edward M. Graham and J. David Richardson
November 1997 ISBN 0-88132-249-0

52 Improving Trade Policy Reviews in the World Trade Organization Donald Keesing
April 1998 ISBN 0-88132-251-2

53 Agricultural Trade Policy: Completing the Reform Timothy Josling
April 1998 ISBN 0-88132-256-3

54 Real Exchange Rates for the Year 2000 Simon Wren Lewis and Rebecca Driver
April 1998 ISBN 0-88132-253-9

55 The Asian Financial Crisis: Causes, Cures, and Systemic Implications Morris Goldstein
June 1998 ISBN 0-88132-261-X

56 Global Economic Effects of the Asian Currency Devaluations Marcus Noland, LiGang Liu, Sherman Robinson, and Zhi Wang
July 1998 ISBN 0-88132-260-1

57 The Exchange Stabilization Fund: Slush Money or War Chest? C. Randall Henning
May 1999 ISBN 0-88132-271-7

58 The New Politics of American Trade: Trade, Labor, and the Environment
I. M. Destler and Peter J. Balint
October 1999 ISBN 0-88132-269-5

59 Congressional Trade Votes: From NAFTA Approval to Fast Track Defeat
Robert E. Baldwin and Christopher S. Magee
February 2000 ISBN 0-88132-267-9

60 Exchange Rate Regimes for Emerging Markets: Reviving the Intermediate Option John Williamson
September 2000 ISBN 0-88132-293-8

61 NAFTA and the Environment: Seven Years Later Gary Clyde Hufbauer, Daniel Esty, Diana Orejas, Luis Rubio, and Jeffrey J. Schott
October 2000 ISBN 0-88132-299-7

62 Free Trade between Korea and the United States? Inbom Choi and Jeffrey J. Schott
April 2001 ISBN 0-88132-311-X

63 New Regional Trading Arrangements in the Asia Pacific?
Robert Scollay and John P. Gilbert
May 2001 ISBN 0-88132-302-0

64 Parental Supervision: The New Paradigm for Foreign Direct Investment and Development Theodore H. Moran
August 2001 ISBN 0-88132-313-6

65 The Benefits of Price Convergence: Speculative Calculations
Gary Clyde Hufbauer, Erika Wada, and Tony Warren
December 2001 ISBN 0-88132-333-0

66 Managed Floating Plus Morris Goldstein
March 2002 ISBN 0-88132-336-5

67 Argentina and the Fund: From Triumph to Tragedy Michael Mussa
July 2002 ISBN 0-88132-339-X

68 East Asian Financial Cooperation C. Randall Henning
September 2002 ISBN 0-88132-338-1

69 Reforming OPIC for the 21st Century Theodore H. Moran
May 2003 ISBN 0-88132-342-X

70 Awakening Monster: The Alien Tort Statute of 1789
Gary C. Hufbauer and Nicholas Mitrokostas
July 2003 ISBN 0-88132-366-7

71 Korea after Kim Jong-il Marcus Noland
January 2004 ISBN 0-88132-373-X

72 Roots of Competitiveness: China's Evolving Agriculture Interests Daniel H. Rosen, Scott Rozelle, and Jikun Huang
July 2004 ISBN 0-88132-376-4

73 Prospects for a US-Taiwan FTA Nicholas R. Lardy and Daniel H. Rosen
December 2004 ISBN 0-88132-367-5

74 Anchoring Reform with a US-Egypt Free Trade Agreement
Ahmed Galal and Robert Z. Lawrence
April 2005 ISBN 0-88132-368-3

75 Curbing the Boom-Bust Cycle: Stabilizing Capital Flows to Emerging Markets John Williamson
July 2005 ISBN 0-88132-330-6

76 The Shape of a Swiss-US Free Trade Agreement
Gary Clyde Hufbauer and Richard E. Baldwin
February 2006 ISBN 978-0-88132-385-6

77 A Strategy for IMF Reform Edwin M. Truman
February 2006 ISBN 978-0-88132-398-6

78 US-China Trade Disputes: Rising Tide, Rising Stakes   Gary Clyde Hufbauer, Yee Wong, and Ketki Sheth
August 2006   ISBN 978-0-88132-394-8
79 Trade Relations Between Colombia and the United States
Jeffrey J. Schott, editor
August 2006   ISBN 978-0-88132-389-4

BOOKS

IMF Conditionality* John Williamson, editor
1983   ISBN 0-88132-006-4
Trade Policy in the 1980s* William R. Cline, ed.
1983   ISBN 0-88132-031-5
Subsidies in International Trade*
Gary Clyde Hufbauer and Joanna Shelton Erb
1984   ISBN 0-88132-004-8
International Debt: Systemic Risk and Policy Response*   William R. Cline
1984   ISBN 0-88132-015-3
Trade Protection in the United States: 31 Case Studies* Gary Clyde Hufbauer, Diane E. Berliner, and Kimberly Ann Elliott
1986   ISBN 0-88132-040-4
Toward Renewed Economic Growth in Latin America* Bela Balassa, Gerardo M. Bueno, Pedro-Pablo Kuczynski, and Mario Henrique Simonsen
1986   ISBN 0-88132-045-5
Capital Flight and Third World Debt*
Donald R. Lessard and John Williamson, editors
1987   ISBN 0-88132-053-6
The Canada-United States Free Trade Agreement: The Global Impact*
Jeffrey J. Schott and Murray G. Smith, editors
1988   ISBN 0-88132-073-0
World Agricultural Trade: Building a Consensus*
William M. Miner and Dale E. Hathaway, editors
1988   ISBN 0-88132-071-3
Japan in the World Economy*
Bela Balassa and Marcus Noland
1988   ISBN 0-88132-041-2
America in the World Economy: A Strategy for the 1990s*   C. Fred Bergsten
1988   ISBN 0-88132-089-7
Managing the Dollar: From the Plaza to the Louvre*   Yoichi Funabashi
1988, 2d. ed. 1989   ISBN 0-88132-097-8
United States External Adjustment and the World Economy*   William R. Cline
May 1989   ISBN 0-88132-048-X
Free Trade Areas and U.S. Trade Policy*
Jeffrey J. Schott, editor
May 1989   ISBN 0-88132-094-3

Dollar Politics: Exchange Rate Policymaking in the United States*
I. M. Destler and C. Randall Henning
September 1989   ISBN 0-88132-079-X
Latin American Adjustment: How Much Has Happened?*   John Williamson, editor
April 1990   ISBN 0-88132-125-7
The Future of World Trade in Textiles and Apparel*   William R. Cline
1987, 2d ed. June 1999   ISBN 0-88132-110-9
Completing the Uruguay Round: A Results-Oriented Approach to the GATT Trade Negotiations*   Jeffrey J. Schott, editor
September 1990   ISBN 0-88132-130-3
Economic Sanctions Reconsidered (2 volumes)
Economic Sanctions Reconsidered: Supplemental Case Histories
Gary Clyde Hufbauer, Jeffrey J. Schott, and Kimberly Ann Elliott
1985, 2d ed. Dec. 1990   ISBN cloth 0-88132-115-X
      ISBN paper 0-88132-105-2
Economic Sanctions Reconsidered: History and Current Policy   Gary Clyde Hufbauer, Jeffrey J. Schott, and Kimberly Ann Elliott
December 1990   ISBN cloth 0-88132-140-0
      ISBN paper 0-88132-136-2
Pacific Basin Developing Countries: Prospects for Economic Sanctions Reconsidered: History and Current Policy   Gary Clyde Hufbauer, Jeffrey J. Schott, and Kimberly Ann Elliott
December 1990   ISBN cloth 0-88132-140-0
      ISBN paper 0-88132-136-2
Pacific Basin Developing Countries: Prospects for the Future*   Marcus Noland
January 1991   ISBN cloth 0-88132-141-9
      ISBN paper 0-88132-081-1
Currency Convertibility in Eastern Europe*
John Williamson, editor
October 1991   ISBN 0-88132-128-1
International Adjustment and Financing: The Lessons of 1985-1991* C. Fred Bergsten, editor
January 1992   ISBN 0-88132-112-5
North American Free Trade: Issues and Recommendations*
Gary Clyde Hufbauer and Jeffrey J. Schott
April 1992   ISBN 0-88132-120-6
Narrowing the U.S. Current Account Deficit*
Alan J. Lenz/*June 1992* ISBN 0-88132-103-6
The Economics of Global Warming
William R. Cline/*June 1992* ISBN 0-88132-132-X
US Taxation of International Income: Blueprint for Reform*   Gary Clyde Hufbauer, assisted by Joanna M. van Rooij
October 1992   ISBN 0-88132-134-6
Who's Bashing Whom? Trade Conflict in High-Technology Industries
Laura D'Andrea Tyson
November 1992   ISBN 0-88132-106-0

Measuring the Costs of Visible Protection in Korea* Namdoo Kim
November 1996 ISBN 0-88132-236-9
The World Trading System: Challenges Ahead
Jeffrey J. Schott
December 1996 ISBN 0-88132-235-0
Has Globalization Gone Too Far? Dani Rodrik
March 1997 ISBN paper 0-88132-241-5
Korea-United States Economic Relationship*
C. Fred Bergsten and Il SaKong, editors
March 1997 ISBN 0-88132-240-7
Summitry in the Americas: A Progress Report
Richard E. Feinberg
April 1997 ISBN 0-88132-242-3
Corruption and the Global Economy
Kimberly Ann Elliott
June 1997 ISBN 0-88132-233-4
Regional Trading Blocs in the World Economic System Jeffrey A. Frankel
October 1997 ISBN 0-88132-202-4
Sustaining the Asia Pacific Miracle: Environmental Protection and Economic Integration Andre Dua and Daniel C. Esty
October 1997 ISBN 0-88132-250-4
Trade and Income Distribution
William R. Cline
November 1997 ISBN 0-88132-216-4
Global Competition Policy
Edward M. Graham and J. David Richardson
December 1997 ISBN 0-88132-166-4
Unfinished Business: Telecommunications after the Uruguay Round
Gary Clyde Hufbauer and Erika Wada
December 1997 ISBN 0-88132-257-1
Financial Services Liberalization in the WTO
Wendy Dobson and Pierre Jacquet
June 1998 ISBN 0-88132-254-7
Restoring Japan's Economic Growth
Adam S. Posen
September 1998 ISBN 0-88132-262-8
Measuring the Costs of Protection in China
Zhang Shuguang, Zhang Yansheng, and Wan Zhongxin
November 1998 ISBN 0-88132-247-4
Foreign Direct Investment and Development: The New Policy Agenda for Developing Countries and Economies in Transition
Theodore H. Moran
December 1998 ISBN 0-88132-258-X
Behind the Open Door: Foreign Enterprises in the Chinese Marketplace
Daniel H. Rosen
January 1999 ISBN 0-88132-263-6
Toward A New International Financial Architecture: A Practical Post-Asia Agenda
Barry Eichengreen
February 1999 ISBN 0-88132-270-9

Is the U.S. Trade Deficit Sustainable?
Catherine L. Mann
September 1999 ISBN 0-88132-265-2
Safeguarding Prosperity in a Global Financial System: The Future International Financial Architecture, Independent Task Force Report Sponsored by the Council on Foreign Relations
Morris Goldstein, Project Director
October 1999 ISBN 0-88132-287-3
Avoiding the Apocalypse: The Future of the Two Koreas Marcus Noland
June 2000 ISBN 0-88132-278-4
Assessing Financial Vulnerability: An Early Warning System for Emerging Markets
Morris Goldstein, Graciela Kaminsky, and Carmen Reinhart
June 2000 ISBN 0-88132-237-7
Global Electronic Commerce: A Policy Primer
Catherine L. Mann, Sue E. Eckert, and Sarah Cleeland Knight
July 2000 ISBN 0-88132-274-1
The WTO after Seattle Jeffrey J. Schott, editor
July 2000 ISBN 0-88132-290-3
Intellectual Property Rights in the Global Economy Keith E. Maskus
August 2000 ISBN 0-88132-282-2
The Political Economy of the Asian Financial Crisis Stephan Haggard
August 2000 ISBN 0-88132-283-0
Transforming Foreign Aid: United States Assistance in the 21st Century
Carol Lancaster
August 2000 ISBN 0-88132-291-1
Fighting the Wrong Enemy: Antiglobal Activists and Multinational Enterprises
Edward M. Graham
September 2000 ISBN 0-88132-272-5
Globalization and the Perceptions of American Workers
Kenneth F. Scheve and Matthew J. Slaughter
March 2001 ISBN 0-88132-295-4
World Capital Markets: Challenge to the G-10
Wendy Dobson and Gary Clyde Hufbauer, assisted by Hyun Koo Cho
May 2001 ISBN 0-88132-301-2
Prospects for Free Trade in the Americas
Jeffrey J. Schott
August 2001 ISBN 0-88132-275-X
Toward a North American Community: Lessons from the Old World for the New
Robert A. Pastor
August 2001 ISBN 0-88132-328-4
Measuring the Costs of Protection in Europe: European Commercial Policy in the 2000s
Patrick A. Messerlin
September 2001 ISBN 0-88132-273-3

DISTRIBUTORS OUTSIDE THE UNITED STATES

Australia, New Zealand,
and Papua New Guinea
D. A. Information Services
648 Whitehorse Road
Mitcham, Victoria 3132, Australia
Tel: 61-3-9210-7777
Fax: 61-3-9210-7788
Email: service@dadirect.com.au
www.dadirect.com.au

Canada
Renouf Bookstore
5369 Canotek Road, Unit 1
Ottawa, Ontario KlJ 9J3, Canada
Tel: 613-745-2665
Fax: 613-745-7660
www.renoufbooks.com

India, Bangladesh, Nepal, and Sri Lanka
Viva Books Private Limited
Mr. Vinod Vasishtha
4737/23 Ansari Road
Daryaganj, New Delhi 110002
India
Tel: 91-11-4224-2200
Fax: 91-11-4224-2240
Email: viva@vivagroupindia.net
www.vivagroupindia.com

Japan
United Publishers Services Ltd.
1-32-5, Higashi-shinagawa
Shinagawa-ku, Tokyo 140-0002
Japan
Tel: 81-3-5479-7251
Fax: 81-3-5479-7307
Email: purchasing@ups.co.jp
For trade accounts only. Individuals will find
IIE books in leading Tokyo bookstores.

Mexico, Central America, South America,
and Puerto Rico
US PubRep, Inc.
311 Dean Drive
Rockville, MD 20851
Tel: 301-838-9276
Fax: 301-838-9278
Email: c.falk@ieee.org
www.uspubrep.com

Middle East
MERIC
2 Bahgat Ali Street, El Masry Towers
Tower D, Apt. 24
Zamalek, Cairo
Egypt
Tel. 20-2-7633824
Fax: 20-2-7369355
Email: mahmoud_fouda@mericonline.com
www.mericonline.com

Southeast Asia (*Brunei, Burma, Cambodia,*
Indonesia, Malaysia, the Philippines,
Singapore, Taiwan, Thailand, and Vietnam)
APAC Publishers Services PTE Ltd.
70 Bendemeer Road #05-03
Hiap Huat House
Singapore 333940
Tel: 65-6844-7333
Fax: 65-6747-8916
Email: service@apacmedia.com.sg

United Kingdom, Europe
(*including Russia and Turkey*), **Africa,**
and Israel
The Eurospan Group
c/o Turpin Distribution
Pegasus Drive
Stratton Business Park
Biggleswade, Bedfordshire
SG18 8TQ
United Kingdom
Tel: 44 (0) 1767-604972
Fax: 44 (0) 1767-601640
Email: eurospan@turpin-distribution.com
www.eurospangroup.com/bookstore

Visit our Web site at:
www.iie.com
E-mail orders to:
IIE mail@PressWarehouse.com